Trans* Policies and Experiences in Housing and Residence Life

ACPA BOOKS AND MEDIA CONTACT INFORMATION

ACPA International Office
Tricia A. Fechter Gates
Deputy Executive Director
One Dupont Circle, NW, Suite 300
Washington, DC 20036-1110
(202) 759-4825
FAX (202) 827-0601
pfechter@acpa.nche.edu

ACPA Publications Board
Robert T. Palmer, Editor
Associate Professor
Howard University
2441 4th Street, NW
Washington, DC 20059
robert.palmer@howard.edu

Trans* Policies and Experiences in Housing and Residence Life

Edited by
JASON C. GARVEY,
STEPHANIE H. CHANG, Z NICOLAZZO,
AND REX JACKSON

Foreword by
KATHLEEN G. KERR

ACPA
College Student
Educators International

Sty/us

STERLING, VIRGINIA

Published by Stylus Publishing, LLC.
22883 Quicksilver Drive
Sterling, Virginia 20166-2102

Library of Congress Cataloging-in-Publication Data
Names: Garvey, Jason C., editor.
Title: Trans* policies and experiences in housing and residence life / edited
by Jason C. Garvey, Stephanie H. Chang, Z. Nicolazzo, and Rex Jackson ;
foreword by Kathleen G. Kerr.
Description: First edition. |
Sterling, Virgina : Stylus Publishing, LLC., 2018. |
Includes bibliographical references and index.
Identifiers: LCCN 2017034874 (print) |
LCCN 2017055536 (ebook) |
ISBN 9781620367698 (uPDF) |
ISBN 9781620367704 (ePub, mobi) |
ISBN 9781620367674 (cloth : alk. paper) |
ISBN 9781620367681 (pbk. : alk. paper) |
ISBN 9781620367698 (library networkable e-edition)) |
ISBN 9781620367704 (consumer e-edition)
Subjects: LCSH: Student housing--Social aspects--United States. |
Gay college students--Housing--United States.
Classification: LCC LB3227.5 (ebook) |
LCC LB3227.5 .T73 2018 (print) |
DDC 378.1/9871--dc23
LC record available at https://lccn.loc.gov/2017034874

13-digit ISBN: 978-1-62036-767-4 (cloth)
13-digit ISBN: 978-1-62036-768-1 (paperback)
13-digit ISBN: 978-1-62036-769-8 (library networkable e-edition)
13-digit ISBN: 978-1-62036-770-4 (consumer e-edition)

Printed in the United States of America

All first editions printed on acid-free paper
that meets the American National Standards Institute
Z39-48 Standard.

Bulk Purchases

Quantity discounts are available for use in workshops and for staff
development.
Call 1-800-232-0223

First Edition, 2018

Contents

Part Two
INITIATIVES THROUGH STAFF AND ADMINISTRATION

Foreword

WHEN MY DAUGHTER FIRST met her best friend, he was struggling. He did not publicly express the gender he does now and was not comfortable conforming to the sex that had been assigned to him at birth. He was an awkward teenager, uncomfortable in his own skin. As he transitioned with the support of family and friends to a gender expression matching his gender identity, not surprisingly he gained confidence, and that awkwardness disappeared. As an administrator at the University of Delaware (UD), I frequently saw my daughter and "J" as they both took classes at UD. J joined us on several family vacations, and although he has a terrific mother, I was tickled when he began to call me Mom.

I could never truly know what it is like to be a trans* college student. But I can know the desire as a mother, or surrogate mom, for my children to have all the opportunities available to them so they can be successful. Every summer, I tell parents at New Student Orientation that our residence halls are their students' homes. I also tell them that the halls are an integral part of a UD education, and significant learning occurs because of the experiences students have in the halls. I do not just want some of the students to feel like their residence hall is home, I want all the students to believe it.

We can desire terrific learning outcomes on intercultural competence, self-efficacy, and self-awareness; however, the reality is that learning is unlikely to occur if students do not feel like they matter, if they do not feel like they belong. All students should be able to view their residence hall not only as their home but also as a sanctuary from a difficult day where they can recharge, regroup, and start the next day ready to learn anew. As student affairs practitioners, how can we believe we are offering that to our trans* students if they feel invisible? How can we believe that they know they matter and they belong if their gender nonbinary identities do not have places and spaces within our walls?

The purpose of this book is to show us a path forward. For some, it will lead to an important first step, for others, an advancement of current efforts. The team of editors has created a masterful tool for change with this book. Their knowledge of the scholarship combined with the ability to identify schools willing to share their experiences implementing trans*-inclusive practices and policies epitomize a scholar-practitioner mind-set. Their work serves as a response to what we know, what we do about it, and how we do it.

The book begins with a preface by Jason C. Garvey, who provides important context, including the editors' objectives, the book's organization, and the reason for choosing Nash's (2004) scholarly personal narrative format that is so effective in later chapters. The introduction by Stephanie H. Chang and Craig Leets Jr. is an invaluable review of relevant language and issues related to campus climate.

The chapters that follow are vibrant examples of the work being done to turn residence halls into homes. The shared struggles, processes, politics, and insights will assist the staff of any institutional department seeking to advance. The personal narratives are powerful vehicles to convey the nuances of personal, department, and institutional change that must be navigated and achieved.

In the epilogue, Z Nicolazzo writes about the practice and process necessary for trans* equity. It will require ongoing work at multiple levels, and Z challenges all of us to not believe that creating all-gender or gender-inclusive housing is the end point. It is only the beginning of a cultural shift that must occur on college campuses.

Although it would be ideal for this cultural change to overtake an entire campus at once, I recognize the impossibility of that. Cultural change does not happen suddenly and completely. Instead, within our sphere of influence, we must remove those structural artifacts that perpetuate a culture, support a gender binary, and are not gender inclusive. Our students deserve all our focus and energy to dismantle those artifacts piece by piece. Making sure every student has a residence hall home to return to at the end of the day is the least we can do. This book gives us the tools needed to accomplish that.

Kathleen G. Kerr
Associate Vice President for Student Life
Executive Director of Residence Life and Housing
University of Delaware

Preface

Jason C. Garvey

G ENDER-INCLUSIVE HOUSING PRACTICES AND policies are becoming more prevalent in U.S. higher education. Administrators, educators, and practitioners of higher education and student affairs are facing growing needs in recognizing and understanding the challenges the campus environment presents to trans* students.[1] Housing and residence life (HRL), an essential student affairs functional area for residential colleges and universities, plays an important role in the safety, well-being, and ultimate sense of belonging for college and university students (Strayhorn, 2012). However, little is known about the experiences of trans* students in HRL. Currently in the United States, the Trans Policy Clearinghouse identifies 265 colleges and universities as having gender-inclusive housing options in which students can have a roommate of any gender (Campus Pride, 2017). This book presents the processes and steps that select institutions of higher education are undertaking to develop and implement trans* practices and policies in HRL

PURPOSE

This edited volume examines how HRLs develop and implement trans*-inclusive HRL policies. What are the institutional politics associated with fostering trans*-inclusive policies? When formalizing a policy, what unanticipated challenges may emerge? How are students, particularly trans* students, influenced by the implementation of gender-inclusive housing practices and policies? Also, what are campus administrators and practitioners learning from their involvement with the development of trans* work on campus? Gender-inclusive policies and practices in HRL are largely underexplored in student affairs and higher education publications. Consequently, there is a strong need for an edited collection to share the experiences and narratives of practitioners advocating for gender-inclusive housing.

Five key objectives guide this volume. First, it aims to promote and challenge student affairs and higher education staff's knowledge about trans* students' identities and experiences. Second, this book supports and celebrates the accomplishments of educators and professionals in their strides to promote trans*-inclusive policies and practices. Third, it highlights the unique role housing and residence life plays in creating institutional change and serving trans* student populations. Fourth, we hope it demonstrates the value and use of scholarly personal narratives (SPNs; Nash, 2004), particularly regarding experiences related to implementing trans*-inclusive policies in housing and residence life. Fifth, this book aims to create a strong partnership between scholarship and student affairs practice by developing an avenue for practitioner scholars to publish their experiences related to gender-inclusive policies in housing and residence life and for others to use these stories to improve their practice.

ORGANIZATION OF CHAPTERS

The chapters are organized around the multiple facets of developing, implementing, and negotiating trans*-inclusive policies and practices in housing and residence life. Each chapter was written by a practitioner or a group of practitioners who have direct experience with trans*-inclusive policies. Contributors offer their experiences with gender-inclusive housing policies, with specific focuses on the following: campus environments (e.g., What led to the creation of a gender-inclusive policy in housing and residence life?), politics (e.g., How did you navigate the campus politics when developing such a policy?), policy (e.g., How did you develop the policy?), implementation (e.g., How was the policy put into action? How were students, and in particular trans* students, affected by the implementation?), and future recommendations (e.g., What did this experience teach you, and what recommendations do you have for target audiences that are considering developing gender-inclusive policies in housing and residence life?).

WRITING STYLE

The chapters were written in the format of SPNs (Nash, 2004). Contributors were asked to integrate and acknowledge their own social identities, experiences, and institutions in their chapters in a manner that also includes relevant scholarship on trans* experiences and the practices of housing and residence life in higher education.

According to Nash (2004), SPNs are critical intellectual reflections of personal experiences. Although SPNs contain references to the current literature, most important, they place the writer at the forefront. Nash stated, "Writers are always an integral part of what they observe, study, interpret, and assert" (p. 26). In addition to describing the implementation and evaluation of a new policy, the editors were interested in individual and collective stories behind wrestling with inclusive gender, gender identity, and gender expression practices. The contributors were encouraged to write their chapters with the belief that their stories are important, relevant, and will help to enhance the experiences of student affairs and higher education educators, and also advance knowledge of trans* communities. Nash stated, "Your own life tells a story (or a series of stories) that, when narrated well, can deliver to your readers those delicious aha! moments of self and social insight" (p. 24). Through SPNs, the editors aim to allow readers to explore their individual "aha" moments with issues on gender identity and expression while also recognizing how aha moments happened for the chapter contributors.

PROCESS OF SELECTING INSTITUTIONS AND CONTRIBUTORS

Chapter proposal submissions were by invitation only. The editors carefully reviewed all institutions with gender-inclusive housing policies and determined which institutions have exceptional policies and practice for trans*-inclusive housing and residence life. Invitations for chapter abstracts and proposals went to select institutions, requesting contributors to provide a one-page abstract of a chapter for review.

Chapters were selected based on specific criteria. As this edited volume is intended to inform practice, the editors intentionally sought chapters from a diverse representation of institutions (e.g., research intensive, liberal arts, size of undergraduate enrollment) and locations (e.g., urban or rural, geographic region). The editors accepted chapter proposals with unique and compelling stories to share. Exceptionalism was based on several parameters including the diversity of contributors' perspectives and voice, participating undergraduate student authors, unique policies, political context, date of implementation, formality of assessment, and critical approach to the topic.

Contributors whose chapters were accepted were paired with a primary editor to work with throughout the editing process. Each chapter draft was reviewed by a secondary editor, who also provided feedback. Two editors read and provided feedback to all contributors, creating continuity throughout the entire volume. To provide writing assistance, the editors developed a document with writing guidelines and tips. Additionally, the contributors attended video conference sessions and an in-person meeting during the 2014 ACPA: College Student Educators International annual conference.

EDITORIAL TEAM

This edited book is cosponsored and edited by members of ACPA's Coalition for LGBT Awareness and Commission for Housing and Residential Life. Editors were selected based on their varied experience and perspectives as scholars and practitioners, with careful consideration for representing voices across social identities. Jason C. Garvey is assistant professor of higher education and student affairs in the Department of Leadership and Developmental Sciences at the University of Vermont. Stephanie H. Chang is a PhD candidate in the college student personnel administration program at the University of Maryland, College Park. She serves as an adjunct faculty member in New England College's master of science higher education and administration program, and she is also director of student diversity and inclusion at the University of Delaware. Z Nicolazzo is assistant professor in the Department of Counseling, Adult, and Higher Education and a faculty associate in the Center for the Study of Women, Gender, and Sexuality at Northern Illinois University. Rex Jackson is associate director for residence life at Southern Illinois University Edwardsville.

USES AND INTENDED AUDIENCES

The volume is aimed specifically at student affairs practitioners working in housing and residence life. Particularly, this book is meant to serve as a resource for campus staff and practitioners who are planning to develop and implement gender-inclusive housing policies at their institutions. Additionally, this book is meant to serve as a resource and textbook option for student affairs and higher education graduate preparatory programs. Specific course topics that may benefit from this book include diversity and social justice, student affairs practicum and internship, current issues in student affairs and higher education, and capstone courses, among others. Finally, the book may serve as a beginning point for conversation at institutions that currently do not have gender-inclusive housing policies. Audiences may begin considering moving beyond current gender-inclusive practices and policies in housing and residence life to more fully serve students across all genders.

OVERVIEW OF CONTENTS

This book has two main parts, along with an introduction and epilogue to frame the chapters. In the introduction, Stephanie H. Chang and Craig Leets Jr. provide an overview of trans* student experiences and encourage readers to think critically about the ways colleges and universities foster trans* students' sense of belonging. They present critical questions to consider when reading institutional narratives on gender-inclusive housing initiatives.

The two main parts of the book provide detailed narratives of staff and students from institutions with gender-inclusive housing initiatives. The main intended purpose is to inform practice in higher education and student affairs to make more accessible and equitable housing policies and practices across genders. To facilitate progress at other institutions, each section is framed around the mechanisms used to introduce gender-inclusive housing.

In part one, contributors from six institutions present narratives for the development of policies more inclusive across genders through student organizing and activism. For some institutions, like Roosevelt University and George Washington University, policies were facilitated through individual and group organizing by students. Among other colleges and universities, policies were developed through the leadership of student groups, like the Trans* Advocacy Group at Oberlin College and Students for the Equality of Queers at the University of California, Riverside. Policies at the final two institutions in this section were enacted through activism from student governing bodies, including Dickinson College's student senate and students from the University of Wisconsin–Madison's University Housing Gender and Sexuality Alliance.

In part two, contributors from five institutions provide narratives for gender-inclusive initiatives in housing and residence life developed through staff and administration. For the University of Maryland, efforts were led by staff in the Department of Resident Life. Two institutions, American University and Ithaca College, had housing and lesbian, gay, bisexual, transgender, and queer (LGBTQ) student services working in partnership. The final two institutions, the University of Arizona and University of Oregon, had initiatives that were developed with leadership from LGBTQ student services in collaboration with housing and residence life.

The book ends with an epilogue in which Z Nicolazzo challenges the inclusivity of gender-inclusive housing policies. Z closes with alternative possibilities to expand approaches when working alongside trans* college students.

NOTE

1. The introduction clarifies terminology used throughout the book, including *trans** and *transgender*.

REFERENCES

Campus Pride. (2017). *Colleges and universities that provide gender-inclusive housing.* Retrieved from www.campuspride.org/tpc/gender-inclusive-housing

Nash, R. J. (2004). *Liberating scholarly writing: The power of personal narrative.* New York, NY: Teachers College Press.

Strayhorn, T. L. (2012). *College students' sense of belonging: A key to educational success for all students.* New York; NY: Routledge.

Acknowledgments

FIRST AND FOREMOST, THE editors would like to acknowledge and thank the countless trans* students, student affairs professionals, and faculty whose voices and advocacy continue to push colleges and universities to do better by improving safety, housing, and support for trans* students. The emotional and physical labor of the trans* community has done a lot to shape this book and what many institutions are doing today to address the needs and concerns of their community. The campus changes and policies described in this book would not have been possible without their tireless efforts. We would also like to acknowledge the work done by the countless housing and residential life professionals described in this book. Many doing this work as allies of the trans* community by helping campus administrators hear the trans* voices on their campuses.

In addition, we want to acknowledge each of the chapter authors whose contributions made this book possible. These individuals took a great deal of time over the past few years to collect and share their experiences so others in the profession can learn how to push forward innovative housing policies and procedures to better serve their trans* residents. And finally, we would like to thank ACPA, Stylus Publishing, ACPA's Commission for Housing and Residential Life, and ACPA's Coalition for Sexuality and Gender Identities. Without their support, guidance, and encouragement we would not have been able to complete this book.

Introduction

Stephanie H. Chang and Craig Leets Jr.

PRACTICES AND POLICIES TO support transgender students are becoming more prevalent on college and university campuses, but reflections on the process of implementing these practices and policies are rarely documented by college and university administrators. Higher education administrators have yet to truly state an understanding of what, why, and how barriers to transgender inclusion happen on campus. What challenges exist on and off campus for transgender community members? Why are these challenges left as barriers to transgender students when they arrive on campus? How do the ways barriers are addressed on campus still leave transgender students excluded from the greater campus community? Is it a lack of understanding of transgender culture, identities, and experiences? Is it the rigidity of current societal norms, practices, and traditions around gender? Our guess is that the problem is both—a lack of information about transgender people and the way society defines *sex, gender, gender expression,* and *gender identity.* Thus, generally, educational settings like colleges and universities practice a segregation of gender that makes being transgender uniquely challenging on campus.

The challenges and barriers faced by transgender students are not exclusive to this student population. There is a pattern of exclusion and socialization of gender that can be traced through educational systems and other societal institutions. Harro (2010) describes "this socialization process [as] *pervasive* (coming from all sides and sources), *consistent* (patterned and predictable), *circular* (self-supporting), *self-perpetuating* (intradependent) and often *invisible* (unconscious and unnamed)" (p. 45, emphasis in original). Gender socialization begins prior to birth when children are color coded by pink for girls and blue for boys. This socialization continues in school when boys and girls use separate restrooms, and teenage boys and girls are required to use separate locker rooms. By college, gender separations increase in housing assignments, by room, floor, or even building. The escalating segregation

1

and separation of boys and girls and men and women and labeling of gender as restricted to boys, girls, men, and women enhances the struggles and experiences of transgender students who often do not fit neatly into traditional gender binaries. This poses a challenge, not for transgender students, but for educators and administrators in student affairs and higher education to be proactive and vigilant about changing the practice of exclusion and segregation by gender.

Before moving forward in this chapter, it is important to acknowledge our experiences with transgender students in higher education. Both authors have had differing trajectories through student affairs and higher education, but both of us have centered our higher education work on equity and inclusion and serve as directors of lesbian, gay, bisexual, transgender, and queer (LGBTQ) centers and services on our campuses. In the remainder of the chapter, we use our names in specific instances when writing about our experiences, and when we speak together, we use *we* and other plural pronouns. Stephanie's entry into LGBTQ student services in higher education occurred through serving as a practitioner in the LGBTQ Centers. This included developing and facilitating educational programs, such as Safe Zone and other ally trainings, and promoting annual events in the LGBTQ community, such as National Coming Out Day, Transgender Day of Remembrance, and Pride celebrations in the spring. In addition, she also advocated for LGBTQ-inclusive university and departmental policies and practices. Similarly, Craig has worked in multiple LGBTQ centers. Our experiences during our work in these centers and the anecdotes we present later have informed our understanding of the topic of this book.

In our work with student affairs colleagues outside LGBTQ resource centers, we have found that many colleagues know quite a bit about the issues and challenges facing lesbian, gay, bisexual, and queer students but have limited to no experience with transgender students, which results in minimal awareness relating to the barriers on campus affecting transgender community members. However, there has been a growing body of literature to support and advocate for transgender services on college and university campuses. There are many ways institutions can be even more proactive in meeting the needs of transgender and gender nonconforming students (Beemyn, Curtis, Davis, & Tubbs, 2005; Beemyn & Rankin, 2011; Jardine, 2013).

Many scholars and researchers have demonstrated that transgender students experience college and university campuses as negative and discriminatory environments (Bilodeau, 2005; Dugan, Kusel, & Simounet,

2012). Beemyn and colleagues (2005) suggested that campus administrators "address [transgender] students' needs in areas of campus life where transgender students have unique concerns: programming, housing, bathrooms and locker rooms, counseling and health care, and records and documents" (p. 49). Truly, beyond these areas of campus life, any facet of the institution that segregates and divides individuals by sex and gender can be a barrier to transgender students. In many cases, these barriers, such as a lack of suitable housing options, can adversely affect students' academic performance and sense of belonging on campus (Baumeister & Leary, 1995; Chapman & Pascarella, 1983; Kane, 2013; Pascarella & Blimling, 1996). However, as mentioned earlier, our experience shows that much of the awareness of transgender students' experiences is limited, and we have found that our colleagues' knowledge of transgender communities is often limited to introductory LGBTQ terms and definitions instead of a more nuanced, personal knowledge of the issues facing these students on campus.

Because LGBTQ terminology is constantly evolving and may be new for some higher education practitioners and administrators, we encountered colleagues who found themselves frustrated or challenged by which terms to use to identify LGBTQ students. Our position and response to this type of sentiment is to not only recognize our colleagues' struggles but also challenge them to consider LGBTQ and, more specifically, transgender students' challenges before their own. To us, this means honoring the identities and labels that students use for themselves as opposed to assigning them identities and labels. In this introduction, we provide a working definition for *transgender* as an identity and an umbrella term for the purposes of this book. At times, transgender and trans* may be used interchangeably, but we want to acknowledge that terms to define and describe transgender communities are viewed differently from campus to campus as well as within the transgender community itself. We also review various ways transgender students have experienced the campus environment and highlight the importance of housing and residence life (HRL) as a key component to fostering students' sense of belonging on campus. Our intent in this introduction is to introduce transgender experiences on college and university campuses and encourage educators reading this volume to think critically about the ways campuses are truly fostering inclusion for transgender students and their sense of belonging. We pose critical questions to consider when reading the stories and experiences of individuals who have worked to support transgender students on campus.

A WORKING DEFINITION

There is a degree of subjectivity with the terms and related definitions for the language used within, among, and about the LGBTQ community. Consequently, the terms and definitions we provide are those we see commonly used among LGBTQ student service professionals in higher education. These definitions also align with the meanings used by the other contributors to this book. However, we want to emphasize there are multiple ways of identifying and expressing gender beyond the identifiers we are using here.

The National Center for Transgender Equality (NCTE, 2016) offered the following definition for the term *transgender*: "A broad term that can be used to describe people whose gender identity is different from the gender they thought to be when they were born. Trans is often used as shorthand for transgender."

NCTE's definition is a useful entry point to becoming more informed about transgender identities, and we find this definition valuable as it comes from an organization that advocates for transgender justice on a national scale. However, merely knowing this definition is insufficient when serving transgender communities. Although definitions can place an institution closer to knowing and recognizing possible barriers and challenges for an LGBTQ campus community, we encourage educators to continue in their efforts to understand the unique experiences that transgender students have on campus. In the NCTE definition, *transgender* is viewed as an umbrella term that may also be relevant for people whose current gender identity does not match the sex they were assigned at birth (i.e., genderqueer, nonbinary, agender); this highlights the complex and in flux nature of identity, expressions, and identifying with a particular social identity term.

For our purposes and the purposes of this book, we expand on the NCTE's definition by including *trans**, which has already appeared throughout this introduction. As Tompkins (2014) wrote, *trans* with an asterisk (*) "signals greater inclusivity of new gender identities and expressions and better represents a broader community of individuals" (p. 27). Tompkins further stated that *trans** is "meant to include not only identities such as transgender, transsexual, trans man, and trans woman that are prefixed by trans- but also identities such as genderqueer, neutrios, intersex, agender, two-spirit, cross-dresser, and genderfluid" (p. 27). Using *trans** in place of *transgender* or another gender identity and expression term is an attempt to be inclusive of multiple gender-bending, gender-blending, and genderqueer identities. In addition, the term *trans** also marks a clear distinction between trans* and cisgender identities. *Cisgender* indicates people "[with a] gender identity [that aligns] with the sex they were assigned at birth" (Jardine, 2013, p. 241). When thinking about sex, gender identity, and gender expression for people who are not cisgender, these concepts are not neatly defined or categorized.

It is important to mention there is no community-wide agreement on whether to use the asterisk with trans*. Because the identities, labels, and concepts of the transgender community are so intimately connected to one's sense of personhood, many individuals adopt definitions that most closely align with their personal experience. It is important for educators to be aware of one definition for each LGBTQ term while also being open to someone's disagreement with that definition because it does not align with that person's experience. Similarly, we must remember that experiences shared by one lesbian, gay, bisexual (LGB) or trans* person are not reflective of the entire community. The experiences of an LGBTQ person can inform our understanding of the community but should not be interpreted as an experience that can be expanded to include every LGBTQ person.

Similar to other definitions within the LGBTQ community, opinions vary on using the asterisk. Killerman (2015), a cisgender ally to the trans* community, explained that the asterisk originated from electronic Internet searches where adding an asterisk to the end of a term signals the browser to find the term by itself while also finding words that have the term embedded in a longer word (e.g., *residen** can include *residence* and *residential*). Killerman agreed with Tompkins on why the asterisk makes *trans** more inclusive than *trans*. However, Killerman's use of the word also provides an argument for those who oppose the use of the asterisk. Electronic searches using *trans** would not retrieve words and identities without *trans* and, therefore, would not be inclusive in scope. Some who oppose the asterisk emphasize *trans* and *transgender* as umbrella terms that should not need any additional indicators to emphasize their expansive, inclusive usage (Gabriel, 2014). If *trans* and *transgender* are understood to be inclusive umbrella terms that represent a variety of identities that exist beyond the gender binary of woman and man, then some argue that we should not need the asterisk to overemphasize the inclusion of those identities that do not include *trans* in their label. Nonetheless, in this book *trans** is used as the primary term to refer to the transgender and trans* student community on campus. However, the other contributors to this volume may indicate and explain their decision to use a different primary term or descriptor.

Moving forward with terms and definitions, a solid understanding of the terms *sex*, *gender identity*, and *gender expression* is needed when discussing trans* communities. Sex does not neatly fit into two discrete categories. The

Intersex Society of North America (2008) described *intersex* as "a general term used for a variety of conditions in which a person is born with reproductive or sexual anatomy that doesn't seem to fit the typical definitions of female or male" (para. 1). The Intersex Society clarified that being intersex may become known at birth or later in life with the development of intersex anatomy or other secondary sex characteristics. The purpose of defining sex as beyond female and male and including intersex is to demonstrate how the binaries of male and female and man and woman are inherently flawed because they are based on a binary sex classification system, which ignores the variety of biology represented among human beings.

According to the Center for Gender Sanity (CGS, 2009), assigned sex at birth can be interpreted as male, intersex, or female. Assigned sex at birth is about an individual's anatomy, chromosomes, and hormones and is typically externally defined by others because doctors make a sex designation based on the genitalia they see immediately after a child is born. Working in LGBTQ centers, many trans* students have told us they prefer the use of *assigned sex at birth* over *sex* or *biological sex* to emphasize that the sex designation forced on them at birth does not agree with their gender identity when they are older. According to the CGS, gender identity involves a psychological and internal sense of self and refers to being a man, genderqueer, bigender, or woman. Although gender identity is internal, the expression of gender is external and outwardly communicates gender as masculine, androgynous, and feminine (CGS, 2009). Gender expression is most understood through gendered behaviors and socially accepted or normative gender roles. Generally, the predominant expectation is for females and males to match their socially expected gender identity, expression, and roles. For example, the socially expected gender identity and expression for a person assigned female at birth is for her to identify as a woman and act feminine or at least express herself in feminine ways. Femininity may include wearing makeup, high heels, dresses, and skirts, and acting in ways stereotypically attributed to women. This may not be accurate or real for many people assigned female at birth. Similarly, social expectations and stereotypes of masculinity may not be accurate or real for people assigned male at birth. A fluidity and redefinition of gender identity and expression needs to become part of students' experiences on campus, but this is difficult to achieve when campuses promote and reinforce expected sex and gender binaries. Some examples of where colleges and universities may reinforce social expectations and gender as solely a function of women's and men's spaces include restrooms, locker rooms, athletic teams, sororities and fraternities, demographic questions on campus surveys and questionnaires, and housing. Changes to the ways *gender* is viewed and defined on campus is a must, and for this book we start the process of encouraging and promoting some long overdue changes in HRL. A student affairs functional area focused on providing students with a sense of security and a place to call home while on campus, HRL has historically been one of trans* students' main barriers to fully accessing their institution.

CAMPUS CLIMATE

Existing scholarship in higher education on transgender students, although rare, largely focuses on trans* students' perceptions of campus climate (Brown, Clarke, Gortmaker, & Robinson-Keilig, 2004; Rankin, 2005). Based on climate studies that group transgender students with LGB students (Brown et al., 2004), trans* students are more likely to have negative perceptions of a campus community. According to Rankin (2005), LGB and trans* students negatively experience the campus climate through discriminatory comments, messages, and physical violence. In some cases, higher education administrators respond to these experiences by establishing sexuality and gender diversity resource centers, creating support groups, developing ally trainings, and offering additional institutional changes such as providing gender-inclusive bathrooms and residence halls (Rankin, 2005). However, as Rankin (2005) noted, even with these and other initiatives lesbian, gay, bisexual, and transgender students may still perceive a negative campus climate. Administrators should regularly ask themselves questions such as the following:

 ♦ What is the climate and culture like on your campus?
 ♦ In what ways do you, personally, or your institution formally measure campus climate for LGBTQ students, faculty, and staff?
 ♦ What actions, steps, and measures have been taken on your campus to improve the campus climate and culture for the LGBTQ community? How is the effectiveness of these actions being assessed?
 ♦ Is climate measured specifically for trans* students, faculty, and staff, separately from LGB individuals? How is your institution responding to this information? How is that response being assessed?

In a legal perspective related to serving trans* students, Pomerantz (2009) stated, "The fear and uncertainty surrounding the transgender experience result in part from limited public exposure to individuals in the transgender community" (p. 1216). What aspects of a campus environment communicate to trans* students that the campus is a safe and secure place to be an out trans* student? Unfortunately, it is likely that the symbols, signals, and spaces that communicate a trans*-inclusive campus environment are minimal. A campus environment is often a reflection of the surrounding community or greater society (Kane, 2013; Rankin, 2005; Sanlo, Rankin, & Schoenberg, 2002). Thus, the prejudices, stereotypes, and biases toward trans* communities off campus can be readily found on campus. For example, Lombardi, Wilchins, Priesing, and Malouf (2002) studied gender violence in society and found that because trans* people "are seen as breaking gender norms in a major way, they are most likely to experience extreme sanctions for it, such as violence and discrimination" (p. 100). In their study, Lombardi and colleagues (2002) found that trans* youths "have a greater likelihood of experiencing violence than older people" (p. 98), and violence (e.g., physical, sexual, and verbal) frequently leads to unemployment, homelessness, and "secondary victimization—experiencing other forms of victimization" (p. 99). Trans* students on campus are not protected or sheltered from society's gender violence or the consequences found in Lombardi and colleagues' study. Therefore, institutions should ensure that trans* students have access to additional resources and support by providing trans*-inclusive services on campus to respond to these additional societal consequences faced by these students.

In exploring services available to trans* students, McKinney (2005) found that trans* students felt there were gaps in transgender-specific programming and resources on campus to address their identities and concerns. Specifically, participants in McKinney's study cited concerns related to identifying knowledgeable health-care professionals, student groups that support only trans* (not LGBTQ) students, and campuswide programming that encourages education and discussion related to LGBTQ topics. Similarly, Beemyn (2005) also noted that "health center staff are . . . often not sensitive to or knowledgeable about the medical needs of transgender students" (p. 78), and counseling centers on campus rarely have counselors trained in understanding the specific needs of trans* students. These gaps in services and resources to trans* students communicate noninclusive campus environment messages. Where will our trans* students find health care, psychological services, or housing if they cannot find them on campus? What actions are institutions taking to ensure that trans* students are able to access competent resources similar to those of our cisgender students?

Fortunately, many colleges and universities are offering more services and resources to trans* students by identifying and supporting LGBTQ-specialized psychologists; trans*-specific student groups; and, on some campuses, academic LGBTQ studies programs (Beemyn, 2005; Kane, 2013; McKinney, 2005). Although this is happening on some campuses, there is still much to be learned about trans* students' experiences of campus climates in higher education and much to be done to ensure all campuses offer some level of specific support to these students.

GENDER VIOLENCE

In addition to the perceptions of negative campus climate experiences, the transgender community also faces a great deal of gender violence off campus as well. This type of gender violence needs to be reemphasized to ensure that educators fully understand the importance of supporting trans* students who face a myriad of barriers, challenges, and safety concerns, on campus and off, simply for being who they are. In recent years, more organizations have started to collect data and information on the dangers faced by trans* people in the United States to inform the greater public of the many ways trans* people experience marginalization in society. Nonprofit organizations produce annual reports and maintain online databases to track the violence faced by trans* people as part of their work to achieve the greater goal of ending the marginalization that trans* people experience (Grant et al., 2011; Herman, Haas, & Rodgers, 2014; National Coalition of Anti-Violence Programs [NCAVP], 2014). These documents present a harsh climate for transgender people in our country and present a clear answer to the question of who suffers when higher education institutions do not work to intentionally and specifically welcome, support, and include trans* students in all aspects of university life.

In 2010 the National Coalition for Transgender Equality and the National LGBTQ Task Force (formerly the National Gay and Lesbian Task Force) conducted the largest and most comprehensive study of trans* people in the United States. These two organizations worked together to collect information about the lives of transgender people through the National Transgender Discrimination Survey, which was repeated in the summer of 2015, but results had not been released at the time of this.

The lead researchers compiled a report from the 2010 survey data that depicts the harsh realities transgender people face in their daily lives and

throughout their lifespans (Grant et al., 2011). This report highlighted significant disparities faced by trans* people in employment, income, education, housing, health care, and public accommodation. A reader could stop
after the report's executive summary and get a strong understanding of the
discrimination, exclusion, and violence faced by transgender people in the
United States.

One of the most staggering statistics in this report is that "41% of respondents reported attempting suicide compared to 1.6% of the general population" (Grant et al., 2011, p. 2). The overrepresentation of transgender people
attempting suicide shows a clear outcome resulting from the marginalization
trans* people are facing in almost every part of their lives. Following the
release of this report and the attempted suicide statistic, the American Foundation for Suicide Prevention and the Williams Institute further analyzed the
results of the National Transgender Discrimination Survey to better understand the prevalence of suicide attempts among transgender people (Herman
et al., 2014). Through further investigation, these scholars found that suicide
attempts were more prevalent at intersections of transgender identities and
other factors, including youth status, lower educational attainment, lower
economic status, level of outness, HIV-positive status, and lack of acceptance
by family (Herman et al., 2014).

Although the two previous reports focus on discrimination and the
resulting challenges for trans* people, the NCAVP specifically focuses on
and reports the hate-related violence faced by LGBTQ people annually. In
its latest report, the NCAVP (2014) places trans* people first in the list of
the most affected communities. The NCAVP reported that trans* women,
trans* people of color, and trans* people with HIV experience more violence than their cisgender, White, and HIV-negative peers (NCAVP, 2014).

Although this information is not limited to college students and is not
put in the context of higher education, it is important to remember the
ways trans* students are facing the same challenges, barriers, and dangers
reported in the previously mentioned documents. Before trans* students
come to our campus, they face many challenges in their homes, schools,
jobs, and other parts of their lives. Additionally, when transgender students
come to our campuses they face these challenges in the classroom, on campus, and in their lives outside the institution. Our campuses are not immune
to the interpersonal, systemic, and societal marginalization that those reports
help us to understand. We must also remember that trans* students will
be facing these barriers when they leave our universities. Considering this,
HRL professionals have a unique opportunity to create a living environment

that might be safer and more positive and inclusive than trans* students will experience in other times of their lives.

HOUSING OPTIONS

For campuses with residential facilities, the safety, security, and comfort offered by an inclusive on-campus housing option cannot be overemphasized for transgender and trans* or LGB students. HRL plays a critical role in students' success and livelihood while they are in college. The primary role and responsibility of HRL is to provide students with a safe living environment that can reasonably feel like home while living on campus. A secondary role and concern of HRL is the promotion of curricular and cocurricular programs to support students' academic interests. However, for trans* students, finding a physically and psychologically safe place to live is not always possible. Some questions considered by us and the chapter contributors include the following:

- How are HRL professionals understanding transgender student identities and experiences?
- What options exist for trans*-inclusive housing on campus?
- What happens when transgender students have no on-campus living options?
- How can trans* students pursue their academic interests when basic housing needs cannot be met?

These questions position administrators, practitioners, and educators in HRL units as key players in meeting the needs of trans* students on campus.

Much is at stake for transgender students when it comes to identifying physically and psychologically safe living conditions. Beemyn (2005) noted the importance of creating transgender-inclusive housing options but also discussed the complexities of creating trans* housing options given the politicized nature of trans* identities and experiences. For example, Beemyn (2005) cited Wesleyan University's efforts to offer a "gender-neutral hallway" (p. 80), but "school administrators disbanded the hallway [after] they were concerned about segregating the students" (p. 80). The University of North Carolina's (UNC's) board of governors blocked a trans* housing option for the Chapel Hill campus (Owens, 2013). The trans*-inclusive housing option was approved by Chapel Hill's board of trustees but ultimately rejected by the board of governors (Owens, 2013). Also complicating services to trans* students (and faculty and staff) on North Carolina campuses is the state law challenging the existence of all-gender bathrooms. This type of legislation and governing from UNC's board of governors demonstrates persistent trans* exclusion in higher education and society. The exclusion of transgender services, policies, and practices is pervasive.

Tilsley (2010) wrote about Amanda Stevens, a trans* woman at the State University of New York at Albany, who recalled her experiences with on-campus housing in "special accommodations in the dormitories" (para. 7). Amanda stated, "Eventually, I had to out myself" and "It was kind of embarrassing" (para. 3). Amanda's situation illustrates how trans* students often are required to disclose their identity (referred to as *coming out*) to university professionals to be able to apply for trans*-inclusive housing. In many cases, like Amanda's, a trans* student may first be required to come out to receive any notice of acquiring adequate accommodations. HRL administrators need to consider the following questions:

♦ How many times must a trans* student come out to receive an inclusive, affirming housing assignment?
♦ Will the students be made aware of anyone else in the department who is aware of their housing request, and how will the department maintain the students' confidentiality if they have not come out to certain people in their lives, such as their family, and they are worried about those people knowing they are trans*?
♦ What will happen from one year to the next? Will Amanda and other trans* students in similar situations have to repeatedly apply and reveal their trans* identities again each year?

We think it is important for HRL professionals to consider the ways that this process might be extremely stressful for a trans* student. When approaching every new person to whom they have to come out in their journey to inclusive housing, trans* students face the stress and worry that comes with not knowing if the next person will be transphobic and add to the discrimination they face in other areas of their life. Also, if HRL departments are not aware of this issue and have not created a process for this situation, trans* students are often faced with the stress of educating others on their experience, and these others often find subtle or overt ways to invalidate or question trans* identities and experiences. If there is a preliminary application and request process that requires students to disclose their identity to receive appropriate housing, the foregoing questions and factors should be considered.

Even if an HRL department is supportive and creates trans* housing options, the type of housing option may still be a problem. As suggested in the example of Wesleyan University (Beemyn, 2005), establishing a hallway or floor of a residence hall to be trans* inclusive may be a solution, but what are the risks of isolating trans* and LGB students in one location on campus? Does one designated hallway send the message that the campus is trans* friendly? Or, does a separate hallway reveal trans* or LGB students and isolate them from the rest of the campus population? According to Beemyn, Domingue, Pettitt, and Smith (2005), an advanced level of serving trans* students would be to provide "gender-neutral bathrooms and private showers in existing and newly constructed residence halls" and "establish a LGBT and Allies living-learning program" (p. 91). This creates a housing option that is open to any student interested in using gender-inclusive bathrooms and showers. The result of this option is a space not only designated for trans* and LGB students but also where trans* students are included as part of the community.

In yet another option, Beemyn (2005) suggests that transgender students' needs can be addressed on a case-by-case basis, which has two benefits. First, given the physical configuration of residence halls, dedicating a hallway or floor to trans*- and LGB-themed housing may not be an option. Second, trans* students may not want to live in trans*-designated spaces if they desire to pass or appear cisgender (Beemyn, 2005). The complexity of offering trans* housing options illustrates the important role the functional area of HRL plays for trans* students' livelihood, sense of safety, and sense of belonging on campus. Without suitable living arrangements on campus, how are colleges and universities actually demonstrating their support for the academic success and well-being of trans* students?

SENSE OF BELONGING

Strayhorn (2012) described perception of *social support on campus* as "a feeling or sensation of connectedness, the experience of mattering or feeling cared about, accepted, respected, valued by, and important to the group (e.g. campus community) or others on campus (e.g. faculty, peers)" (p. 3). Hurtado and Carter (1997) referred to *sense of belonging* as a psychological dimension that relates to underlying feelings and assumptions of being part of a campus environment or community. The development of the literature on sense of belonging in higher education largely concerns that of marginalized student populations. For instance, Hurtado and Carter studied the experiences of Latino students, and Strayhorn (2012) explored the experiences of African American students. For trans* students, sense of belonging is frequently integrated into LGB students' experiences. As already noted, trans* students are more likely to have negative perceptions of climate and feel less belonging as compared to their cisgender and LGB peers (Brown et al., 2004; Rankin, 2005). This is a clear indication that more attention needs to be paid to trans* students' experiences and campus policies such as HRL trans*-inclusive housing options.

Baumeister and Leary (1995) reviewed literature on belonging and concluded that the need to belong requires positive interpersonal interactions and sustained stability of relationships with peers. They stated, "The perception of the bond is essential for satisfying the need to belong" (p. 500). Although Baumeister and Leary referred to the relationships individuals have with one another, their suggested criteria for belonging can be easily translated into social settings, such as campus environments. Ostrove and Long (2007) suggested that "social structures inform who belongs and who does not in any given context" (p. 364). As social structures, college and university campuses communicate messages regarding learning objectives, institutional priorities, and future aspirations. Many of these messages reveal how campuses relate and respond to diversity and inclusion. For example, nondiscrimination policies frequently include sexual orientation and, at times, gender identity or expression. The existence of a nondiscrimation policy is a great way of protecting LGB and trans* students, faculty, and staff on campus, but how nondiscrimation policies are implemented or practiced may drastically differ from the intent of the policy. In any case, a nondiscrimination policy is a symbolic gesture of inclusion and can relate to notions of belonging for the trans* campus community.

However, there are also symbols, practices, and policies on college and university campuses that signal exclusion and a lack of stablity for trans* students, such as not offering gender-inclusive bathrooms, locker rooms, or housing options. What messages are sent to trans* campus communities when there is a lack of trans*-inclusive options on campus? How do these messages set trans* communities apart from the greater campus environment? By not offering some form of trans*-inclusive environments on campus, it is easy to imagine that members of the trans* community will have negative campus climate perceptions.

CONCLUSION

Throughout this introduction we review a number of concepts to set the context for the chapters to follow in which colleagues from a variety of institutions share their experiences of shifting the culture of their HRL departments to be more inclusive of trans* students. Taking the expanded view of gender described earlier, these professionals seek to create housing options that lead trans* students to perceive a more positive campus climate and sense of belonging at their institutions. Given the information and statistics presented earlier, we cannot overemphasize the importance of making intentional change on multiple levels of an institution to create more inclusive, welcoming environments for trans* students.

In addition to a dedication to inclusive environments, HRL department staff should consider their legal obligations to accommodate trans* students. The Civil Rights Division of the U.S. Department of Justice and the Office for Civil Rights of the U.S. Department of Education's Dear Colleague Letter focuses on the protections for trans* students under Title IX of the Education Amendments of 1972 (Lhamon & Gupta, 2016). The letter includes a section that states specific expectations for HRL departments and their obligations in including trans* students. HRL administrators should consider how their campuses will comply with the expectations set by this letter under Title IX.

HRL professionals are uniquely situated in their institutions to have a great impact on trans* students, and we encourage them to use this book as a tool to create change on their campuses. We hope the questions we pose, the experiences related in the following chapters, and the recommendations throughout this book will prompt readers to find concrete strategies to lead change on their campuses. We assert that the inclusion of trans* students is not a possibility to choose out of goodwill but is, instead, a necessity for higher education professionals to immediately address to ensure that this growing student population on campus is able to access opportunities in the institution and succeed in the same way their cisgender peers are able to. As Beemyn and colleagues (2005) stated,

> If college administrators are to continue to meet the changing needs of students, they must develop procedures that recognize diverse gender identities and expressions. This professional obligation is also a legal requirement at institutions where state or municipal laws or college politics ban discriminating against their gender identity or expression. (p. 52)

Whether through legal obligation, a desire to ensure equitable access to the institution for all students, or both, HRL professionals can be an essential, positive contributor to the success of trans* students on campus.

Finally, although much of this chapter discusses the challenges facing transgender people and trans* students and affecting their experiences on campus, we do not want readers to perceive trans* people solely as victims on campus and in society. Trans* people are rich contributors to our classrooms, campuses, and society. Trans* students are leaders and are leading great change at our institutions and in our nation, and higher education has the ability to encourage the success of trans* people through ensuring our institutions are as inclusive as possible for this vibrant community.

REFERENCES

Baumeister, R. F., & Leary, M. R. (1995). The need to belong: Desire for interpersonal attachments as a fundamental human motivation. *Psychological Bulletin, 117*, 497–529. doi:10.1037/0033-2909.117.3.497

Beemyn, B., Curtis, B., Davis, M., & Tubbs, N. J. (2005). Transgender issues on college campuses. *New Directions for Student Services*, 111, 49–60. doi:10.1002/ss.173

Beemyn, B. G. (2005). Making campuses more inclusive of transgender students. *Journal of Gay & Lesbian Issues In Education, 3*, 77–87.

Beemyn, B. G., Domingue, A., Pettitt, J., & Smith, T. (2005). Suggested steps to make campuses more trans-inclusive. *Journal of Gay & Lesbian Issues in Education, 3*, 89–94.

Beemyn, G., & Rankin, S. (2011). *The lives of transgender people*. New York, NY: Columbia University Press.

Bilodeau, B. (2005). Beyond the gender binary: A case study of two transgender students at a Midwestern research university. *Journal of Gay & Lesbian Issues in Education, 3*, 29–44.

Brown, R. D., Clarke, B., Gortmaker, V., & Robinson-Keilig, R. (2004). Assessing the campus climate for gay, lesbian, bisexual, and transgender (GLBT) students using a multiple perspectives approach. *Journal of College Student Development, 45*, 8–26.

Center for Gender Sanity. (2009). *Diagram of sex and gender*. Retrieved from http://www.gendersanity.com/diagram.html

Chapman, D. W., & Pascarella, E. T. (1983). Predictors of academic and social integration of college students. *Research in Higher Education, 19*, 295–322.

Dugan, J. P., Kusel, M. L., & Simounet, D. M. (2012). Transgender college students: An exploratory study of perceptions, engagement, and educational outcomes. *Journal of College Student Development, 53*, 719–736.

Gabriel. (2014). *The trans asterisk and why we need to stop using it.* Retrieved from www.thepulpzine.com/the-trans-asterisk-and-why-we-need-to-stop-using-it

Grant, J. M., Mottet, L., Tanis, J. E., Harrison, J., Herman, J., & Keisling, M. (2011). *Injustice at every turn: A report of the national transgender discrimination survey.* Washington, DC: National Center for Transgender Equality and National Gay and Lesbian Task Force. Retrieved from www.thetaskforce.org/static_html/downloads/reports/reports/ntds_full.pdf

Harro, B. (2010). The cycle of socialization. In M. Adams, W. J. Blumenfeld, C. Castañeda, H. W. Hackman, M. L. Peters, & X. Zúñiga (Eds.), *Readings for diversity and social justice* (2nd ed., pp. 45–51). New York, NY: Routledge.

Herman, J. L., Haas, A. P., & Rodgers, P. L. (2014). *Suicide attempts among transgender and gender non-conforming adults.* Retrieved from queeramnesty.ch/docs/AFSP-Williams-Suicide-Report-Final.pdf

Hurtado, S., & Carter, D. F. (1997). Effects of college transition and perceptions of the campus racial climate on Latino college students' sense of belonging. *Sociology of Education, 70*, 324–345. doi:10.2307/2673270

Intersex Society of North America. (2008). *What is intersex?* Retrieved from www.isna.org/faq/what_is_intersex

Jardine, F. M. (2013). Inclusive information for trans* persons. *Public Library Quarterly, 32*, 240–262. doi:10.1080/01616846.2013.818856

Kane, M. D. (2013). Finding "safe" campuses: Predicting the presence of LGBT student groups at North Carolina colleges and universities. *Journal of Homosexuality, 60*(6), 828–852.

Killerman, S. (2015). What does the asterisk in "trans*" stand for? Retrieved from itspronouncedmetrosexual.com/2012/05/what-does-the-asterisk-in-trans-stand-for

Lhamon, C. E., & Gupta, V. (2016). *Dear Colleague Letter on transgender students.* Washington, DC: U.S. Department of Education, U.S. Department of Justice.

Lombardi, E. L., Wilchins, R. A., Priesing, D., & Malouf, D. (2002). Gender violence: Transgender experiences with violence and discrimination. *Journal of Homosexuality, 42*(1), 89–101. doi:10.1300/J082v42n01_05

McKinney, J. S. (2005). On the margins: A study of the experiences of transgender college students. *Journal of Gay & Lesbian Issues in Education, 3*, 63–75.

National Center for Transgender Equity. (2016). *Understanding transgender people: The basics.* Retrieved from http://www.transequality.org/issues/resources/understanding-transgender-people-the-basics

National Coalition of Anti-Violence Programs. (2014). *Lesbian, gay, bisexual, transgender, queer, and HIV-affected hate violence in 2013*. New York, NY: Author.

Ostrove, J. M., & Long, S. M. (2007). Social class and belonging: Implications for college adjustment. *Review of Higher Education, 30*, 363–389.

Owens, C. (2013, August 9). UNC board bans "gender-neutral" housing on campuses. *News & Observer*. Retrieved from www.newsobserver.com/2013/08/09/3095006/unc-board-bans-gender-neutral.html

Pascarella, E., & Blimling, G. S. (1996). Students' out-of-class experiences and their influence on learning and cognitive development: A literature review. *Journal of College Student Development, 37*, 149–162.

Pomerantz, L. E. (2009). Winning the housing lottery: Changing university housing policies for transgender students. *University of Pennsylvania Journal of Constitutional Law, 12*, 1215–1255.

Rankin, S. R. (2005). Campus climates for sexual minorities. *New Directions for Student Services, 111*, 17–23.

Sanlo, R. L., Rankin, S., & Schoenberg, R. (2002). *Our place on campus: Lesbian, gay, bisexual, transgender services and programs in higher education*. Westport, CT: Greenwood Press.

Strayhorn, T. L. (2012). *College students' sense of belonging: A key to educational success for all students*. New York, NY: Routledge.

Tilsley, A. (2010, June 27). New policies accommodate transgender students. *Chronicle of Higher Education*. Retrieved from chronicle.com/article/Colleges-Rewrite-Rules-to/66046

Tompkins, A. (2014). Asterisk. *Transgender Studies Quarterly, 1*, 26–27.

Part One

Initiatives Through Student Organizing and Activism

1

Walking the Talk

Gender-Inclusive Housing at Roosevelt University

Bridget Le Loup Collier, Ellen O'Brien, Jennifer Tani, Bob Brophy,
Brenden Paradies, and Brandon Rohlwing

THE GENDER AND DIVERSITY Inclusion Learning Community at
Roosevelt University (Roosevelt) was initially created to help trans*
students experience a greater sense of belonging in the on-campus
community. According to a report by Rankin, Weber, Blumenfeld, and
Frazer (2010), about 39% of transgender and gender-nonconforming students, faculty, staff, and administrators have experienced harassment on
campus—a rate that is significantly higher than the 20% experienced by
their cisgender lesbian, gay, and bisexual counterparts. The focus of this
chapter is the deliberate and philosophical process that Roosevelt undertook
to create a partnership among students, faculty, staff, and university leadership to create a gender-inclusive housing option in residence life.

The chapter begins with an introduction of the contributors and their
roles in creating a gender-inclusive housing option at Roosevelt. Roosevelt's
campus environment is described and culture of residence life examined
through a student's narrative. The majority of the chapter outlines the process of developing the gender-inclusive housing policy at Roosevelt, followed
by recommendations for practice and closing remarks. Appendix 1A provides an abbreviated time line for developing and implementing Roosevelt's
gender-inclusive housing policy.

The contributors to this chapter were instrumental in bringing about the changes in the housing policy and the development of the gender and diversity inclusion community at Roosevelt. Bridget Le Loup Collier and Ellen O'Brien provided the oversight and leadership for the transformational changes that took place related to gender-inclusive policies in residence life.

Jennifer Tani was an active member of the task force, initially named the Gender Neutral Housing Task Force and later renamed the Gender Inclusive Housing Task Force, and helped conduct research on other universities' policies. Bob Brophy advised the task force on the future possibilities of implementing a gender-inclusive housing option at the University Center of Chicago (UCC). Brenden Paradies was a student leader who continuously advocated for gender-inclusive housing policies and brought the topic to the forefront of discussion with university leadership. His personal story is told in this chapter and highlights the need to support all students in the university community. Brandon Rohlwing, the first resident assistant on the gender and diversity inclusion floor of Roosevelt's Wabash Building, provided insight on how to prepare students and the community to ensure the safety and inclusion of students who choose a gender-inclusive space.

CAMPUS ENVIRONMENT

It is important for residence life practitioners to understand the history of the institution and the housing and residence life program where policies are being evaluated to create effective cultural and structural changes. Roosevelt's mission maintains a social justice orientation, which is a central tenet that guides policies and practices. Roosevelt's founding in 1945 as an independent, private, coeducational institution of higher learning was a feat requiring considerable courage. The university was born in a dispute between the board of trustees of Chicago's Central Young Men's Christian Association (YMCA) College and its president Edward J. Sparling over equality of opportunity and academic freedom. In 1945 the board of the Central YMCA College mandated quotas to be placed on the admission of minority students, not an uncommon practice at the time. Sparling, a man of uncompromising principles, defied this mandate and was fired as a result. In a remarkable vote of confidence, 92% of the faculty and 97% of the students left the school with him. Together, they established a different kind of academic institution, one committed to equal access to higher education for all Chicago citizens.

The boldness of Roosevelt's founding and its explicit mission to promote social justice attracts and inspires Roosevelt students, faculty, and staff. It can also be a source of frustration when institutional practices fail to live up to students' expectations of their experience at a social justice university. Although the university has never had a majority of full-time residential students as it has historically served primarily adult learners, the institution has been innovative with each of its major student housing developments. In 1970 Roosevelt opened the 364-student Herman Crown Center, which was the first college residence hall located in downtown Chicago. This facility served as the main residence hall for Roosevelt until it was closed in the spring of 2008, when the costs of improving the building and bringing it up to code were untenable.

In 2004 Roosevelt formed a partnership with DePaul University and Columbia College of Chicago to build the UCC, a residence hall in the South Loop area of Chicago with 18 stories housing 1,700 students and a large conference center. The UCC is the first residence hall of its kind that provides housing for students from three different institutions. The complexity of having three different institutions with three different missions adds a unique dimension when evaluating and implementing housing and residence life policies and practices.

When the Herman Crown Center closed in 2008, Roosevelt had just reached its highest student enrollment in history with more than 7,600 students. The university administrators made the decision to demolish the residence hall and committed to building a new facility that would bring much needed classroom and other spaces to the campus. In the summer of 2012, the university opened the Wabash Building, a 32-story vertical campus, the second tallest academic building in the United States. A residence hall occupies the top half of the high rise with 611 beds, and the rest of the building houses student services and student-life facilities, classrooms, and offices.

The physical and cultural transformation of the residence life program and evolution of the university environment were part of the organizational changes that led to the development of a gender-inclusive housing policy. In 2012 the Roosevelt Office of Residence Life did not have an explicit policy that stated assignments would be made based on binary genders; however, in practice students were only assigned in that manner. The Office of Residence Life did offer limited co-ed options in Fornelli Hall, which was a third-party privately managed apartment building located six blocks north of the campus. The co-ed option was not designed for trans* students and still restricted the students to identify in a binary manner.

While physical, structural, and cultural changes were taking place at the university, trans* students who had experienced limitations in housing options because of their gender identity began to organize and call attention to the discrimination they were experiencing at a social justice institution. The students met with various members of the administration and reported a lack of understanding from faculty and staff and unsupportive policies for trans* students on campus.

BRENDEN'S STORY

Brenden Paradies is a 2014 graduate of Roosevelt and is a transman who at the time of this writing is presurgery and has participated in one year of testosterone treatment. He discussed his experiences as a trans* student and expressed feeling there was not a sense of place for him in the Roosevelt on-campus community in the following:

> My involvement with the gender neutral housing initiative really started when I was personally discriminated against at Roosevelt during an on-campus housing living experience. I was essentially kicked out of the two-bedroom female on-campus housing option I was assigned to for the summer. I was not comfortable with the living arrangement in the first place because it was a requirement for individuals to live with individuals of the same biological sex as them if they wished to stay on campus. I was unable to afford rent at the time in the Chicagoland area, and moving home with Mom and Dad was an even more undesirable option. I had no choice but to share a bedroom with a biological and female-identified roommate. Within three days, I was reported to the UCC management office and was notified that my roommates were uncomfortable living with me and felt sexualized due to my gender identity.

Brenden was an active student and well known to faculty, staff, and students. Brenden and other trans* students who shared similar experiences began to tell their stories more broadly with faculty in the women's and gender studies program and staff on campus who were viewed as allies. The storytelling led to calls to action, and students began to build connections between faculty and staff allies and key student groups such as Feminists in Action and RISE, which is a student leader group that evaluates and challenges policies on college campuses.

The student leaders organized the university's first Safe Zones workshop in April of 2012, which was attended by more than 40 faculty, staff, and students. This event generated even more support for efforts to bring the discussion on gender-inclusive housing to the forefront. As they continued their work, students began to focus their efforts on addressing the housing policy by making specific requests to members of the student affairs administration who were in decision-making roles regarding policy. The students were guided by faculty to take a learning-centered approach to their activism, which is a framework often applied at Roosevelt, particularly for students who minor in social justice studies.

In 2011 the Student Government Association passed a resolution calling on residence life to implement a gender-inclusive housing option. The resolution expressed an explicit need to confront the gap between the social justice mission of the university and the notable absence of gender justice as an expressed priority throughout the university. Although the resolution passed, administrators in residence life and student affairs did not take immediate action to address the students' request. The significant structural changes taking place at the university, particularly related to the physical and cultural transformation of the residence life program, had limited the ability of the administrators in residence life and student affairs to move the initiative forward at that particular point in time.

In April of 2012 a change in leadership in residence life brought Bridget Collier to Roosevelt as assistant vice president of residence life. Collier met with student leaders who expressed frustration that the gender-neutral housing option resolution had not been adopted. Collier then met with several members of the university's administrative leadership to understand the obstacles to making changes to the way students were assigned to housing.

Through her conversations, Collier first noticed a lack of understanding between the distinction of gender-inclusive and co-ed housing options, particularly regarding the fluidity of gender identity and the social justice mission of the institution. This lack of understanding was evident to her from the perspectives of the students as well as members of the university administrative leadership. Additionally, university leaders and members of the president's cabinet expressed concerns related to managing the media attention this type of housing option would attract. Administrative leaders cited examples of other universities that faced criticism in a public forum. Some members of the leadership were concerned about the reaction of parents and members of the board of trustees, and others posed questions related to risk management and the ability to provide nontargeted safe spaces for students on campus.

PROCESS OF DEVELOPING THE POLICY

Collier determined the need for a deeper exploration of what the students were asking. She also understood that research needed to be conducted on policies and practices at other institutions as well as an evaluation of the areas of risk that had been suggested. Collier worked with the student leaders to identify a broad group of stakeholders who would be asked to serve on what was initially called the Gender Neutral Task Force.

In the fall of 2012 a 19-member task force was formed. Membership was intentionally broad and inclusive and was composed of faculty; student development professionals; administrative leaders from areas such as admissions and community relations; members of student government; student leaders and activists; members of the university's lesbian, gay, bisexual, and transgender community; and the institution's contractual partners in housing at the UCC.

Collier charged the group to evaluate the feasibility of a gender-neutral policy that was mission driven, addressed the concerns of the administration, and was tailored specifically to the needs of the Roosevelt student population and community. The goal was to compile a report and make a recommendation to the university administrative leadership for a gender-inclusive housing option to be implemented by the fall of 2013.

The task force began with the charge from Collier but initially did not have a defined process. A participatory action research framework was used to first understand the needs of trans* students. According to Tolman and Brydon-Miller (2001), the general guidelines of participatory action research include focusing on communities and populations that have traditionally been exploited or oppressed, addressing the specific concerns of the community members and fundamental causes of oppression with the goal of achieving positive social change, and conducting research, education, and action with unique contributions from all participants and through which all participants learn and are transformed. The final process that the task force went through, described next, includes defining terminology, conducting assessment, researching best practice, writing the policy, outlining the housing assignments process, and preparing the report for the university administrative leadership.

Defining Terminology

The first focus of discussion by the task force was the determination that the term *gender neutral* did not accurately describe the needs of the students or the intent of the housing option. Members of the task force felt that using the term *neutral* took away someone's gender expression. After several meetings of discussion on the vernacular, the task force unanimously voted to change the term to *gender inclusive*. This was a defining moment of the task force as it provided clearer language that best described the intention to create an inclusive community for all students.

The discussion related to the name of the initiative also revealed that many members of the task force were not familiar with terms that are used to identify gender. This revelation led to the development of a gender-inclusive dictionary used by the members of the task force and remains a tool that is used by students, faculty, and staff in educational programs related to gender identity.

Conducting Assessment

To demonstrate community support for a gender-inclusive housing option, the task force gathered data that were included in the final report submitted to the university's administrative leadership. The annual Residence Life Educational Benchmarking survey, which is administered by Educational Benchmarking, included a question related to students' interest in and support for the housing option, and focus groups were conducted with residence hall students to gather their experiences. Additionally, a brief description of gender-inclusive housing with an option to provide feedback, ask additional questions, or express concerns was included in the parents' newsletter sent by the university.

The data that were gathered provided the task force with rich information related to the students' experiences and the level of support for this option. Eighty-three percent of the students that responded to the annual survey indicated they supported a gender-inclusive housing option on campus. Powerful narratives from students also highlighted the need for a gender-inclusive housing option such as in the following:

> As an out and proud gay man who believes that individuals should not be punished or discriminated against for their choice in who they love and how they express their love, it gives me great pleasure to support the Gender

Inclusive Housing option on campus. . . . I believe that this issue is of such great importance in our community. Gender Inclusive options may help to break down the boundaries and fears that cause this type of defacement and inconsiderate attack upon others in the community. (Roosevelt University Task Force, 2013, p. 4)

Another student commented on the relevance of creating an inclusive community at a social justice institution.

I believe Gender Inclusive Housing is a way for Roosevelt to really showcase their dedication to modernity and diversity. A lot of colleges talk about how they respect the queer community, but GIH is a real, concrete, and lasting way to demonstrate [Roosevelt's] progressive mindset (Roosevelt University Task Force, 2013, p. 4)

The survey responses, the narratives that were collected from the focus groups, and communications sent to the residence life staff were included in the final report that was provided to the university leadership.

Researching Best Practice

Another learning tool for the members of the task force was researching housing policies at other institutions. Members of the task force were assigned to investigate institutions that had embarked on this process in recent years to identify their successes and challenges. The group used a list published by the Association of College and University Housing Officers-International (2011).

The task force members presented their findings and determined that there was wide variance in the policies, including determining who could participate in gender-inclusive housing as some institutions did not allow first-year students to participate. For example, students at Purchase College must be 21 years old or have completed 36 credit hours, and the University of Chicago requires students to be in their second, third, or fourth year to participate in gender-inclusive housing. There was also wide variance in the housing assignments process. Some institutions, such as the University of Illinois at Chicago, require students to speak with a staff member before signing up for a gender-inclusive space. The differences in the application of policies at other institutions provided the opportunity for the members of the task force to consider the specific needs of the Roosevelt student body.

Writing the Policy

The knowledge the task force accumulated through the process of defining terminology, conducting assessment, and researching best practice provided the foundation for the creation of the written policy. The policy had several iterations and was revised several times. The final Roosevelt University's Gender-Inclusive Housing Policy was formally approved in January of 2013 and includes the following:

> Gender Inclusive Housing reflects Roosevelt University's social justice mission through support of our diverse student body. This community promotes ethical awareness by providing a safe and supportive environment for students of all gender identities, gender expressions, and sexual orientations.

Students interested in this housing option may include, but are not limited to, those who identify as transgender, gender nonconforming, intersex, genderqueer, and allies.

Students in this community agree that

◆ individuals have the right to identify themselves as any gender or sexual orientation and have the right to not identify, and
◆ individuals may change the way they identify their gender or sexual orientation.

All residents are expected to be active members of this community by providing support and encouragement to each other both in and outside of the residence hall environment, and by participating in continuing education surrounding gender and sexual identity (Learning and Theme Communities, 2015).

Outlining the Housing Assignments Process

The review of policies from other institutions provided the task force with an opportunity to debate and make decisions on important considerations for the assignment process that would support the policy. The task force formed a housing assignment working group that also used the gender-neutral housing list from the Association of College and University Housing Officers-International (2011) to review the assignment process at other institutions. The working group determined that the best model for Roosevelt would be to offer a gender-inclusive housing option to students

in a Gender and Diversity Inclusive Learning Community on a designated floor in the Wabash Building that is operated by the university.
This model allowed the residential life staff in the learning community to
be trained appropriately and offer tailored support to the residents. This
model also allowed a formal partnership with the women and gender studies and social justice programs to offer clustered courses for students and
to support programmatic efforts.

Roosevelt's gender-inclusive housing option is open to all students,
regardless of their year, although students under the age of 18 must provide
parental consent. The Gender and Diversity Inclusion Learning Community
provides options for trans* students, students in the process of discovering
their gender identity, gay or bisexual students, students who feel uncomfortable rooming with members of the same sex, intersex students who do not
wish to be identified by any sex, and students who feel they would be more
comfortable with a roommate of a different gender. Allies are also welcome
to live in the community. The diversity inclusion component of the floor
allows the students to examine topics of diversity that are broader than gender, such as the intersection of gender with race and ethnicity.

Students who apply for gender-inclusive housing are encouraged, but not
required, to self-select their roommate. If students are unable to identify a
roommate and would like to live in the gender-inclusive community, residence life staff will make a roommate selection during the assignment process.

Preparing the Final Report and Recommendations to University Leadership

In the spring of 2013 the task force submitted its final report and recommendations to university leaders, which included the president's cabinet and
administrative leaders in student affairs. The report contained the membership list of the task force, which demonstrated broad stakeholder support as
it demonstrated representation from students, faculty, and staff across the
institution; data from the assessment; highlights from institutional benchmarking; and the recommendation to create the Gender and Diversity Inclusion Learning Community.

The university leadership unanimously supported the implementation of a
gender-inclusive housing option, and Collier was charged with managing the
implementation. The Gender and Diversity Inclusion Learning Community
and a gender-inclusive housing option was promoted during the spring 2013
housing assignments process in the 2013–2014 school year. The community

successfully launched in the fall of 2013 and is currently one of Roosevelt's most robust residential learning communities. The intentional outreach and support provided by resident assistant Brandon Rohlwing and the support of the faculty in the gender studies program and key student affairs administrators have helped trans* students and students with varying gender identities to feel a greater sense of belonging and inclusion at the university.

RECOMMENDATIONS FOR PRACTICE

Residence life practitioners need to take into account a variety of considerations to successfully implement a gender-inclusive housing option. It is recommended for practitioners to create an inclusive process that provides opportunities for students, faculty, staff, and key stakeholders to discuss the needs of the university community and allows individual and organizational learning to take place. Components of the process should include identifying a broad and representative stakeholder group to participate in the process, conducting assessment with the community and any stakeholders, benchmarking other institutional models and policies, determining the specifics of the housing assignment process, and providing a recommendation to university leadership.

It is also recommended to establish a time line to ensure that the process moves forward and the campus community does not become mired in the discussion. The process can be used as a way to garner support from the community and to help manage the change in the on-campus housing community. The process can be viewed as part of the communication plan in the change management process.

CONCLUSION

Housing and residence life programs serve critical roles in helping students of all identities feel safe and have a sense of belonging on campus. It is imperative to consider the needs of trans* students living in campus housing and ensure that inclusive housing options are provided. Residence life practitioners are often challenged with managing change surrounding progressive housing options, and this change can be successful when practitioners understand the cultural environment of the institution and use the process as a way to garner the support of the campus community.

REFERENCES

Association of College and University Housing Officers-International. (2011). *Gender-neutral housing institutions.* Retrieved from genderinclusivehousing .wikispaces.com/file/view/Gender+Neutral+Housing+Institutions+-+ACUHO-I.pdf

Collier, B. (2013). *Roosevelt University Task Force report on gender-inclusive housing.* Unpublished manuscript.

Rankin, S., Weber, G., Blumenfeld, W. & Frazer, S. (2010). *2010 state of higher education for lesbian, gay, bisexual & transgender People.* Retrieved from Campus Pride website: www.campuspride.org/wp-content/uploads/campuspride2010lgb treportssummary.pdf

Roosevelt University. (2015). *Learning and theme communities.* Retrieved from www .roosevelt.edu/student-experience/residence-life/living-learning

Tolman, D. L., & Brydon-Miller, M. (Eds.). (2001). *From subjects to subjectivities: A handbook of interpretive and participatory methods.* New York, NY: New York University Press.

APPENDIX 1A
Time Line for Gender-Inclusive Housing Policy at Roosevelt University

Date	Process
August 2004	The University Center of Chicago opens and houses 1,700 students from the three member institutions including Roosevelt University, DePaul University, and Columbia College of Chicago.
May 2008	Herman Crown Center, Roosevelt University's main residence hall, closes because of untenable costs for improving the building.
April 2011	Student Government Association passes a resolution calling on residence life to implement a gender-inclusive housing option.
March 2012	Trans* students begin telling their stories about their experiences with residence life at Roosevelt University with faculty in the women's and gender studies program and staff on campus who were viewed as allies.
August 2012	Roosevelt University opens the Wabash Building, a 32-story vertical campus and the second tallest academic building in the United States.
April 2012	Student leaders organize Roosevelt University's first Safe Zones workshop, attended by more than 40 faculty, staff, and students.
August 2012	The Gender Neutral Task Force, which was later renamed the Gender Inclusive Task Force, forms with 19 members and the goal to compile a report and make recommendations to university administrative leadership for a gender-inclusive housing option.
October 2012	Staff conducts an assessment related to gender-inclusive housing options, including the annual Residence Life Educational Benchmarking survey conducted by Educational Benchmarking, focus groups with residence hall students, and feedback through parents' newsletter.
October 2012	Task force members research housing policies at benchmark institutions that had embarked on gender-inclusive housing policies.
January 2013	The task force submits its final report and recommendations for gender-inclusive housing to university leaders, and the implementation of a gender-inclusive housing option is unanimously supported.
March 2013	The Gender and Diversity Inclusion Learning Community and gender-inclusive housing option is promoted during the housing assignment process.
August 2013	The Gender and Diversity Inclusion Learning Community and gender-inclusive housing option formally launches.

2

Student Advocacy, Campus Consensus, and Evaluation

Introducing Trans*-Inclusive Housing Policies at George Washington University

Seth Weinshel, Andrew Sonn, Robert Snyder, Timothy Kane, Kristen Franklin, and Chantal (Champaloux) Mosellen

L OCATED FOUR BLOCKS FROM the White House, George Washington University (GW) attracts students who have a passionate interest in public service, public policy, and social justice. One such student, Michael Komo, leader of Allied in Pride, GW's lesbian, gay, bisexual, and trans* (LGBT) student organization, sought institutional support in 2009 to establish gender-neutral housing (GNH) policies and align housing options with GW's commitment to diversity and inclusion. Komo researched GNH policies, engaged stakeholders, and introduced student government legislation to implement a GNH pilot program at GW. A university-wide committee then considered the research, investigated implementation logistics, engaged members of the GW community, judged the level of institutional risk, and created recommendations approved by executive leaders to introduce a successful program.

Ultimately, the committee and GW's executive leaders agreed with a student who wrote, "As a university, GW should be [as] open as possible to fulfilling the needs of all students" (Anonymous, personal communication,

April 9, 2010) and an alumnus who stated GNH would "enhance GW's reputation as an open, welcoming campus for all students and be attractive to students in LGBT community" (Anonymous, personal communication, April 23, 2010). GW's contribution to the discussion of practices and policies to support transgender students focuses on three themes: listening to student voices throughout the decision-making process, engaging diverse stakeholders to form campus consensus, and using benchmarking to inform implementation and subsequent evaluation of the policy's effectiveness.

Each of the contributors to this chapter has a connection to GNH policy review and implementation. Robert Snyder, Andrew Sonn, and Seth Weinshel all served on the GNH Review Committee, representing the Office of the President, Division of Student Affairs, and GW housing. Timothy Kane currently directs GW's LGBT Resource Center, Kristen Franklin is associate director of GW housing, and Chantal (Champaloux) Mosellen, a graduate student in GW's higher education administration program, has researched gender-neutral housing policies.

CAMPUS ENVIRONMENT

GW's city environment, progressive campus climate, and varied housing inventory provided the context for establishing GNH. Enrolling more than 20,000 students from all 50 states and more than 130 countries, GW is the largest higher education institution in Washington, DC, and encompasses three campuses and several graduate education centers in the DC metropolitan area and Hampton Roads, Virginia (GW, 2014a, 2014f).

Located four blocks from Dupont Circle, a historically LGBT neighborhood, GW has been considered an LGBT-inclusive community for decades. This open and affirming LGBT campus environment was confirmed in 2011 when GW received a near perfect rating (4.5 out of 5 stars) as being LGBT friendly by Campus Pride (2014). GW earned this rating by providing strategic LGBT student services, programs, and activities through the GW LGBT Resource Center, established in 2008 (GW, 2014e). GW also offers an LGBT and sexuality studies minor, which offers opportunities to explore theory and applied research. Campuswide events such as National Coming Out Day, Rainbow Graduation, and LGBT community service projects are sponsored annually. Several LGBT student organizations conduct educational, political, and social programs for the GW community, and the LGBT Alumni Association builds connections among LGBT students and alumni.

The final contextual feature conducive to GNH was the variety of housing configurations that allowed GNH options to be introduced without disrupting other residents who elected to live in single-sex apartments or residence halls. The Foggy Bottom and Mount Vernon campuses provide flexibility for housing assignments and programs housing for about 7,500 students on both campuses (GW, 2014f). GW's 48 residential options range from traditional coed halls and apartment-style halls with private bathrooms, to four- to eight-person townhouses for upperclass students and independent-living high-rises (GW, 2014b).

By 2001–2002, GW had opened 10 mixed-gender Scholars' Village townhouses on the Foggy Bottom Campus, housing about 70 students. The townhouses were popular housing options for sophomores, juniors, and seniors, and were structured as living and learning communities. In 2009–2010 one of the townhouse themes, Escaping Gender, focused on providing trans* students with a gender-neutral safe and comfortable location. The townhouses were not designed as GNH options but nonetheless ended up being gender-inclusive living environments. GW's housing inventory, especially the prevalence of private bathrooms and townhouses, offered a flexible platform for GNH options.

CAMPUS POLITICS

In fall 2009 Michael Komo, along with his peers, translated the vision for GNH policies into action. Komo researched the existing 50 higher education institutions with GNH policies; met with GW students, faculty, and administrators; and secured the endorsement of GW's Residence Hall Association (M. Komo, personal communication, October 1, 2014). His hard work paid off when the GW Student Association's Senate passed a resolution recommending that GW consider implementing GNH ("Gender-Neutral Housing Coming to GW," 2010). This resolution called for GW to study GNH and introduce options for the 2011–2012 academic year. It also set in motion GW's actions to consider and make recommendations on GNH policies for GW residence halls. Appendix 2A lists the milestones for GW's GNH policy review and implementation.

GW acted on the GW Student Association's resolution by creating a university-wide GNH Review Committee of students, staff, and faculty members to examine the issue and consider stakeholder perspectives. Committee members brought varied perspectives to the group, including those of the GW Student Association, GW Residence Hall Association, president's office, housing office, chief student affairs officer's office, the GW Multicultural Student Services Center, parent services office, media relations, faculty senate, Office of the General Counsel, admissions, and development and alumni relations. The committee's membership symbolized GW's intention to study this issue from many perspectives. The committee's composition was also useful in keeping stakeholders apprised of its progress. Student representatives, especially the GW Student Association president, showed other student leaders the university was responding to the resolution. Meanwhile, staff representatives, especially those from the president's office, Office of the General Counsel, and media relations, provided informal updates to campus leaders so the final recommendations were not a surprise to them.

POLICY DEVELOPMENT

GW's 15-member Review Committee addressed its charge from GW's chief student affairs officer to explore the viability of GNH and offer recommendations on how to proceed. The policy development process had five main stages that were completed over the course of seven months. During these five stages, the committee met biweekly and participated in a series of activities that built a well-functioning team marked by a high level of trust among its participants.

The committee's first stage involved defining and educating members about the project's terms, understanding the needs of trans* students, and considering GNH logistics. Terminology on Brandeis University's (2014) website formed the foundation for how the committee defined *gender-neutral housing*. Brandeis University (2010) described GNH as "a housing option in which two or more students share a multi-occupancy bedroom, in mutual agreement, regardless of the students' sex or gender" (para. 3). At the time GW was considering changing its housing policies, the term *gender-neutral housing* was adopted because most higher education institutions in 2009–2010 used this term. Brandeis's clear description of the term proved useful when committee members discussed the project with other stakeholders.

Research continued during the second stage to gather sources on GNH policies and trans* students' needs. In 2010 the empirical research on GNH was limited. As a result, the committee distributed to its members practitioner-based articles and periodicals on GNH and trans* students (Kalawur, 2009; Lipka, 2006; Schnetzler & Conant, 2009; Schwartz,

2010). Although these sources provided anecdotal information, they also expanded the committee members' knowledge base. The articles featured trans* and LGBT students and provided insight into individuals' holistic needs and the challenges posed by their institutions and peers. These personal accounts delineated the barriers many trans* students face on a daily basis and how important GNH options were for many trans* students. During the third stage, GNH policy analysis, the committee collected and analyzed policies at other private research universities. Committee members confirmed the institutions with GNH policies and supplemented the research by discussing the policies with colleagues at other institutions. The committee found 54 institutions at the time had introduced GNH policies, including 10 of the 36 (28%) institutions listed among GW's peer and aspirational institutions. About one-quarter of the 54 institutions permitted first-year students to live in GNH (GW, 2010). The committee determined several peer institutions and many prestigious U.S. colleges and universities had already introduced GNH policies.

During the fourth stage, the committee collected input from more than 75 GW students, faculty, staff, alumni, and parents. The committee determined the campus's pulse on GNH from oral and written testimonies. Committee members also visited administrative meetings to discuss GNH terminology and gather faculty and staff members' opinions. This qualitative approach served as an informal means of information gathering from key campus constituencies.

To solicit students' viewpoints about GNH, the committee invited students to submit anonymous testimonies or meet with committee members for 5- to 10-minute semistructured interviews. Students provided opinions on the policy, which were overwhelmingly in favor of GNH and made suggestions for implementation. Of the 40 student testimonies, 38 individuals were in support of GNH. The vast majority of the testimonials were from self-identified gay males and their allies, and most testimonies focused on providing more housing options for them. At the time, there were very few GW students who identified as trans*. Therefore, few testimonies considered the needs of trans* students. The implications were that the policy transcended the concerns of trans* students to include all students' housing needs.

Common themes emerged among the students who were in favor of GNH. Students explained this policy would enhance the comfort and safety they felt in the residence halls, be inclusive of the needs of all students, and be in line with best practices nationally for LGBT-friendly institutions. Additionally, a majority of the students felt their peers, especially first-year students, were mature enough to make their own decisions regarding GNH options.

Several students produced compelling oral and written testimony. One student reflected on the role of residence halls in the collegiate experience in the following:

> It is easy to think of dorms as impersonal and utilitarian. A student's room becomes a place of sanctuary between classes, for studying, and sleeping. A major disruption in a living situation can be disruptive to all aspects of our lives. (Anonymous, personal communication, April 9, 2010)

It was evident in this testimonial that access to a safe living environment was highly valued.

Another student commented on the importance of trans* students feeling comfortable. This testimony addressed the challenges that a traditional single-sex room can present for students who identify as trans*, for example,

> Students who are gender queer should not have to go through additional barriers . . . trying to define themselves as "male" or "female" during this housing process, especially in hir own room. It is difficult enough for a gender-queer person to make these decisions in public (choosing a restroom, for example), so being able to feel comfortable in hir own room is a crucial part of hir lifestyle. (Anonymous, personal communication, April 9, 2010)

Two students were opposed to GNH based on perceived logistical challenges. One of them wrote, "The logistical problems . . . would include more housing swaps and roommate complaints every year" (Anonymous, personal communication, April 9, 2010). The other student thought that GNH "could put further stress on the housing system" (Anonymous, personal communication, April 9, 2010), referring to a possible scenario wherein heterosexual couples who choose to live together break up and need to find new accommodations. The committee members believed that students opposed to GNH masked their opposition in their statements in logistical terms to avoid appearing homophobic or transphobic.

Committee members encouraged students to share their ideas on GNH policy implementation. The majority of students recommended making gradual changes, suggesting that a pilot program should be administered before adopting GNH. The majority of students also emphasized that GNH should be offered across the housing system and not be confined to one residence hall or floor to avoid singling out GNH participants. Committee members also spoke with faculty, staff, parents, and alumni and recruited parents and alumni from existing advisory boards. Overall, these stakeholders were supportive of GNH. Each group had similar reasons for supporting GNH policies. One parent was in favor of the GNH initiative because it helped "support who they [students] are" (Anonymous, personal communication, April 16, 2010). Likewise, faculty, staff, and alumni supported GNH because of its inclusiveness and fit with GW's diverse student body.

A few disquieted parents and alumni expressed common concerns. Some parents did not think students were mature enough to make their own decisions about GNH options; another parent was concerned with "how this would play out with parents from 'Middle America'" (Anonymous, personal communication, April 16, 2010). Alumni were also concerned that GNH would present logistical challenges, upset parents, and be perceived as an overly radical policy.

As far as implementation, many of the parents, alumni, faculty, and staff questioned whether GNH was a suitable option for first-year students because they thought first-year students were not developmentally ready for this living environment. Many also thought that implementation should be kept low-key. Such an implementation was important to respond to GW's decision-making culture, which traditionally introduces major policy changes as pilots to test effectiveness and generate acceptance from stakeholders. Furthermore, the committee's work occurred relatively early in the tenure of GW's new president and provost, requiring sensitivity to make significant policy changes on a gradual basis to avoid controversy.

Identifying the committee's findings and recommendations formed the fifth and final stage. Committee members found the number of students (38) in support of GNH far exceeded those in opposition (2), and judged that the social justice stances of those in support outweighed the concerns of those opposed to the policy. GNH policies of peer institutions, as well as practitioner-based research, supported policy implementation. The profiles of the institutions with GNH policies, particularly the numerous private research universities, supported GW's decision to adopt GNH. Committee members from the housing office also confirmed that GW housing software and mainframe systems could accommodate GNH assignments. By adding a question to the online application, the housing office could easily identify students who requested GNH and assign the students to the same room or apartment.

In the end, the committee recommended that GW should offer GNH options for all student classes in all residence halls (GW, 2010). The moving testimonies of GW students swayed committee members to permit first-year students to participate in GNH. The recommendations of the committee called for GW to introduce GNH policies as a four-year pilot program for campus residence halls for the next academic year. To educate the campus on the policies, the committee recommended GNH to be defined as a way of expanding housing options for all students, and GNH assignments were to be mutual roommate requests only. To address the concern that heterosexual couples would select GNH options, the housing office's educational programs would emphasize that romantically involved individuals should not select GNH assignments.

POLICY APPROVAL AND IMPLEMENTATION

The communication of the committee's recommendations included informal and formal approaches. The informal approach involved committee members providing stakeholders with a preview of the committee's recommendations. This was an important step to understand how the recommendations would be received by these constituencies.

The committee also took a formal approach to communicating the recommendations to GW's executive leaders. This approach was managed apart from the committee by the student affairs vice president, who reported to the president and provost. Consistent with GW's decision-making structure, the president, provost, and student affairs vice president discussed the recommendations with the rest of the president's executive leadership team and also the board of trustees' Student Affairs Committee. The president's senior staff, which includes the president, the provost, and the university vice presidents, endorsed the recommendations. This was an important milestone because major policy changes are not implemented at GW without seeking and receiving collective approval from the executive leaders.

Once the executive leadership authorized the recommendations, GW followed communications procedures. The Division of External Relations published a GNH story in *GW Today*, the university's official online news source, which served as an official statement on the committee's recommendations and next steps ("Expanding Housing Options," 2010). The story was used to respond to media inquiries, in addition to being a resource for students and others interested in GNH. This concluded the committee's work: The story recapped the committee's efforts and informed the university community about GW's GNH policy.

In spring 2010 during the housing assignment process for the 2011–2012 academic year, students and parents received information about GNH options, and information was posted on the housing website. GW (2014c) provided GNH information with the housing selection information and created a website titled "GNH Frequently Asked Questions" to answer student and parent questions about the policy.

GW introduced GNH as a multiyear pilot program to evaluate and adjust GNH to best meet GW students' changing needs. If the policy proved to be unsuccessful, it would also be possible to end the program at any time during this period. Beginning with the 2015–2016 academic year, the program moved from pilot status to a permanent program and policy.

IMPACT ON TRANS* STUDENTS

Based on survey and anecdotal data, GW's GNH participants have been primarily heterosexual and have had positive experiences. Trans* students have also had positive reactions to GNH (Anonymous, personal communication, February 3, 2014; George Washington University, 2014g), although the number of GNH participants from the GW community has been low. Based on conversations with housing staff members, most GW trans* students prefer single rooms for a variety of reasons, for example, they have not identified themselves as trans* to their peers, or they are more comfortable in a single room with a private bathroom (Anonymous, personal communication, July 23, 2013; Anonymous, personal communication, February 24, 2014).

Since its inception, GW's GNH program has grown from about 50 to 60 initial participants to about 150 participants, representing about 2% of the on-campus population. In the 2013–2014 academic year, there were 168 participants, making the pilot program successful. For the 2015–2016 academic year, GNH was formally in place as a housing policy.

In responses to the annual surveys, GNH residents shared their reasons for choosing the housing options and reflected on their experiences. About one-quarter of the students who participated in GNH during the 2013–2014 academic year based their decision on wanting to feel comfortable with their roommates based on their sex, gender, or sexual orientation. To illustrate, one student stated,

> It is important for me to have the option to live with someone of the opposite sex. As a gay man, I often find it easier to be comfortable around women.

> Being randomly assigned to live with another man could . . . leave me in a situation where I am living with someone who is uncomfortable with my sexual orientation, which . . . creates an unsafe living environment. (Anonymous, personal communication, December 1, 2013)

Many LGBT students also reported that living in a GNH environment creates a safer living environment than being paired with a random roommate (George Washington University, 2014g).

Additionally, GW (2014d) has a website that identifies staff members who have participated in an LGBT Safe Zone training session to answer GNH questions. In response, many students have contacted these staff members, stating that this helps them feel supported and that they find comfort in staff who are trained to create a positive housing experience.

GNH participants have also offered suggestions for improvement, including providing better education about the program; many students felt that GNH options were not well publicized. In addition, students living in gender-neutral rooms have said that they have been asked inappropriate questions about their sexual orientation by students and staff unaware of GNH policies, possibly because of the high number of heterosexual students who participate in GNH. Students would also like to have an option to be assigned roommates also interested in a gender-neutral room, as many students feel the program is inaccessible for first-year or transfer students who have not identified roommates.

FUTURE RECOMMENDATIONS

Reflecting on GW's review and implementation of the GNH policy from 2010 to the present, we have the following recommendations for other institutions:

- Prioritize students above all constituents by giving them an important role and voice in the process of policy formation.
- Educate committee members and key stakeholders early on in the discussion regarding GNH key concepts and terminology.
- Promote trust among committee members through best practices of creating safe spaces for discussing new or sensitive topics related to GNH.
- Involve diverse key stakeholders throughout the process, including students, parents, alumni, faculty, and staff members.

+ Use data and empirical research to support decision-making.
+ Adapt benchmarking data and content to your campus culture to create a GNH policy that is best for your institution.
+ Secure support of executive leaders, including senior administration and members of the board of trustees.
+ Evaluate the program on an annual basis.

GW's GNH committee members spoke with more than 70 individuals representing diverse key stakeholders and carefully reviewed their testimonials during the GNH policy review. Biweekly committee meetings encouraged a collaborative approach while laying the foundation for securing support of senior administration and the board of trustees. Review of the committee's recommendations by these executive leaders occurred apart from the committee and was balanced with considerations of institutional culture and needs. Providing information about the context for the recommendations was an essential element of this stage of GNH policy review.

Although there were few, if any, empirical studies available at the time we conducted the review, practitioner-based articles were useful in educating members of the committee on baseline topics such as gender-based definitions and trans* students' experiences. Today, there are many more peer-reviewed sources to use in policy review and implementation. In addition, trends of peer and aspirant institutions were very important considerations, especially because these institutions had similar Carnegie Classifications as private research universities and were among the universities prospective GW students often apply for admission. Ultimately, GW crafted a GNH policy most appropriate to our campus culture.

Finally, we have surveyed GW's GNH program participants on an annual basis to determine the success of the GNH pilot policy and to introduce tweaks to the program. Survey results have helped the housing office administer GNH and have led GW to continue to offer GNH.

CONCLUSION

The following comment by an alumnus sums up why the committee recommended that GW implement GNH: "GNH is in the spirit of human dignity and raises the comfort level of all students" (Anonymous, personal communication, April 23, 2010). This statement encapsulates the rationale behind trans* housing policies in supporting academic achievement for all students, especially trans* students, that is rooted in individuals being comfortable in their living environments so that they can succeed in all collegiate endeavors. At GW this effort was started by a student who wanted to change the world, supported by a university that wanted to do what it determined to be the right thing, occurred within a context that was receptive to the policy, and used an approach that respected the university's decision-making process. These are all important lessons for other institutions contemplating trans* housing policies, in that such policies need to be considered in the context of the institution's culture and with respect to how decisions are typically made and how change occurs in higher education.

REFERENCES

Brandeis University. (2010). *Gender neutral housing.* Retrieved from web.archive.org/web/20100130081353/http://www.brandeis.edu/studentaffairs/dcl/roomselection/genderneutral.html

Brandeis University. (2014). *Gender neutral housing.* Retrieved from www.brandeis.edu/studentaffairs/dcl/roomselection/genderneutral.html

Campus Pride. (2014). *LGBT-friendly campus search.* Retrieved from www.campusprideindex.org/search/index

Expanding housing options. (2010). *GW Today.* Retrieved from gwtoday.gwu.edu/expanding-housing-options

Gender-neutral housing coming to GW. (2010, December 3). Retrieved from news.gwradio.com/2010/12/03/gender-neutral-housing-coming-to-gw

George Washington University. (2010). *Expanding GW students' choices and increasing housing assignment flexibility: Gender neutral housing summary document.* Washington, DC: Author.

George Washington University. (2014a). *About.* Retrieved from www.gwu.edu/about

George Washington University. (2014b). *Campus life.* Retrieved from www.gwu.edu/campus-life

George Washington University. (2014c). *Gender neutral housing FAQs.* Retrieved from living.gwu.edu/gender-neutral-housing

George Washington University. (2014d). *Housing resources.* Retrieved from living.gwu.edu/housing-resources

George Washington University. (2014e). *LGBTQIA Resource Center.* Retrieved from mssc.gwu.edu/lgbtqia-resource-center

George Washington University. (2014f). *Our location*. Retrieved from www.gwu
.edu/our-location

George Washington University. (2014g). *2013–2014 gender neutral housing survey*.
Washington, DC: Author.

Kalawur, Y. (2009, December 10). University considers "gender-neutral" housing. *CNN*. Retrieved from www.cnn.com/2009/LIVING/12/10/columbia.coed
.dorms/index.html

Lipka, S. (2006, September 29). "Advocate" guide profiles 100 best colleges for gay
students. *Chronicle of Higher Education*. Retrieved from chronicle.com/article/
Advocate-Guide-Profiles-100/11618

Schnetzler, G. W., & Conant, G. K. (2009, October 11). Changing genders, changing policies. *Chronicle of Higher Education*. Retrieved from chronicle.com/article/
Changing-Genders-Changing/48733

Schwartz, J. (2010, April 16). Finding a gay-friendly campus. *New York Times*.
Retrieved from www.nytimes.com/2010/04/18/education/edlife/18guidance-t
.html?pagewanted=all

APPENDIX 2A
Gender-Neutral Housing Milestones

Date	Process
2008–2009	Escaping Gender living and learning community is established.
January 2010	Allied in Pride introduces proposal to Student Association Student Life Committee. Committee passes proposal 7 to 1. Bill passes Student Association Senate 19 to 11. Student Association president signs bill.
January–February 2010	GW forms GNH Review Committee.
February–April 2010	Committee meets biweekly and researches GNH policies and best practices.
April–May 2010	Committee gathers testimonials from campus constituents.
May–September 2010	Committee analyzes testimonials and other institutions' policies, writes report, and presents findings to student affairs leadership.
September–November 2010	Report findings and recommendations are provided to senior leadership.
December 2010	GNH policy is announced as a housing option for the 2011–2012 academic year.

3

Beyond Coeducation

The Politics and Representation of Gender

Adrian Bautista, Rebecca Mosely, and Maura Sternberg

According to the U.S. Census Bureau (2015),

> Colleges and universities with both male and female students are the norm today. But in 1833, only a few women went to college and the idea of coed classes was a social innovation. On this date that year, Oberlin College in Ohio opened its doors to both sexes.

In December 1833, 29 men and 15 women began classes as the first students at the Oberlin Collegiate Institute. Although Oberlin was coeducational from its founding in 1833, the college regularly admitted African American students beginning in 1835. According to Baumann (2010),

> Filled with utopian enthusiasm and encouraged by passionate liberators like eastern merchant-philanthropists Arthur and Lewis Tappan, Oberlinians took seriously their covenant to improve the human condition, and they proceeded to implement their visionary principles of race and gender equality in education during the middle and latter decades of the nineteenth century. (p. 6)

Simply put, Oberlin was and continues to be a college and a cause, committed to creating an inclusive and culturally diverse campus community.

Oberlin has continued to evolve and construct learning environments that reflect the demands and needs of its undergraduates. Informed by new approaches to address pluralism in Oberlin's student community, efforts continue for the college's administrators to be informed by the intersections of identities, frequently on the intersection of racial and sexual identification (Baumann, 2010). Campus Pride, a nationally recognized organization dedicated to making campuses friendlier to lesbian, gay, bisexual, and transgender (LGBT) students, ranked Oberlin in its top 25 institutions for LGBT students, specifically citing its annual speaker series, My Name Is My Own: Queering the Intersections of Race, Gender, Class, and Sexuality, which provides institutional support to Oberlin communities "that identify as queer and of color" (Pires, 2014). This inclusive and intersectional perspective informs the residential experience at Oberlin.

The purpose of this chapter is to present the history of gender-inclusive housing practices and policies at Oberlin, intertwined with Oberlin's commitment to diversity and social justice. We discuss distinctive gender-inclusive housing options offered by the college's Office of Residential Education and suggestions for advocating for gender-inclusive practices or policies in a campus setting. A brief time line outlining the major policy changes in residential education related to gender inclusivity is presented in Appendix 3A.

We are two Oberlin College administrators and a recent graduate of Oberlin. Adrian Bautista is assistant vice president of student life and senior associate dean for strategic initiatives. Rebecca Mosely is director of the office of equity, diversity, and inclusion, and Title IX and ADA coordinator. Maura Sternberg is a 2014 graduate of Oberlin with a degree in dance and comparative American studies.

HISTORY OF INCLUSIVITY

In 1833 evangelical enthusiasm generated a collegiate model for the joint education of men and women in the rough country of Ohio. The Oberlin way of educating men and women (and soon thereafter, Black students in addition to Whites) provided a source of inspiration and support for educators introducing or struggling with coeducation at a variety of secular institutions. Admitting women was a bigger step than the founders fully understood because evangelical leaders intended no more than to better prepare men and women for duties in life. But without precedents for joint collegiate instruction, the faculty and administrators developed patterns that made plain the inherent paradoxes of Oberlin's nineteenth-century coeducation (Solomon, 1987). For example, early Oberlin has frequently been faulted for its manual labor system, with its clear sexual division of labor with women who generally did the sewing, laundry, and prepared and served meals (Ginzberg, 1987).

Yet, what made the Oberlin experiment interesting was the tendency for men at Oberlin to assume women's standards for their own behavior. In 1835 moral reform societies were formed in Oberlin, with the first male society to become an auxiliary to a national female organization. Abolitionist, suffragist, and Oberlin student Lucy Stone noted that male students participated in "female" work (Ginzberg, 1987, p. 71).

Ultimately, Oberlin students pursued the development of a community in which men and women were held accountable to a single standard of traditional Christian values while still promoting traditional gender roles and women remaining in the domestic sphere. By 1841 Oberlin conferred bachelor's degrees to three of the women who first enrolled, marking Oberlin as the first institution in the United States to grant bachelor's degrees to women. Oberlin's coeducation model spread in the 1840s, 1850s, and the early 1860s to colleges such as Grinnell in Iowa, Knox in Illinois, and Antioch College and Wilberforce, a historically Black university, both in Ohio.

The influence at Wilberforce serves as a reminder that evangelical Oberlinians also disagreed with the basic premise of nineteenth-century colonizationists. Thus, on the grounds of Christian obligation and opposition to slavery's economics, Black students were admitted "even when few black students cried out for admittance" (Baumann, 2010, p. 26). Free from difficult petitioning processes, Black college students in the South transferred to Oberlin. Recognized for its liberal racial policies, empowering Black abolitionists alongside White abolitionists, Black Americans in slavery-era United States came to Oberlin "in search of identity, self-betterment, and self-emancipation through education as well as a safe place to live" (Baumann, p. 28). In the post–Civil War period, Black graduates of Oberlin provided leadership at schools for freed men and women. According to Solomon (1987), "Oberlin black women like Mary Jane Patterson, Fanny Jackson Coppin, and Anna Julia Cooper transmitted this heritage to the black high-school students they prepared for college attendance" (p. 84).

COEDUCATIONAL REVOLUTION?

Oberlin's decision to create coed living and 24-hour visiting privileges was made famous by an article in *Life* magazine that featured two Oberlin students, one male and one female, on the magazine cover (Thorsen, 1970). The two students lived in the same dorm and maintained a close personal relationship. Although the concept of coed residence halls might seem like an obvious fit for an institution that was the first to award degrees to women, the change was radical considering that until the late 1960s, women at Oberlin College and at campuses across the country had to abide by curfews. In the nineteenth century, interaction among Oberlin's men and women was limited to classes and eating at the same tables. In the 1930s a "drastic change" (Thorsen, 1970, para. 2) occurred when men and women could sit next to each other in the chapel. During this time, college officials strategically choreographed students' living and social arrangements. Women's housing units were located exclusively on the south end of campus, and men's housing units were on the north side.

Unfortunately, racially segregated college housing also existed in the female student community. Mary Church Terrell, one of the first African American women in the United States to obtain a bachelor's degree (1884), documented the quality of life for Black students at Oberlin and the developing Jim Crowism in dining halls and a growing number of Black-only rooming houses on campus (Baumann, 2010). In Terrell's era, Black female students were petitioning for the right to reside in college boarding houses or cottages "because they wanted to share in an environment in which the intimacies and informalities of family life prevailed" (Baumann, 2010, p. 108). As the 1920s arrived, such concerns became prominent on campus, and racially segregated dormitories presented something of a crisis in race relations as many students questioned Oberlin's commitment to racial equality.

The sociopolitical environment of the 1960s, reflecting an antiestablishment cultural phenomenon, was very active in response to the civil rights movement and Vietnam War protests. This brought a new wave of student discontent in response to the in loco parentis community model that called on faculty and staff to serve as parents to students. By 1968 Oberlin's faculty yielded their bylaw to govern student life, and college officials adopted an open dorm policy permitting visitation at men's and women's residences by any member of the opposite sex, anytime throughout the day (Baumann, 2010). A year later students and administrators agreed to create several coeducational residence halls. The spirit of the era also led to a reevaluation of Oberlin's legacy of racial tolerance, and in 1968 the college's first iteration of the Afrikan Heritage House was created on campus. Support for other program houses followed, and today residential education offers options in nine language or cultural heritage program houses, which is unique to a small number of liberal arts colleges.

BEYOND COEDUCATIONAL RESIDENCE HALLS

Throughout the remainder of this chapter, we focus on the latest gender-inclusive practices such as voting on the gender designation of bathrooms, adopting the use of preferred pronouns, initiating all-gender housing policies, and working with themed living-learning communities that were developed from gender inclusion. Each of these practices, policies, and programs has helped Oberlin to continue its legacy and goals toward creating a more inclusive, diverse, and social justice–oriented campus community.

Unfortunately, there is not a lot of information about when some of the practices discussed later in this chapter began at Oberlin. Some of the changes may have occurred in an organic way, which means as students wanted to see a change, they just made it happen. This method often happens at Oberlin and leaves administrators to later discover that what the students were doing was in the end a good idea. Thus, administrators subsequently supported students' initiatives by continuing the process or idea in a more structured way. As policies and procedures are discussed, when possible time frames are included in the development of each policy or procedure.

All-Gender Bathrooms

At the beginning of each semester, a unique and long-standing practice at Oberlin is the process of voting on the gender designation of residence hall bathrooms. This practice has been in place since at least the 1990s but was not formalized as a policy until 2011. The policy was made formal when Trans* Advocacy Group, a registered student organization, approached Rebecca Mosely as an administrator of residential education to put a policy in place. Prior to the formal policy, there was no standard for how bathrooms would be labeled or assigned in the residence halls. There were also no standards for how voting should occur, how to discuss concerns related to bathroom designations in different types of buildings, or the role of the student staff member in the process. So although student staff members led these discussions, the lack of consistency or clarity made many of the discussions contentious and at times left students and staff members feeling unheard and unsupported. In 2011 administrators and students were able to formalize a process in which all students' voices were heard, and students could have bathrooms that met their needs when they arrived on campus.

Currently, the formalized policy ensures that each residence hall will take votes from residents at the beginning of each semester to determine the gender assignment of each bathroom. Residential education staff quickly realized that to ensure that resident advisers (RAs) were capable of leading the discussions concerning bathroom voting, RAs needed more training regarding gender diversity. Thus, a training program cosponsored by Oberlin's Multicultural Resource Center staff is now offered. During training each fall semester, all residential education staff members and RAs attend a session titled Trans* Ally, which educates residential education staff and RAs on the importance of bathroom spaces and the bathroom vote. The training educates students on the current bathroom policy, gives them an opportunity to practice leading the conversation, and provides a basic understanding on why this policy is important to students. Even after this training, some students may not feel prepared to lead the conversations by themselves. Therefore, if a student is unprepared to lead the conversation, other student staff members or members of the Multicultural Resource Center staff offer assistance.

At the end of the voting process, all students in the building must have a bathroom where they feel comfortable. For many of the residence halls on campus, there are minimal issues with this practice, but when concerns arise, they are mostly related to the proximity of a bathroom. However, in some of the smaller buildings, more issues concern number of bathrooms available. This makes meeting all students' needs nearly impossible, but the students at Oberlin were able to devise a system called the E System in which the letter E is placed on a sign outside the bathroom door. If the sign is an E, everyone can use the bathroom. However, if the E is turned clockwise to face down, it becomes an M, meaning only men can use the room. If the E is turned counterclockwise, facing up, it becomes a W and only women can use the space. Finally, if the E is turned backward, it means that an individual is using the bathroom and prefers to use the space alone. This type of creative problem-solving illustrates the ingenuity of Oberlin students and an ongoing focus on inclusion.

In practice, the policy and procedures regarding bathroom voting work, but there are still concerns from people whose religious, cultural, or personal practices make them feel uncomfortable using bathrooms with someone of a different gender. Although some concerns have prompted residential education to make accommodations when appropriate, residential education has noted relatively few concerns. Additionally, the number of students who now feel comfortable in bathrooms at Oberlin is significantly higher.

I Like My Gender This Way, Please

Another way Oberlin builds inclusivity and challenges binaries is by encouraging sharing of preferred gender pronouns (PGPs) as often as possible. For example, meetings of all types—student organizations, administration, faculty—generally start by having those present give their names and their PGPs. This represents an attempt to recognize the oppression that can occur when people are not recognized in the way they identify themselves. Members of the Oberlin community can name and define their own truths and identities by sharing their PGPs with others. For Maura, when asked for PGPs, the response is, "My name is Maura Sternberg, I am a fourth-year student majoring in dance and comparative American studies, and I like she, her, and hers." The phrase "I like she, her, and hers," is how Maura communicates to others her PGPs.

Asking for gender pronouns prevents people from wrongly assuming someone's gender. Some additional gender pronoun responses may be *he, him, his*; *they, them, theirs*; *ze, zir, zirs*; and "I don't identify with gender pronouns," among many others. In this way, asking for pronouns also gives individuals the freedom to identify themselves outside the gender binary. In society people are socialized to feel confusion, anxiety, discomfort, and sometimes hatred when faces with people who present themselves in non-gender-conforming ways. Asking for gender pronouns helps us at Oberlin to respect the nonbinary genders that society frequently deems unreadable and thus invisible.

Residential education staff ask students to self-identify their gender in their own words on the housing application form. Rather than placing preset options such as *man, woman,* and *other* as choices, residential education asks students to use their own words to write how they identify their gender. The hope is that this practice does not reinforce gender norms. Prior to making this change on the form, housing decisions were based on sex rather than gender. The preset options were limiting and did not allow students to fully identify their gender. This sometimes led to problems when a cisgender student was placed with a trans* student unknowingly because there was no way to know that the two students did not identify with the same gender or to know that either one of them would be uncomfortable living with a person who identified as a different gender.

To prevent problems in the housing placement process, residential education now also asks students if they are willing to live with someone who identifies with a gender different from their identified gender. In general, first-year students are housed with people who identify with their same gender, as the vast majority of students still specify man or woman as their gender. However, if students list something other than their assigned gender on the form, it allows residential education to work proactively to find roommate pairings that will make both roommates comfortable. Residential education is thus able to provide students of any gender with the opportunity to have a roommate in their first year of college and not just place those students who are transitioning or who do not identify as cisgender into single rooms.

All-Gender Housing

Another way that Oberlin is able to provide flexibility and inclusivity to students of all genders is through all-gender housing. According to Hansen (2006), "In 2004, the College designated Noah [Hall] as what was then called a 'gender-neutral' dorm, meaning that students were able to choose their roommates regardless of their sex. 'All-gender' has since replaced 'gender-neutral' as a more accurate term" (para. 3). After two years of a single all-gender residence hall, students came to administrators in residential education to ask if all-gender housing could be expanded to other parts of campus. This expansion happened through consultation with students who were involved in a housing policies committee in fall 2006, and all-gender housing increased to four wings in residence halls located throughout campus. Finally, in fall 2007, all-gender housing was expanded to include any space in all residence halls.

One issue that is frequently addressed by administrators is whether there was an increase in student concerns about living near mixed-gender rooms. It is not completely clear what concerns people might envision students living near mixed-gender rooms might have, but in the years since all-gender housing was started on campus, concerns from students regardless of room type most commonly involve roommate disagreements. In addition, roommate disagreements for those in all-gender rooms have mirrored the roommate issues of students in single-gender rooms. Residential education staff members have also found that students who live in these spaces are less likely to have roommate issues because they almost always request to live with each other and are there-fore less likely to be placed with a person they do not know and with whom they do not get along. In Rebecca's 10 years of working at Oberlin, she can recall only two conflicts in mixed-gender housing spaces. One conflict was the result of parents who were unaware that their student was living with someone of a different gender and demanded an immediate change, and the other was the result of the relationship between the roommates that ended.

Another issue fielded by Oberlin administrators is how unmarried couples are allowed to live together. This is a presumptuous question because it fails to realize that not all romantic relationships are heterosexual. In fact, this may be one of the weakest arguments because it favors same-sex couples being able to live together while not allowing couples that are not the same sex to do the same. Whatever the reason that people choose to live together, college adminis-trators need to recognize that undergraduates are adults who should be allowed to make their own decisions regarding their living arrangements.

The main ongoing obstacle residential education staff members have to overcome with all-gender housing is often a result of parents' confusion or concern. Rebecca Mosely has been working at the college since the beginning of all-gender housing and has spoken with several parents who were concerned about these policies, but she has never known of a single student who voiced these concerns to any staff member of residential education. Many times, par-ents do not understand why gender-inclusive policies exist and are concerned for the needs of their child. Although this is understandable, residential educa-tion staff members have found that in most circumstances the concerns of the parents are not reflective of the student. Residential education staff members encourage students to be up front and honest with their parents about their plans if they are choosing to live with someone of a different gender, but this does not always happen. If there are issues regarding parents and all-gender housing, residential education staff members work with the students and par-ents to come to some sort of solution to the problem.

Baldwin Cottage

Although Oberlin has worked creatively to provide flexibility and inclusivity in all the housing spaces on campus, it is also important to note that these policies only go so far to address gender issues. With this in mind, Oberlin officials have also worked to address gender inclusion by creating and sustain-ing two residential communities whose missions involve gender inclusivity. The first of these is Baldwin Cottage, the women's and trans* collective on campus. Baldwin was established to work against patriarchal social structures. Maura Sternberg was randomly placed in Baldwin Cottage her first year at Oberlin and found that even though Baldwin houses cisgender women and trans* folks of any sexuality, countless incorrect stereotypes circulated about Baldwin, including the notions that only lesbians live there, only queer people live there, only women and transwomen can live there, no cisgender men are allowed inside, and everyone in Baldwin hates men. These stereotypes are indicative of the discomfort and confusion about spaces that aim to support oppressed communities. In these situations, it is clear that Oberlin's commitment to inclusivity is still a struggle, a work in progress, and a series of imperfect attempted solutions to ease students' experiences.

The majority of the first-year students placed in Baldwin the year Maura lived there happened to be heterosexual cisgender women, most of whom experienced some transition issues and culture shock entering Baldwin's space, which included becoming aware of intersectional approaches to feminism to include more identities than those of White cisgender men and women. Even though Baldwin served the trans* community, during Maura's first year in Baldwin, on all official documents it was referred to as the women's collective.

Through discussions among Baldwin's residents and the RAs, one of whom was Maura, Baldwin staff and its residents made it clear to residential education that the women's collective marker was inadequate. Historically, trans* issues are swept to the margins of feminist movements; the people in Baldwin wanted to shift that pattern. Baldwin's RAs looked through official documents and websites and alerted residential education when the women's collective misnomer was listed so that it could be changed. Throughout this process, Baldwin became officially the Women and Trans* Collective. Residential education responded quickly to these requests with no argument or burdensome bureaucracy. Residential education's flexibility in this instance was and is crucial in developing trans*-inclusive spaces.

Edmonia Lewis Center for Women & Transgender People: Activist-Themed Living

In March 2014 students working with the Edmonia Lewis Center (ELC) for Women & Transgender People planned a series of events to commemorate the one-year anniversary of Oberlin's Day of Solidarity, organized in response to persisting hate-related incidents during the 2013–2014 academic year (Weinstein, 2014). Classes were canceled on March 4, 2013, and various student groups, faculty, and staff coordinated a collective demonstration of solidarity, including musical performances by campus groups, speeches by campus leaders, and a community convocation titled We Stand Together (Ly, 2013). The events highlighted the efforts of student activists working from a unique, hybrid residential and administrative space, known more frequently as the ELC.

A student-led collective that works to transform existing systems of oppression across sex, gender, race, and sexuality, the ELC is named after sculptor Mary Edmonia Lewis, a Black female student who arrived at Oberlin in 1859 and was accused in 1862 of poisoning two White female students. Charged by local authorities, Lewis was later forced to leave Oberlin without graduating. Although the ELC board is made up of students, it is a hybrid administrative and residential unit, not funded like a student organization but like any student life office through divisional resources.

Founded in 1997 as the Women's Resource Center, it was located in the downstairs section of a college-owned house, with the second floor closed for zoning reasons by the city of Oberlin. A series of events in 2001, particularly a string of vandalism incidents resulting from a decision to change an all-male residence hall to a coed facility, as well as increased board membership from LGBT and queer communities of color, sparked a movement to transform the center in 2002 into the ELC. In recognition of the ELC's important work on campus, which included student-facilitated Trans 101 trainings, for-credit student-taught course offerings, and cocurricular activities such as the Indigenous Women's Speaker Series, the ELC was relocated to its present dual-purpose facility in 2005.

The two-story duplex that houses the ELC is an interesting hybrid, with one side serving as the administrative unit run nearly exclusively by a student board. The adjacent unit is a four-bed residential facility that is designated as a safe space for women and trans* students of color. The student ELC board members coordinate the application and selection process with support from residential education professional staff. The ELC's cocurricular offerings and the center's accompanying partnerships with academic departments like comparative American studies and gender, sexuality, and feminist studies; administrative offices such as the Multicultural Resource Center; and numerous student organizations demonstrate inextricable ties between Oberlin's culture of diversity and social justice and gender sensitivity.

The ELC's shift from a women's center that served primarily White students to a trans* students of color activist space reveals the importance of flexibility and creativity by the residential education office as additional, intersecting identities expand a limiting gender binary to a gender spectrum to a gender continuum. The ELC represents a living example of intersectionality as trans* activist students of color use a hybrid residential space to illuminate and counter the various forms or systems of oppression. The ELC also represents Oberlin's evolving and progressive support and direction for intersectionality in extending learning beyond the classroom. This complicated approach reflects the way feminists can explore how gender, race, class, and sexuality are represented in relation to ethnicity, nationality, politics, and other categories of human experience.

FUTURE GOALS

As one can see from what we have presented here, Oberlin College is fortunate to have a student body that is forward thinking and solution oriented. Although the staff members in residential education are happy to know that Oberlin College has made major strides in making housing spaces more gender inclusive, there is still much work to be done. There are many on campus and in the broader community who do not recognize the normative nature of gender in society. Oberlin College administrators need to continue to do work with students, faculty, and staff to help all community members become capable of creating a wholly gender-inclusive community. Although students and staff are making strong efforts toward this in our residential spaces, the same is not always true in classes or classroom buildings. By educating all Oberlin College community members, college administrators may be better able to serve all our students.

Students often refer to Oberlin as living in a bubble, and the outside world is less understanding of and celebratory about diversity of all kinds but most specifically regarding gender. Through educating the Oberlin community about various gender identities, students may begin to create a change in the world outside Oberlin. Oberlin's staff and students hope that one day no person will feel excluded because of that individual's gender identity.

REFERENCES

Baumann, R. (2010). *Constructing Black education at Oberlin College: A documentary history*. Athens: Ohio University Press.

Ginzberg, L. D. (1987). The "joint education of the sexes": Oberlin's original vision. In C. Lasser (Ed.), *Educating men and women together: Coeducation in a changing world* (pp. 67–80). Urbana: University of Illinois Press.

Hansen, J. (2006, May 26). All gender housing expands: Students push for all-gender dorms. *Oberlin Review*. Retrieved from www.oberlin.edu/stupub/ocreview/2006/05/26/news/article1.html

Ly, L. (2013, March 5). Oberlin College cancels classes to address racial incidents. *CNN*. Retrieved from www.cnn.com/2013/03/04/us/ohio-oberlin-hate-incidents

Pires, R. (2014, February 19). The 25 best colleges and universities for LGBT students. *Buzzfeed*. Retrieved from www.buzzfeed.com/clairepires/the-25-best-colleges-and-universities-for-lgbt-students

Solomon, B. M. (1987). The Oberlin model and its impact on other colleges. In C. Lasser (Ed.), *Educating men and women together: Coeducation in a changing world* (pp. 81–90). Urbana: University of Illinois Press.

Thorsen, K. (1970, November 20). Co-ed dorms: An intimate campus revolution. *Life*. Retrieved from www2.oberlin.edu/175/didyouknow-coed.html

U.S. Census Bureau. (2015). *U.S. Census Bureau daily feature for December 3: First coed college*. Retrieved from www.prnewswire.com/news-releases/us-census-bureau-daily-feature-for-december-3-first-coed-college-300367991.html

Weinstein, R. (2014, March 9). One year later, campus commemorates March 4. *Oberlin Review*. Retrieved from oberlinreview.org/5117/news/one-year-later-campus-commemorates-march-4

APPENDIX 3A
Time Line of Gender Inclusivity at Oberlin

Date	Process
1834	Oberlin becomes the first institution to have a female seminary as part of a college.
1837	Oberlin becomes the first college to admit women to a collegiate course of study in classes with men.
1841	Oberlin becomes the first college to graduate women from a coeducational college.
1969	Oberlin first allows coeducational residence halls with 24-hour visitation for different genders.
1990s	Oberlin students vote on the gender designations of bathrooms allowing single-gender or gender-neutral bathrooms. (This voting process may have occurred earlier, but no official record can be found of this happening.)
1997	The Women's Resource Center is founded.
2002	The Women's Resource Center changes its mission to support women and lesbian, gay, bisexual, transgender, and queer communities and is renamed the Edmonia Lewis Center.
2004	Oberlin creates the first gender-neutral residence hall on campus.
2007	All residence halls at Oberlin become all-gender buildings with the exception of a few remaining all-female spaces.
2008	Oberlin removes predefined gender options from the housing registration form in favor of a write-in spot to allow students to self-define gender. This allows students to word their gender identity their way.
2011	The Women's Collective votes to become the Women's and Trans* Collective.
2011	A formal policy regarding bathroom voting is created.

4

Gender-Inclusive Housing Inside and Outside an LGBTQ Residential Living Community

James C. Smith and Nancy Jean Tubbs

IN 2005 THE UNIVERSITY of California, Riverside, (UCR) became the first public university in the nation to offer a gender-inclusive housing option to all students. All housing applicants, including students entering their first year at UCR, could select a gender-inclusive housing living option in Pentland Hills or placement in Stonewall Hall, a new lesbian, gay, bisexual, trans, intersex, queer, questioning, and allies (LGBTIQQA) intentional living community, which also featured gender-inclusive housing. Like other theme communities (e.g., Honors Hall, Pan-African Theme Hall), Stonewall Hall includes intentional programming and education. The gender-inclusive housing option simply allows any student to live with any other student. It does not have any special programming.

In this chapter, Nancy Jean Tubbs, director of the UCR LGBT Resource Center since 2000, provides background on the extent of trans inclusion at UCR prior to the proposal for Stonewall Hall and gender-inclusive housing as well as the research and development required to launch the new living options. James C. Smith, associate director for residential life, provides details on staff responsibilities related to gender-inclusive housing and explores community issues in the residence hall. Both of us reflect on how gender-inclusive housing has affected prospective and current trans students at UCR and discuss the continuing challenges for trans inclusion in housing. Please see Appendix 4B for a time line for creating gender-inclusive housing at UCR.

Although the original proposal for Stonewall Hall uses *LGBTIQQA*, our current campus staff usually use *LGBTQ* as an umbrella term and *trans* to refer to diverse gender identities including transgender, genderqueer, non-binary, intersex, and so on. Therefore we use LGBTQ or trans throughout this chapter. In addition, our campus has changed terminology from *gender-neutral housing* to *gender-inclusive housing*.

CONTEXT PRIOR TO 2004

When I (Nancy Jean Tubbs) arrived at UCR in January 2000 as director of the LGBT Resource Center, I brought with me a basic understanding of gender identity and expression from my previous institution. This informed the content of the first educational projects I introduced at UCR, from a Transgender 101 educational handout to inclusion of gender identity issues in a new allies training program. In addition, the University of California LGBT Association, the systemwide group for LGBT students, staff, faculty, and alumni, was going through a period of education regarding the intersex community and voted to change the association's name to include intersex people in 2002.

However, trans students at UCR were not visibly connecting with the LGBT Resource Center in my first few years as the center's director; no students were sharing trans identities in one-on-one interactions, in Tuesday Talks (a staff-facilitated discussion group), or on speakers' bureau student panels. Trans students' experiences and needs remained theoretical. In February 2003, UCR hosted the University of California Lesbian Gay Bisexual Transgender Intersex Association Conference and General Assembly during which more than 700 students and other guests visited our campus for three days. During the conference, a University of California, Santa Barbara student asked where the gender-neutral restrooms were located because a fellow Santa Barbara student did not feel safe using the gendered multistall restrooms on our campus. For the first time in my professional life, the specific needs of a trans student stood in front of me in reality and not just in theory.

The following academic year, the center hired two new half-time professional program coordinators who were both trans-identified. The center also welcomed a new trans-identified graduate student. For the first time during

my UCR tenure, students accessing the LGBT Resource Center were interacting with *out* trans people. In addition, the program coordinators launched
new trans-focused projects such as the Trans Remembrance Display and the
Trans Allies program. Many students began to embrace a genderqueer self-
identity and learned to use gender-neutral pronouns such as *ze* and *hir*. At
our annual LGBT student leadership winter retreat, also known as Snow
Camp, students challenged each other and staff to expand our understanding of gender identity and expression in new ways. Conversations about
men's experiences and women's experiences broke out of a binary framework.
Rather than caucusing on how society defined their gender, students created
space around self-identities that were more fluid. Awareness of trans issues
and lives were at an all-time high on our campus.

Thus, in March 2004 when Students for the Equality of Queers (SEQs)
submitted a proposal to housing services at UCR for a new LGBTIQQA
theme hall, the students who wrote the proposal presented the need for
gender-neutral roommate pairing and an application form allowing students
to select nontraditional gender identities. My own perception is that the
students proposing the new theme hall, including gender-neutral roommate
pairings, expected housing services to resist the idea. Instead, Andy Plum-
ley, assistant vice chancellor for housing, dining, and residential services,
requested a working group to spend the summer researching the proposal to
create an implementation plan.

2004–2005: RESEARCH AND DEVELOPMENT

The working group included myself, LGBT Resource Center program coordinator Eric Peterson, full-time professional staff residence life leadership
coordinator Mary Tregoning, three student members of SEQs who had
cowritten the original LGBTIQQA theme hall proposal (Clare Gmur, Bryon
Nuttall, and Donovan Jones), and summer graduate intern for housing and
LGBT concerns Chad Wilson.

Over the course of the summer, this working group gathered information at UCR, at the University of California system level, and from similar
campuses across the United States. We contacted members of the Consortium of Higher Education LGBT Resource Professionals to learn about
campus housing policies regarding gender identity and expression, as well
as the wisdom of other campuses offering LGBTQ theme halls or housing
accommodations for trans students. We researched pertinent UC policies

and verified our campus has the authority to create new housing options without seeking approval from the Office of the President. In addition, UCR already offered several intentional living communities, including the Honors Hall and Pan-African Theme Hall. Creating a new LGBTQ theme hall to enhance the educational and community-building experiences for a particular student population would build on current UCR practice.

We researched state laws such as the California Fair Employment and Housing Act (2003), which prohibits discrimination based on gender identity or gender expression, and also learned California does not have any anti-cohabitation laws that would prevent men and women from living together. We took an inventory of the building facilities for on-campus residential life at UCR, after other campuses shared that one of their biggest challenges to establishing gender-inclusive housing was the lack of available facilities with private restrooms and showers.

The UCR residence hall Pentland Hills not only offered single-occupancy restrooms and showers but also used a floor plan of three suites of four double-occupancy rooms. This floor plan proved practical as we began to address the relationship between gender-inclusive housing and an LGBTQ theme hall. We could designate a building of 48 beds to be gender-inclusive housing, and Stonewall Hall (also gender-inclusive) could expand or contract to fill one, two, or more suites if demand were high enough. Yet if less than 48 students requested gender-inclusive housing or Stonewall Hall, housing services staff could fill a suite of eight beds with all men or all women who indicated on their housing application that they were open to living in gender-inclusive housing but had not identified mixed-gender roommates. Housing services staff did not apply gender-inclusive housing roommate selection but rather matched students with roommates using other criteria and then moved them into the same building as the gender-inclusive housing suites.

As we made progress over the summer, working group members agreed the most interesting and needed task ahead was the implementation of a gender-neutral housing option (later named *gender-inclusive housing*). As we researched other theme halls in the University of California system and beyond, we were struck by how many did not allow trans students to be placed in a room based on their gender identity rather than their legal sex. The *T* in the LGBT theme halls seemed to represent a naming norm rather than indicate a truly trans-inclusive living community.

We were determined to make sure the needs of trans students were met by the new housing option, including the housing application process. The online UCR housing application asked students to provide their gender, rather than accessing data from the student information system (containing information from the UC admissions application). This allowed us to recommend new ways of requesting gender information during the application process.

By the end of summer 2004, the working group submitted recommendations to the assistant vice chancellor for housing, dining, and residential services on how the original student proposal for an LGBTQ theme hall that was also trans inclusive could be implemented successfully at UCR. The recommendations included the following:

1. A UCR Housing Policy on Gender Identity and Expression (see Appendix 4A) that was largely modeled on language used by Ohio State University (OSU, 2014) was proposed.
2. UCR housing services should offer two new living options on campus: Stonewall Hall and gender-inclusive housing.
3. Stonewall Hall should use gender-inclusive housing, but students could live outside Stonewall Hall and still select gender-inclusive housing.
4. Both living options should be located in Pentland Hills to take advantage of the flexible suites and the private restrooms and showers. Each Pentland Hills suite includes four double-occupancy rooms, two private showers, and two private restrooms. A Pentland Hills building could expand or shrink its Stonewall Hall and gender-inclusive housing living options in groups of eight residents.
5. Staffing for Stonewall Hall should echo that of other intentional living communities, including a resident adviser (RA), program coordinator, and hall mentor.
6. Some Stonewall Hall programs should be open to all on-campus residents to educate all residents regarding sexual orientation and gender identity.
7. The online UCR housing application should allow students to select M, F, or Other with an open text box, allowing students to state a different gender identity.
8. The online UCR housing application should include a link to the UCR Housing Policy on Gender Identity and Expression.
9. The online UCR housing application would allow students to indicate whether they required gender-inclusive housing because of their gender identity or expression, if they and their roommate requested

the gender-inclusive housing option, if they and their roommate were open to gender-inclusive housing, or if an individual was open to gender-inclusive housing placement but had not yet identified a roommate.

10. A housing professional staff person should be responsible for roommate matching for gender-inclusive housing placement, including interviews if necessary to gather information on residents' preferences.

11. UCR housing services should provide required training for housing staff at all levels prior to the launch of marketing and implementation of Stonewall Hall and gender-inclusive housing.

The actual implementation of Stonewall Hall and gender-inclusive housing closely followed these recommendations. In December 2004, housing services considered the kinds of questions that its staff, other campus community members, and off-campus people such as parents and media representatives might ask. The information presented next helped frame the new housing options for campus stakeholders and the public and were integrated into housing services staff training to increase staff understanding and comfort levels when talking about the new housing options.

The general questions included the following:

♦ What are the differences between Stonewall Hall and gender-inclusive housing? Stonewall Hall is a residential living option that brings together the LGBTQ community. Like other theme communities (e.g., Honors Hall, Pan-African Theme Hall), it includes intentional programming and education. The gender-inclusive housing option simply allows any student to live with any other student. It does not have any special programming.

♦ Are bathrooms coed? All bathrooms are private, single-occupancy facilities that any resident may use.

♦ Are public restrooms gender neutral? The UCR campus has several unisex restrooms, although most public restrooms are gendered (labeled *Men* or *Women*).

♦ What is Stonewall? Stonewall Hall is named after an important landmark in LGBTQ history. In 1969, patrons (including many people of color and trans people) at the Greenwich Village club Stonewall Inn rioted against a New York City police raid. Following the Stonewall riots, LGBT people felt empowered to organize for equal rights, and the modern liberation movement was born.

+ How much does it cost to live in Stonewall Hall or gender-inclusive housing? Located in Pentland Hills, Stonewall Hall residents pay the same rate as any other Pentland Hills resident. However, the rates to live in Pentland Hills are higher than the cost to live in the other residential halls.
+ Will there be gender-inclusive apartments? All UCR-owned apartments allow gender-inclusive housing for students who identify their roommates before jointly requesting to live together on their housing applications. Apartments are only available to second-year and older students.

Questions about placement included the following:

+ Can you automatically be placed in Stonewall Hall or gender-inclusive housing? No, students must request the option.
+ Can students move out of Stonewall Hall midyear? Yes, any student in on-campus housing may request roommate changes using standard residence life policies and procedures. However, the approval is based on availability of space and a contract change cost may apply.
+ Can you live with your significant other? Yes.
+ Can brothers and sisters live together? Yes.
+ Can a parent influence placement? UCR respects the decisions and confidentiality of students as they complete their housing contract.

Questions for parents and families included the following:

+ Can students or their families request to *not* be placed in Stonewall Hall? Placement is always optional and never required. Students who do not want to live in Stonewall Hall do not select it on their contract, and thus they are not placed in Stonewall Hall.
+ What info is protected by the Federal Educational Rights and Privacy Act (FERPA)? Is the fact that a student lives in Stonewall Hall protected information? Yes, this information is protected by FERPA.
+ As a parent, I am concerned that UCR is allowing men and women to live together on campus. Why would you allow this? UCR believes that Stonewall Hall and gender-inclusive housing offers important living options that meet the diverse needs of UCR students. In addition, the residential life mission encourages an educational and supportive living-learning environment. Students uncomfortable with this living option may choose to not select it on their housing contract.

♦ Why is UCR allowing living options that are against my religious beliefs? Students with religious concerns need not request these living options.

♦ Isn't this going to be contagious or corrupting for other students? Students are entitled to their personal opinions. However, other students require this accommodation based on their gender identity, or they simply support this living option as a comfortable space for them and their roommate. Since establishing this living option more than 10 years ago, no one else has exhibited concern about the influence of gender-inclusive housing on students' living options.

Other questions included the following:

♦ Isn't this segregation? No. No student is ever required to live in Stonewall Hall or gender-inclusive housing.

♦ What about safety and security? The building is located next to the resident services office. There is triple-key security (a separate key for rooms, suites, and the building). Stonewall Hall has not experienced any unusual or more frequent incidents.

♦ Will there be an LGBTQ resident assistant? Student staff positions will be open to every student, regardless of sexual orientation or gender identity. A commitment to the mission and goals of residence life is important.

♦ What does LGBTQ stand for? LGBTQ stands for lesbian, gay, bisexual, transgender, queer. Please see the LGBTQ terminology handout from the LGBT Resource Center website at out.ucr.edu for more information.

Although these frequently asked questions were never published for the public, the UCR staff used them to answer questions from students, staff, faculty, parents, and the media once housing services integrated general descriptions of Stonewall Hall and gender-inclusive housing into their on-campus housing marketing in 2005.

STAFF RESPONSIBILITIES FOR GENDER-INCLUSIVE HOUSING

I (James Smith) began working at UCR housing services as the residence life coordinator for academics and programming in fall 2004. This position involved oversight of the living-learning programs and special interest communities. I was to work with the resident directors in these areas as well as the campus partners who worked with us to develop these programs. Because gender-inclusive housing is part of Stonewall Hall and is a special interest community, it was part of my responsibility to ensure that the community was established. In addition, it was part of my job to work with campus partners and stakeholders to develop training programs on gender-inclusive housing because it was so new to campus and relatively new to campus housing programs across the United States.

The training and development of all housing staff members who had a connection with the gender-inclusive housing community was especially important. As a department, it was imperative for all housing staff to be aware of the LGBTQ population and the needs and issues that may be associated with this community. Housing services and the LGBT Resource Center formed a partnership to create a variety of training sessions for the professional staff members in assignments, residence life, housing administration, maintenance, and housekeeping. Our student staff members received separate training that was a part of their annual LGBTQ allies training sessions. The trainings ranged from one to two hours and the crux of the training for professional staff members centered on the student population in this community and some of the ways the residents may have different needs or require additional support.

Topics for training included an introduction to various identity development theories, LGBTQ history, LGBTQ community signs and symbols, and interactive activities. The training sessions generally lasted about two hours and were interactive to give the audience a better understanding of the population. Each training session opened with a welcome from the assistant vice chancellor for housing, dining, and residential services, who was a major support in the initiation of this community.

The assistant vice chancellor for housing, dining, and residential services not only welcomed the group but also spoke about the commitment to UCR's residential students and the expectation to continue to create inclusive communities for UCR students. The professional staff members in the resident service and assignment areas were required to attend, and those in housekeeping and grounds maintenance were requested to attend. Since the housing assignments, team members had the most direct contact with students and their living options (in terms of answering students' questions, placing students in their rooms, and sending out assignments), it was imperative for them to understand gender-inclusive housing so they could answer questions and assist students who requested this option.

The only resistance to the training seemed to come from one member of the resident services team who did not understand the concepts of gender identity. After a separate follow-up meeting with this staff member, she seemed to be in a better place to assist students. The training sessions seemed successful, and many staff members gained insight into gender-inclusive housing and the LGBTQ community. Unfortunately, the training did not continue for many years for a number of circumstances, including increased workloads for personnel and finding available times to bring all staff together. However, training sessions are now scheduled for specific audiences such as housing placement staff.

Over the years, many on the UCR campus have increasingly assumed that the campus is inclusive and have therefore believed that training sessions are not needed or are forgotten by various members of training teams. Much of the burden was placed on residential life to train staff members, and when staff training time became more limited, training on gender-inclusive housing was a lower priority. Questions such as, "We are diverse, who needs diversity training?" plague the educators who work in student affairs. Although the commitment to the community did not waver, the time and energy needed to continue education waned. As an item for the future, one specific goal in housing is to go back to the training files, review previous materials, and create new training sessions. Because of a great deal of staff turnover in many of the housing departments, what may seem like a refresher session will be brand new for many.

In addition to the training of professional staff in the Department of Housing Services, residence life staff have also asked all student staff members to go through an LGBTQ 101 training, with an optional session titled Part Two Allies Program. This training is sponsored and directed by the LGBT Resource Center, and RAs, program coordinators, and assistant resident directors participate. The department has found the training sessions beneficial not only for those who participate but also for the residents in the communities they serve. LGBTQ students may live in any community and it is up to the staff members to ensure they provide safe and inclusive communities. There have been some years where this training did not occur because of changes in training priorities in housing services. Although the campus has not experienced significant issues when staff were not trained annually, housing services has found it is often needed for smaller staff audiences when specific issues arise. For example, some staff require new training on terminology, handling roommate conflicts, or why UCR offers gender-inclusive housing when the living option is unfamiliar to new staff.

COMMUNITY ISSUES

The housing services department has received numerous calls over the years from staff at many colleges and universities regarding the implementation of gender-inclusive housing practices and policies. Many of the staff members in residence life have also talked with the media including NBC, CNN, and the Associated Press. The questions that always seem to garner the most attention are those on community issues such as, "Has there been an increase in sexual assaults?" or "Are students choosing this community to have more sex with each other?" or "What about straight couples?"

In response to these questions, the Department of Housing Services looks holistically at the community and balances the problems in all the halls. Problems may include but are not limited to roommate issues, student conduct situations, or a shortfall in requests for housing in this community. Questions of sexual activity or conduct issues are not only connected to one hall but also a part of the college experience across all residential communities. Whether students are learning about who they are or how to manage their emotions, they often go through a myriad of experiences during their tenure on campus. It seems natural for folks to focus negative attention on the trans community and gender-inclusive housing specifically because of stigma, marginalization, and discrimination historically affecting trans people. It is as though people were looking for reasons not to implement this type of community on their campus.

Overall, there have been a number of positive interactions, and because the gender-inclusive housing community is located in the same building as Stonewall Hall, there is a synergy of education on all populations. For example, lesbian, gay, and bisexual students are able to garner a better idea of the struggle of trans students because of the programming. At UCR, the department is aware that housing services provides an accommodation for students who want to live on campus, and programs and services are based on resident needs. Housing services surveys students each year using the Educational Benchmarking Index, which is part of the national survey through SkyFactor, and after each large-scale housing event or program. The results of the surveys show that students appreciate Stonewall Hall and gender-inclusive housing as an accommodation.

Yet, there have been some minor bumps along the way, and each year housing learns better ways to navigate those issues. Some of these issues involve RAs not identifying with the LGBTQ community or placing students in this community who do not necessarily identify with or understand the needs of the LGBTQ community because of occupancy demands. Because students request gender-inclusive housing on their own, they must indicate this on their contract. When RAs who do not identify as LGBTQ are in the community, residents seem less likely to interact with them, based on feedback housing services received in surveys. Although staff applicants are not asked about their sexual orientation on their application, the housing services department staff work to continue to make contact with those who identify with the community based on feedback from residents.

The RA, who is also a student, may or may not identify with the LGBTQ community. This means there are times when we may not have an RA available who is LGBTQ identified to serve the community. Housing services tries to hire people who identify as LGBTQ so they can better assist residents who may share similar experiences. This can, at times, be a challenge for the residents in the community who are LGBTQ. The residents often have high expectations of their RA, and some build identity into those expectations.

Some residents have felt if we hire a straight RA for the community, the RA cannot possibly identify with LGBTQ experiences and are therefore dismissed when it comes to community development. This can be trying for the RA who is attempting to build community and to be an ally for LGBTQ people. At times, housing services will ensure the RA receives appropriate ally training as well as education on the LGBTQ community, but this may not always be possible particularly when it comes to midyear replacement hires. However, housing services and the LGBT Resource Center work in tandem to help the staff member as well as the students in the community work together to bring some level of cohesion.

Although it is never for the Department of Housing Services to ask for reasons students choose to live in gender-inclusive housing, some do in fact identify as heterosexual and are of different genders. This is demonstrated by RA inquiries when getting to know the residents in their community. Housing staff have not experienced a great number of heterosexual students living with a different gender partner, but it does happen. As with any living experience, there have been minor issues when couples choose to live in this community because they are together. In some cases, the couples have alienated other community members by not participating in programs or affecting the community negatively when disagreements with each other occur. Again, these are normal situations in many communities, but the issues are sometimes heightened because it happens in gender-inclusive housing.

Overall, the community continues to thrive, but the number of requests ebbs and flows each year. Some years housing services has had as many as 40 different requests for gender-inclusive housing, whereas other years there are as few as 4 requests; no reason has yet been determined why this happens. Housing services continually markets its options to this community as well as to other special interest communities.

As the department looks to the future, there have been requests to make the gender-inclusive housing option available in other residence hall communities outside Pentland Hills. UCR housing services expanded gender-inclusive housing to university-owned apartments in 2012 as long as residents select their roommates and apply together. In other words, no roommate matching is required. Apartment living is only available to second-year and higher students.

Although it is feasible to make gender-inclusive housing available in additional residence halls, there are a number of minor issues that prevent this from happening. For instance, facilities in most communities do not provide private showers or restrooms; the current location for gender-inclusive housing involves suite-style living where single-occupancy restrooms and showers are shared among no more than eight students. However, the question of creating additional gender-inclusive housing options will continue to be asked because the lack of gender-inclusive housing in special interest housing outside Stonewall Hall forces students to choose between gender-inclusive housing and accessing those intentional living communities.

INFLUENCE ON TRANS STUDENTS AND PROSPECTIVE STUDENTS

In 2005–2006, the first academic year UCR offered the new housing options, 40 students selected gender-inclusive housing, with 8 of those in a Stonewall Hall suite. This filled 5 of 6 suites in one Pentland Hills building. The non-gender-inclusive housing suite residents were all female. Student staff included an RA for the building and a Stonewall Hall programming coordinator. The number of Stonewall Hall residents has gone up and down, but UCR has successfully filled the building with students requesting gender-inclusive housing or open to it every year.

The implementation of gender-inclusive housing in 2005 has affected the reputation of UCR in a positive manner. An increasing number of prospective students who are trans e-mail, call, or personally visit the LGBT Resource

Center to inquire about housing options. An increasing number of parents also contact the LGBT Resource Center to make sure their family member will be able to live in a trans-inclusive housing environment. UCR's housing options also contribute to UCR being named a top 25 LGBT-friendly college campus (Nichols, 2013) and a top 10 transgender-inclusive campus by Campus Pride (Beemyn & Windmeyer, 2012).

A few challenges, however, exist for trans students seeking on-campus housing. First, gender-inclusive housing is located in the most expensive residence hall on campus; however, this is the only facility with private restrooms and showers. Second, students wishing to live in the Honors Hall (a requirement for first-year Honors Program students), Transfer Hall, another cultural-based hall such as Mundo (a residential community exploring Chicano/Chicana culture) or the Pan-African Theme Hall for students who want to expand the consciousness of or identify with pan-African culture, or an academic-based hall such as Enginuity or Pre-Business, do not have access to gender-inclusive housing. Third, some trans students have struggled living with hallmates who selected gender-inclusive housing to live with a significant other, sibling, or best friend but do not begin the academic year with any knowledge of gender identity issues. Basic issues of respect such as using chosen names and pronouns must be learned by new residents, and trans students report stress from this period of adjustment. This dynamic also is found in Stonewall Hall, as many lesbian, gay, and bisexual students also lack trans awareness. Fourth, many parents are involved in students' completion of the online housing application, so students who are not out to their family may not be able to request Stonewall Hall or gender-inclusive housing as a first-year student.

Despite these challenges, UCR administrators believe the gender-inclusive housing option has allowed the campus to be proactive in meeting the needs of many trans students. A journey begun by student activists inspired by trans role models 10 years ago has left a legacy of inclusion that makes UCR proud.

REFERENCES

Beemyn, G., & Windmeyer, S. (2012). *The top 10 trans-friendly colleges and universities*. Retrieved from www.advocate.com/politics/transgender/2012/08/15/top-10-trans-friendly-colleges-and-universities

California Fair Housing Act. (2003). *State law prohibits discrimination in housing*. Retrieved from www.dfeh.ca.gov/Housing

Nichols, J. (2013). *Campus Pride releases 2013 "Top 25 LGBT-Friendly Universities and Colleges" listing.* Retrieved from www.huffingtonpost.com/2013/08/20/campus-pride-lgbt-colleges-2013_n_3781950.html?utm_hp_ref=gay-voices

Ohio State University. (2014). *University housing.* Retrieved from housing.osu.edu/living-on-campus

University of California. (2003). University of California Lesbian, Gay, Bisexual, Transgender Intersex Association historical documents 1991–2013. Retrieved from out.ucr.edu/docs/uclgbtia_historicaldocs.pdf

University of California, Riverside. (2004). UCR Housing Policies on Gender Identity/Expression. Retrieved from out.ucr.edu/ourcampus/Pages/Housing.aspx

APPENDIX 4A
University of California, Riverside Housing Policies on Gender Identity and Expression (Approved Fall 2004)

Consistent with university policy and practice, University of California, Riverside (UCR) housing staff responds to student needs and works to develop a nurturing community atmosphere that values diversity and promotes the dignity of all people.

Housing seeks to meet a range of student needs, which can include those related to physical ability, gender identity/expression, medical condition, dietary request, and so on.

The University of California, in accordance with applicable federal and state law and university policy, does not discriminate on the basis of race, color, national origin, religion, sex, gender identity, pregnancy, disability, age, medical condition (cancer-related), ancestry, marital status, citizenship, sexual orientation, or status as a Vietnam-era veteran or special disabled veteran. The university also prohibits sexual harassment. This nondiscrimination policy covers admission, access, and treatment in university programs and activities.

In order to provide support to students who, for whatever reason, need special accommodations due to gender identity/expression, housing needs to know that a student requires such accommodations. Current and incoming residence hall students with concerns of any kind relating to their gender identity/expression are urged to identify themselves to housing staff. Staff will not ask for any more information than is required to meet students' housing needs and all disclosed information will be kept strictly confidential.

Gender inclusive housing placement priority will be given to students who notify UCR housing in a timely manner that they require accommodations based on their gender identity or gender expression. Students must meet all housing contract and payment deadlines.

If housing is able to accommodate a student request, we do so. In meeting the needs of students, Housing consistently recognizes and respects the gender identity that the student has established with university housing.

Recognizing that students are not all alike, but have different needs and desires, housing addresses their concerns on a case-by-case basis. But at no time will housing force a student, who has followed housing procedures, to have to find a comfortable, welcoming housing assignment on their own.

If any student has a conflict with a roommate because of their gender identity or expression, the student should see their resident director (RD) first. RDs are full-time, professional staff members. RDs have taken part in training specifically on gender identity/expression issues. If talking with the RD brings no resolution, a student can discuss the matter with senior Residence Life staff and/or with the Director of the Lesbian Gay Bisexual Transgender Resource Center.

If at any time a student needs to discuss issues in housing related to gender identity or gender expression, the following UCR professional staff may be contacted: Assistant Director for Residence Life Director, Lesbian Gay Bisexual Transgender Resource Center.

REFERENCE

University of California, Riverside. (2004). UCR Housing Policies on Gender Identity/ Expression. Retrieved from http://out.ucr.edu/ourcampus/Pages/Housing.aspx

APPENDIX 4B
University of California, Riverside, Gender-Inclusive Housing Inside and Outside an LGBTQ Residential Living Community

January 1993	UCR LGBT Resource Center is established, the first on a college campus in California with professional staffing.
September 1993	Pan-African Theme Hall opens for UCR student residents, establishing the first intentional living community on campus.
January 2000	Nancy Tubbs is hired as third director of the UCR LGBT Resource Center.
August 2003	California Fair Employment and Housing Act specifically provides protection from harassment or discrimination in employment because of "Gender, Gender Identity, and Gender Expression" (University of California, 2003).
September 2003	Eric N. Peterson and Eli R. Green are hired as part-time temporary program coordinators in the UCR LGBT Resource Center. Both are trans identified and increase resources and programming related to gender identity and gender expression in the center and across campus.
January 2004	University of California adds gender identity to nondiscrimination statement (University of California, 2003).
March 2004	SEQs (Students for the Equality of Queers) submits a proposal to the Department of Housing Services for an LGBTIQQA theme hall.
June 2004	LGBTIQQA Theme Hall Work Group is established to inventory housing facilities, develop policies, and recommend changes to the online housing application form. The group includes staff from the Department of Housing Services and the LGBT Resource Center, as well as student members of SEQs. Residence life leadership coordinator Mary Tregoning chairs the work group.
Summer 2004	M. Chad Wilson, the first UCR graduate intern for housing and LGBT concerns, begins a six-week internship. He conducts research on gender-inclusive housing, takes an inventory of UCR housing facilities, and serves on the LGBTIQQA Theme Hall Work Group.

Summer 2004	Residence life coordinator for academics and programming James Smith is hired. His responsibilities include the coordination of special-interest and living-learning communities, including Stonewall Hall and gender-inclusive housing.
Fall 2004	UCR housing policies on gender identity and expression approved.
Fall 2004	Housing staff training regarding gender-inclusive housing begins.
Winter 2005	Stonewall Hall and gender-inclusive housing marketing begins.
Winter 2005	Housing student staff recruitment includes resident adviser and program coordinator positions for Stonewall Hall and gender-inclusive housing.
Spring 2005	Online UCR housing applications open. Form includes an option to write in a gender identity other than *M* and *F* and to request gender-inclusive housing and Stonewall Hall as special-interest housing.
Summer 2005	Gender-inclusive housing placement begins.
Summer 2005	Internal training conducted for all housing frontline staff on terminology used in the LGBTQ community, the purposes of gender-inclusive housing and Stonewall Hall, and who may sign up for these living options.
Fall 2005	UCR becomes the first public university in the United States to offer gender-inclusive housing to all students, including first-year students, with 40 residents in gender-inclusive housing (including 8 in Stonewall Hall).
Fall 2005	Housing staff training continues. Training begins with student staff and filters out to others, including housekeeping and maintenance staff members.
Winter 2006	Members of UCR housing staff are interviewed for a segment on the NBC *Today* show discussing gender-inclusive housing.

5

Redefining Community Through Collaboration

Defining Gender-Neutral Housing for a Four-Year Residential Liberal Arts College

Brian J. Patchcoski and Angie M. Harris

D ICKINSON COLLEGE (DICKINSON), FOUNDED in 1773, is a highly selective, private residential liberal arts college located in central Pennsylvania. As an institution steeped in history, its grounds have been the site of notable revolutionary experiences, and its limestone buildings are monuments of classic architecture. The college's mission is to offer students a useful education in the arts and sciences that will prepare them for lives as engaged citizens and leaders.

In this chapter, we discuss the process of defining a gender-neutral housing policy at Dickinson. We address the common misconceptions we faced in developing and implementing an all-inclusive policy applicable to incoming first-year students and the rest of our student community and how we moved beyond these misconceptions through community conversations and education. This chapter also discusses the unique approaches toward gender-neutral housing at a liberal arts institution, particularly the need to obtain faculty commitments, all-college committee representation, student engagement, and administrator support. As Dickinson is a historic institution with aging residential facilities, we also address issues pertaining to housing stock and the approaches we took to design a policy reflective of our living and learning environment.

Alongside the policy, we also address parental concerns, communication and marketing procedures, and the residential curriculum, all devised to ensure our campus partners understand the needs and expectations for this work on our campus. As our policy is relatively new to our campus at the time of writing this chapter, we also discuss our first-year assessments as well as highlight some of the areas of growth we have uncovered.

Although Dickinson has worked to create a housing policy inclusive of the spectrum of gender identities and expressions, we understand that trans* inclusion does not stop inside our residential facilities. We conclude our chapter by addressing the education and much needed advocacy by student affairs practitioners to ensure a holistic approach toward trans* and gender-nonconforming inclusion.

OUR CAMPUS ENVIRONMENT: WHAT LED TO THIS POLICY'S CREATION?

During August 2012 Dickinson College opened the Office of Lesbian, Gay, Bisexual, Transgender, Queer, and Questioning (LGBTQ) Services. During the first year on campus, the LGBTQ services office conducted an assessment of climate, culture, and experiences related to gender and sexuality issues. Through focus groups, campus climate surveys, and data from other campus assessments, we were able to gain a better understanding of the Dickinson culture. After reviewing the range of experiences of those on the campus, a clearer picture began to form that students, staff, and faculty were searching for resources supportive of gender identity and expression. Specifically, students seemed to be seeking housing assignments that allowed transgender and nonbinary individuals the safety they deserved on campus. In an effort to respond to these concerns, it was determined that a working group on transgender and gender-nonconforming issues would be formed to create a set of recommendations on the inclusion of gender identity and expression at the college. Various members of the Dickinson community were selected to participate in the working group based on their positions and ability to contribute to the conversation, including the director of student activities, assistant director of housing, director of the Women's and Gender Resource Center, director of the Office of Diversity Initiatives,

policy. With this in mind, the working group framed their efforts in the context of community understanding and education related to the diversity of genders and sexualities represented at the college. This policy was meant to acknowledge, appreciate, and respect the diverse nature of the Dickinson student body while giving students more options in finding a roommate who is compatible outside the realm of gender and sexuality.

Dickinson's policy allows two or more students to share a multiple-occupancy bedroom, suite, or apartment regardless of students' sex or gender. It also acknowledges that gender-neutral housing is not intended for romantic couples, similarly referred to in other housing placements, but all students at the college are welcome to use these processes regardless. The policy states that Dickinson specifically honors the experiences of students who feel uncomfortable rooming with members of the same sex, transgender students in the process of defining their gender identity, students who feel they would be more compatible with a roommate of a different sex or gender, and students who do not want sex or gender to be a primary factor in choosing a roommate. For Dickinson, gender-neutral housing is part of the larger dedication toward a campus climate that is welcoming, inclusive, and supportive of all students.

Residential Facilities and Safety Concerns

Although Dickinson aspires to make all spaces gender inclusive and safe, as a campus with aging facilities, the policy needed to address faults relative to building structure and monetary constraints regarding renovations. Knowing the campus community and after reviewing feedback from focus groups with members of the trans*, gender nonconforming, and gender queer student community, administrators at Dickinson wanted to be sure that student experiences and concerns were addressed in the policy. Students presented two primary areas of concern: bathroom and shower access and learning community involvement. Students wanted to be sure the policy detailed where gender-neutral bathroom and shower facilities were relative to housing placements, and they wanted to make sure the process did not punish or ostracize students from their learning communities by choosing gender-neutral housing. In an effort to be transparent and authentic with policy and procedures, both these areas are addressed to assist students in their decision to choose this option.

Generally, two types of bathrooms are found in residential facilities at Dickinson: single-person and group bathrooms. All single-person bathrooms (one toilet, one sink, and one shower) are gender neutral or all-gender open to use by anyone in the space. Group bathrooms contain multiple toilets, sinks, and showers. These bathrooms are designated at the beginning of each academic year as male or female, but residents are given the opportunity to review and determine the final designation of these bathrooms. At the beginning of each semester, the resident advisers on each floor or wing with group bathrooms discuss the possibility of designating the group bathrooms as gender specific or gender neutral or all-gender. If the community is not fully supportive of group bathrooms becoming gender neutral, then students are encouraged to discuss the larger issues of use, accessibility, and diversity. This practice has been in place for several years at Dickinson; however, with the implementation of gender-neutral housing, these conversations and open designations as gender-neutral or all-gender bathrooms have increased.

The primary distinction between upper-class and first-year student policies pertains to content and how administrators specifically define places that are optimal in terms of building architecture, bathroom and shower access, and larger living-learning community issues and places that are not conducive to gender-neutral living arrangements. Currently, about 58 unique, general, and special-interest residential options are available on campus, including traditional residence halls, houses, and apartments. As the college encourages students to take into account their needs relative to their room selection, policy creators did not want to limit student experiences in specific residential living situations by narrowly confining them to a certain building or floor. Rather, the policy was meant to enable students to engage with all that Dickinson's on-campus community has to offer.

The first-year and transfer student policy also considers the unique housing challenges that these students might encounter. All first-year students live together in traditional residence halls. Most of these facilities are traditional college residential facilities with group bathrooms. In addition to living in close proximity to other first-year students, first-year students are housed close to others who are in their first-year seminar or learning community. Learning communities provide opportunities for clusters of students in first-year seminars to live in the same building or on the same floor. When creating the policy, again the college did not want to limit student experiences in these programs and opportunities but to point out the potential for a less than optimal placement.

Selection of Gender-Neutral Housing

In crafting the procedures for students to elect gender-neutral housing options, the college wanted to ensure ease and privacy. During the planning process, students expressed discomfort and dissatisfaction with the traditional housing protocol. Students believed that requiring them to come to the housing office to define and defend why they needed a certain living environment was unacceptable, and the working group wanted to be sure to provide a process where students felt comfortable with open housing selection.

Incoming first-year and transfer students receive housing selection information each May that includes detailed information about all living options including gender-neutral housing. First-year and transfer students who express an interest in gender-neutral housing on their online housing application have a phone conversation with a professional staff member so the college can provide housing that best meets the needs of the student. Professional staff are trained and receive an outline of questions to ask each student regarding their understanding of gender-neutral housing, roommate preferences, specific needs for academic success, bathroom and shower needs, seminar preference relative to gender-neutral housing, as well as any further information they believe is beneficial for the staff working on housing placements. Given the nature of first-year housing at Dickinson, these phone conversations are invaluable in assisting the college with the placement of students while considering their needs, bathroom and shower access, as well as their first-year seminar. The working group decided that first-year students, without existing college-specific knowledge, would benefit from a conversation with staff or current students to assist them in making the best possible housing selection.

Assuming that upperclass students know campus and college housing better than first-year students, upper-class students can opt into gender-neutral housing on their own. If a student is a rising sophomore, junior, or senior, they simply self-select roommates and a housing location through the online system during the spring room selection process. The gender-neutral housing option is available in all residential facilities, which avoids segregation and offers students gender-neutral housing in all housing styles and at various housing price points. Once a room, apartment, or suite is made gender neutral, that space will continue to be gender neutral as long as the residents can maintain the full occupancy of the living space.

Vacancy Management

When there is a vacancy in a gender-neutral double-bed room, the student remaining in the room may elect to recruit any new roommate as long as both students agree to live together. If a roommate cannot be identified, the room will default to single-sex or single-gender status. In this case, the Office of Residence Life and Housing may place a student of the same sex or gender in the room if the space is needed and after consultation with the existing resident.

When there is a vacancy in a gender-neutral triple, apartment, or suite, the residents may recruit any new roommates to fill the space. If the residents in a triple, apartment, or suite cannot fill the vacancies, the Office of Residence Life and Housing first attempts to find students who are interested in living in a gender-neutral space. If the office needs to maximize use of available spaces on campus and the preceding solution is not possible, then they will work closely with the residents in the space to determine next steps that are best suited and agreed on by all residents in the space. These steps have included, but are not limited to, relocation of all residents to smaller inclusive rooming assignments, living option designation changes for the entire space, or conducting a larger residential community outreach to find interested residents who may not have appeared in the initial search.

Common Concerns: Addressed

While the working group was creating and drafting the policy, its members also felt a need to address specific misconceptions about gender-neutral housing that other individuals had raised on campus in previous conversations. One of the most important clarifications related to the differences between coed or mixed-gender and gender-neutral housing. The working group clarified this misconception with the following statement:

> The terms co-ed/mixed-gender operate on the assumption that there are two genders: male and female. It leaves no room for those who do not identify as their biological sex or those who are transgender or gender non-conforming. This idea is based on the notion that there are more than two genders, in fact an infinite amount. Allowing for gender-neutral housing, as opposed to co-ed /mixed-gender, shows more inclusiveness and room for diverse identities. (Transgender Law Center, 2005, p. 2)

Another concern that was addressed related to fear. Students wanted to know what would happen if a student chooses to live with someone in a gender-neutral arrangement and becomes uncomfortable with the situation. As with any roommate or housing issue, the college's established room change process allows reassignment in any living situation where there is a problem that cannot be resolved, depending on the spaces available at that time.

Finally, some were concerned about parental involvement in the policy. Students requested staff to address what would happen if their parents did not want them to live in a gender-neutral housing space, and more specifically, they wanted to know if their parents would be notified. Dickinson's policy is that students 18 years of age and older may make decisions about their housing assignment without parental consent. Students are encouraged to maintain an open dialogue with their families so they can be supportive of students' housing decisions, but it is the students' choice whether to tell their parents or guardians. Students under 18 are encouraged to discuss housing plans with their families if possible, but if there are concerns, students are encouraged to approach a staff member to learn about other options to enhance their residential experience.

EDUCATION: IN POLICY AND PRACTICE

Keeping in mind the common concerns that were voiced by the community during the planning and writing process, the working group believed in using the policy as an educational tool and that on-campus educational initiatives were a necessity.

In the Policy

The policy was created under the assumption that those reading the policy had little or no knowledge regarding gender-neutral housing or why Dickinson supports this initiative. The working group specifically crafted the policy by answering some of the most common questions sought by students, faculty, staff, and administrators in the planning process. Writing the policy in an easily accessible format allows community access and engagement. The working group also added definitions from the National Center for Transgender Equality (see transequality.org) so that individuals accessing this policy could learn more about gender identity and expression.

Over the first year of implementation, students reported that the policy and the availability of options educated the larger college community, inclusive of parents and families, on why ensuring gender-neutral housing is important for the Dickinson community while also encouraging allies in the community to seek and select this option to support community members embodying historically marginalized genders and sexualities.

One first-year student said,

> I'm from Oregon—a very liberal area. I am also straight! The reason I chose this living option was to give someone else a roommate who was comfortable with these issues—unlike some of my friends here. My moms have been a huge influence on my worldview and if I can make small steps to change this campus—I will! (Harris, 2014)

Across the Community

Educating the Dickinson community has been and continues to be an important part of the work in implementing gender-neutral housing on campus. Although the education in the policy has been important, the working group has created ongoing conversations and workshops involving students serving as resident advisers, orientation assistants, and staff who are connected with these issues. These sessions aim to review common myths and concerns, provide accurate language to discuss these issues, and explain policies and procedures to create an inclusive environment for issues of gender identity, gender expression, and sexual orientation. Although these pieces are continuously changing as Dickinson works to make these sessions more valuable to our community, these workshops have allowed staff to be proactive and reduce challenging behaviors and fears around this implementation.

BENCHMARKS AND TIME LINE

The policy and procedures at Dickinson did not arise completely from scratch but were built on the great work of other institutions and organizations seeking to make environments more inclusive and accessible. In the policy, the working group gives credit to other institutions that Dickinson is proud to join in offering some form of gender-neutral housing while also highlighting scholars who have recommended best practices in the past (Beemyn, Dominique, Pettit, & Smith, 2005). Dickinson's policy resembles those at American, Colby, Connecticut, Gettysburg, Hamilton, Oberlin, Princeton, Skidmore, University of

Pennsylvania, Vassar, and Wesleyan as many of these institutions are peer and aspirant colleges and universities. It is important for others to know where Dickinson fits in efforts to make a more inclusive campus community.

Staff at Gettysburg College were most helpful in providing assistance in thinking about how this framework might work and what implementation had been like for them in a geographically close rural Pennsylvania town. The working group has also included links on the college website to gender-neutral housing policies at other institutions by listing the Campus Pride (2017) Trans Policy Clearinghouse, thereby providing parents and others who question this work with a framework for why this is important for residential living environments.

As noted in the history of Dickinson provided earlier, although there had been various conversations regarding the creation of a gender-neutral housing policy, it took several attempts to clearly define a plan of action and implementation. After the ESLC encouraged a fall 2013 gender-neutral housing option, the working group moved quickly over a six-month period, from February 2013 to August 2013, to develop, review, and communicate the policy (see Appendix 5A).

The process began in February with policy drafts and review. After surveying and collecting the views and concerns of the student population, the working group drafted a policy relative to the most commonly asked questions. The working group encouraged participation from various members across the Dickinson community to ensure various departments felt included and part of the process. Two of the most important partners in this work were the Office of Admissions and the Office of Marketing and Communications. Because their staffs conduct most of the outreach to students and families, the working group wanted to be sure this new policy was included in all new student materials as well as released to current students, faculty, staff, and alumni.

In March, the ESLC approved the policy. Shortly after receiving that approval, from April through May, the working group began updating all the housing and orientation Web pages, the student handbook to reflect the policy, and various administrative forms sent to new and current students, and began to think about training and pertinent information staff and other members of the college community might need to make this policy a success.

In June, once the housing information had been received for incoming first-year students, the working group hosted workshops and informational sessions for members of the Dickinson community who had been recruited to connect with first-year students who had elected the new gender-neutral housing option. To prepare these representatives, the working group created a script designed to foster a developmental conversation between staff and the incoming first-year students. The working group wanted to be sure the students understood what gender-neutral housing was and also obtain any information that might help provide the most inclusive housing situation based on their requests.

Throughout late June and July, staff members contacted all first-year students and filtered that information back to housing staff to finalize assignments by early August. Once resident advisers and orientation assistants began to return to campus in mid-August, the working group hosted various workshops and educational sessions so students would have the necessary information to answer questions and make referrals to other members of the Dickinson community.

Although the policy at Dickinson may seemingly be progressive, there are still institutional challenges related to sex or gender bathroom allocation in residential facilities, and these concerns continue to affect this policy. The working group had many conversations about voting procedures and decided it was not the time to remove these conversations but rather conduct some type of substantial education on the importance of having gender neutral options. Dickinson is still a conservative community, but the working group has decided to continue to have training sessions and workshops on this process for resident advisers and have them revisit the bathroom election throughout the semester as the communities build and develop trust with one another. These workshops and conversations are something staff continue to address and will continue to make changes and adjustments moving forward.

CAMPUSWIDE CHANGE

Although the focus of this work has been on housing and residential changes, additional work is needed to make the institution truly inclusive of gender identity and expression. Although outside the purview of this chapter, it is important to highlight continued advocacy and recommendations toward broader inclusion of sexual and gender diversity. The recommendations from the working group, educationally based to share information with the larger community yet centered on policy implementation, have allowed staff to take a holistic look at college procedures as well as the local, regional, and national challenges students may be navigating. This continued work and reflections are meant to challenge the institution to ingrain these identities into the larger Dickinson tapestry.

FUTURE RECOMMENDATIONS

After one year of gender-neutral housing selections, the working group has learned a great deal and received positive feedback from the community at large. Even as plans are made to renovate traditional residence halls, specifically those without gender-inclusive bathroom facilities, there now exists an institutional desire and awareness of creating facilities supportive of gender inclusivity.

A sophomore student wrote,

> While I am not new to campus and everything is not perfect here—I believe administration has tried to make this work for the campus community. I hope the bathroom conversations continue and eventually aren't a concern. Although this worked for me, I think we all could learn from living with people experiencing this campus different[ly] than cisgender people. We just need to keep making this normalized—I'm normal—or at least I think I am. (Harris, 2014)

Of course there are areas for improvement including the management of roommate conflicts, a continued need for education, and review of voting procedures in the traditional residence halls with group bathroom facilities. For example, during the first year of implementation, a situation arose in which a student who desired gender-neutral housing encountered a roommate conflict. This student wanted to move out of the current situation, but staff did not have any gender-neutral vacancies at the time. In the future, Dickinson should be able to offer students in this situation an option as soon as possible, which will now necessitate holding vacant rooms specifically for this process.

Dickinson will also continue to provide education for staff and assess the effectiveness of that education. As this policy is integrated into the community, the required education will also evolve.

As the voting procedures for determining the designation of group bathrooms are not ideal, especially as they are based in the confidence and comfort level of the resident adviser leading the conversation, staff at Dickinson continue to seek ways to meet the needs of the community regarding safety and inclusive environments for trans* and gender-nonconforming students. Moving forward, Dickinson will continue to assess policies and make future improvements based on those assessments and it is hoped will continue to renovate facilities with these ideals for inclusion at the forefront of planning.

CONCLUSION

Through community conversations, education, and assessment, Dickinson has implemented an all-inclusive policy applicable to incoming first-year students and the rest of our student community. The shared governance process provided increased faculty commitments, committee representation, student interest, and administrator support. As a historic institution with aging residential facilities, Dickinson also faced issues pertaining to housing stock but has designed a policy clearly articulating these challenges (Dickinson College, 2013). As the policy is relatively new to campus, staff still have much work to do in order to create a truly inclusive residential experience. Although Dickinson has worked to create a gender-inclusive housing policy, trans* inclusion does not stop inside residential facilities. With these policies in place and the shared institutional work happening across campus, Dickinson has an optimistic perspective on the future of this work in higher education.

REFERENCES

Bartlow, S., Triano, M., & Confer, D. (2011). *President's Commission on Diversity Gender Neutral Housing proposal.* Carlisle, PA: Dickinson College.

Beemyn, B., Dominque, D., Pettitt, J., and Smith, T. (2005). Suggested steps to make campuses more trans-inclusive. *Journal of Gay and Lesbian Issues in Education, 3*, 89–94.

Campus Pride. (2017). *Campus Pride trans policy clearinghouse.* Retrieved from www.campuspride.org/tpc

Dickinson College. (2011). *President's report on the LGBTQ campus climate at Dickinson College.* Carlisle, PA: President's Commission on Diversity.

Dickinson College. (2013). *2013–2014 Dickinson College student handbook.* Carlisle, PA: Author.

Flores, J. C. (2010). *Resolution to endorse the gender-neutral housing option for sopho-mores, juniors, and seniors.* Carlisle, PA: Dickinson College.

Harris, A. (2014). [Dickinson College 2014 housing assessment]. Unpublished raw data.

Nycum, B., & Glatze, M. (2000). *The XY survival guide.* San Francisco, CA: XY.

Patchcoski, B. J. (2013). Enrollment and Student Life Committee resource packet. Carlisle, PA: Dickinson College.

Transgender Law Center. (2005). *Peeing in peace: A resource guide for transgender activists and allies* [Pamphlet]. San Francisco, CA: Author.

Yost, M. R., & Gilmore, S. (2011). Assessing LGBTQ campus climate and creating change. *Journal of Homosexuality, 58,* 1330–1354.

APPENDIX 5A
Time Line on Institutional Implementation and Collaboration

Date	Process
2000–2003	Dickinson is named a gay-friendly campus by *Princeton Review* and other college publications.
2009	Campus climate survey is administered to campus community.
2010	LGBTQ Task Force is organized by the President's Commission on Diversity.
November 2010	Resolution is introduced by the student senate to endorse a gender-neutral housing option for sophomores, juniors, and seniors.
December 2011	LGBTQ Task Force submits recommendations for gender-neutral housing.
Spring 2011	First intended launch of gender-neutral living option; implementation does not occur.
February 2012	LGBTQ Task Force submits new proposal on gender-neutral option to Enrollment and Student Life Committee with two new requests: distinction and clarification of gender-neutral versus mixed-gender living options and the expansion of gender-neutral options to all on campus. Implementation does not occur because of lack of staffing.
August 2012	Office of LGBTQ Services opens, and the first full-time professional dedicated to LGBTQ issues on campus is hired.
February 2013	Enrollment and student life reviews trans* and gender-inclusive practices on campus with the LGBTQ services office and decides that the gender-neutral housing option must launch in fall 2013.
March 2013	New gender-neutral housing option is delivered to Enrollment and Student Life Committee. Policy is approved.
April 2013– May 2013	Updates begin on housing and orientation Web pages, to the student handbook to recognize the policy, and to various forms sent to new and current students. Training and pertinent information that staff and other members of the college needed for successful policy implementation are considered.

Date	Process
June 2013– August 2013	Residential facility audit takes place for gender-inclusive single-stall and multistall restroom and shower rooms. Results are added to housing pages allowing students to make the best choices in living arrangements based on facility construction.
June 2013	Training is conducted for residence life staff and others who will be contacting students regarding gender-neutral housing elections.
Late June 2013–July 2013	Phone calls are made to first-year students who have elected the gender-neutral housing option.
August 2013	Housing assignments are released. Training for residence life student assistants and orientation assistants on gender-neutral housing options takes place.
August 2013	Students arrive on campus, and the staff encounter first experiences with full gender-neutral policy implementation.
August 2013– ongoing	Continued assessment and revisions of policy and training components for the campus community are in place.

6

Open House

Our Gender-Focused Learning Community

Andrew J. Erdmann and Jon Tingley

I N THE FALL OF 2013, Open House, a residential living-learning community at the University of Wisconsin–Madison (UW–Madison), opened
for the first time to a group of 54 students nested in a residence hall of
142 students. The start of Open House not only signified a new era of housing options for students but also was the culmination of several years worth
of coordination on the part of student, staff, and faculty to provide first-year
students with an opportunity to live in an environment that would allow
them to explore the concept of gender with their peers.

This chapter describes the process followed by a group of students and
staff to offer a gender-inclusive housing option and tells the story of the
gender-focused learning community that resulted from this work. Additionally, an analysis of Open House's first year is presented, as well as a view to
the future of Open House, with a special lens on the experiences of trans*
students. To contextualize the significance of Open House, however, it is
important to address the history and culture of UW–Madison, which is a
large Research 1 institution in the south-central part of Wisconsin with an
enrollment of about 43,000 students (University of Wisconsin–Madison,
2017). UW–Madison is the flagship of the University of Wisconsin System
(UW System) schools, and as such, must comply with UW System codes
and policies. This link between UW System policies and the development

of Open House is key to understanding how and why Open House was brought to fruition. Finally, in recognition that the name of Open House has evolved from its proposal stage to its current standing, we refer to the community as Open House throughout the chapter to provide consistency and avoid confusion.

PROPOSAL

In the fall of 2009, Chancellor Carolyn "Biddy" Martin established an initiative to create funding for high-impact practices (Kuh, 2008) for undergraduates called the Madison Initiative for Undergraduates (MIU) ("Madison Initiative," 2015). Concurrently, students from UW–Madison's University Housing Gender and Sexuality Alliance (GSA) presented a proposal to the Department of Residence Life, proposing the idea of a gender-inclusive housing option for students on campus. After this meeting, several staff members in the Department of Residence Life were selected to work with the students to develop the proposal further and submit it to the department for funding by the MIU. Andrew was asked to serve in an ad hoc advisory capacity to help students move through this process. As the group began our work, one challenge to creating such a community was UW System Policy 24-1, which stated, "Coeducational housing in the University of Wisconsin System, as implemented under the conditions of this policy, shall be construed to mean men and women occupying separate living areas by floor or room" (UW System, 1972). This policy limited the group's ability to create a community that would be truly gender inclusive in nature and set up the proposal committee with a unique challenge. Andrew was especially dismayed by this challenge, given the limits it would put not only on the creation of Open House as a space but also on trans* students' ability to live on campus. Additionally, the proposal team feared the UW System policy would severely limit the amount of support staff would be able to lend to trans* students in finding suitable housing on campus.

Andrew and the proposal writing team set forth to conduct research on gender-inclusive housing options across the nation. In addition to outside research, listening sessions were conducted with specific stakeholders on campus, including faculty members, staff from the Women's Center and LGBT (lesbian, gay, bisexual, transgender) Campus Center, and residential students. Much of what was discussed at the listening sessions was focused on current campus culture and climate as well as how various stakeholders viewed the creation of Open House. Additionally, there were extensive conversations about the ideal placement for Open House. Residential communities at UW–Madison are distinctively split geographically. Specifically, the south-east area in downtown Madison has a very urban feel, and the lakeshore area, situated on Lakeshore Path on the western part of campus, has a decidedly rural feel. Members of the listening sessions were split over which area of campus they felt Open House would be best suited. Andrew and other members of the proposal team felt strongly that Open House should be placed in the southeast area of campus in a residence hall that had clustered or individual bathrooms as it would be closer to resources such as the LGBT Campus Center and the Multicultural Student Center, as well as University Housing's Center for Cultural Enrichment. Furthermore, students in the listening sessions were especially concerned about the availability of gender-inclusive bathroom facilities as well as other factors, such as noise, amount of total students per floor, and the layout of the community, which was consistent with Kaya's (2004) research on students' sense of climate in residence halls.

Finally, another significant part of the conversation at listening sessions was whether Open House would only be a safe space for trans* students. Conversations on this particular issue were not quite as divisive as the placement of Open House. Listening session participants felt the space could serve in a similar capacity as other identity-based learning communities on campus as a safe space for the particular community in question. However, participants also felt Open House should also be open for allies and students who wanted to learn more about gender.

The final proposal for the creation of Open House as a living-learning community focused on educating students on gender as a broad topic, connecting how students experience their own gender and how their gender intersects with their other identities as they move through the world. Additionally, Open House was designed to infuse concepts of activism into its curriculum. Four faculty members, including one academic department chair, wrote supporting letters for Open House to demonstrate their willingness to work for the approval of Open House. In a letter of support for the proposed community, Finn Enke, professor of history, gender, and women's studies and director of the LGBT Studies Certificate Program, wrote that "Gender—in tandem with other categories of structural hierarchy such as race, religion, class, ability, and so forth—is a powerful organizing principle that affects the daily lives of everyone in complex ways" (F. Enke, personal communication, December 15, 2010).

PROPOSAL ACCEPTANCE

In February of 2011, Open House was accepted as a new residential learning community funded by the MIU. Approval came with several structural and monetary guarantees. The first was that a formal connection to an academic department was established. The chair of the gender and women's studies department at UW–Madison was enthusiastic about this partnership and eager to commit support, financial and otherwise. Second, the community would be funded at a yearly rate of $30,000 in perpetuity by MIU. This included faculty replacement funding at the rate of $20,000 annually and $10,000 for programming each year. Additionally, there was funding for a half-time program coordinator, valued at about $19,000 annually plus benefits. At this point, the work of coordinating logistics for Open House began.

PREPARING FOR OPEN HOUSE

After the university housing staff approved the creation of Open House and funding was secured, staff worked to bring together all the elements that would make Open House successful. The gender and women's studies department was the named sponsor for Open House, so housing staff worked with the department chair to secure a faculty director and hire a part-time program coordinator. A residence life coordinator was added to the staff, and a student house fellow was hired through the student staff recruitment process. These four staff members, as well as the Open House Steering Committee, worked together to form a leadership team for the residential learning community (Figure 6.1). As recommended as part of the proposal process, the fourth floor of Vel Phillips Hall was assigned to Open House, and it officially became UW–Madison's ninth residential learning community. Using Vel Phillips Hall was significant because it provided all students with access to a private restroom in their assigned room, and public restrooms were modified to be gender inclusive. As typical with residential learning communities not based on a specific academic major, recruitment and marketing became a top priority to make sure all 54 spaces were filled with students who wanted to learn about gender. A specific focus was placed on informing local high school GSAs as an attempt to reach students who needed a community like Open House.

Figure 6.1.   Open House stakeholder perspectives.

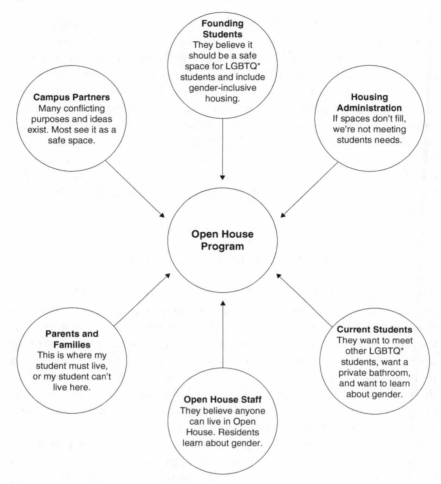

During the academic year and summer of 2013, the Open House program coordinator worked with a student intern to contact high school students involved in GSAs across Wisconsin. A unique partnership between UW–Madison and Gay Straight Alliance for Safe Schools (GSAFE), a Wisconsin nonprofit, made this recruiting effort possible. Open House staff thought it was critical to inform students coming to UW–Madison that a community focused on gender exploration was opening and that incoming students would have the opportunity to be part of its inaugural class. Open

House staff wanted to make sure that incoming trans* students knew they would have a safe place to explore their identities in the residence halls. In addition to working with high schools, the program coordinator and intern went to UW–Madison courses to discuss Open House, held individual meetings with students to discuss the community, and recruited from those students who had already decided to return to living on campus. Through these recruitment efforts, Open House started its first year with students who self-identified across a range of identities including trans* and cisgender, as well as students who identified as questioning their gender.

FIRST YEAR OF OPEN HOUSE

When Open House opened, it was filled completely with students who chose it as their first and second choice, an incredible feat for a learning community in its first year in a system where students make their preference for place-ment known across 10 learning communities and 17 residence halls. Before the students arrived, the Open House program coordinator and house fellow surveyed residents for their preferred names to create door decorations that included the most accurate information. The community's early focus was building allyship and awareness on gender issues, including ally training and gender workshops with staff from UW–Madison's LGBT Campus Center as well as information presented in a seminar course in Vel Phillips Hall. This was an important introduction to the Open House community, given the wide variety of identities present in the learning environment.

Most students in Open House participated in the first-year seminar led by the Open House faculty director, which focused on representations of gen-der in the media. Based on university housing assessment data, Open House staff knew students enrolled in a learning community are significantly more satisfied and exhibit a higher level of engagement and learning than their peers living in general university housing ("Residential Assessment," 2014). Thus, the seminar became a critical component of the Open House pro-gram, providing a safe space for students to explore foundational concepts of gender identity while also exploring their own identity. Open House pro-gramming quickly incorporated intersections with gender based on feedback from students living in the community. Films from the seminar, including *TransGeneration* (Simmons, 2005), sparked conversations about the inter-sections of multiple identities including gender, sexuality, race, ability, and health status. From research on student success and high-impact practices, we knew students benefitted greatly from interaction with faculty and staff (Kuh, 2008), and these activities were some of the ways Open House staff encouraged student success throughout their gender-based programming curriculum. One trans* student shared their experience with this curriculum in the following:

> I came to college thinking I knew all there was to know about LGBTQ+ issues, racism, and other social aspects. After all, I was trans, that meant I knew it all, right? I could not have been more wrong. The people and faculty I met because of Open House taught me so much. (Anonymous, personal communication, April 23, 2017)

Open House's partners from around the university were integral to these conversations and helped provide professionally facilitated discussions about these topics and recruit outside presenters to conduct workshops.

Presenters were brought into the community to help Open House staff meet their goal to expose residents to gender-based concepts and ideas. These events ranged from informal meals with professionals working in a social justice–related field to large-scale, multievent visits with nationally known authors, artists, and performers. Events in the fall semester included a convocation ceremony with campus partners, a lunch with professionals from GSAFE, a gender poetry workshop with a spoken-word artist, a workshop on gender and sexuality fluidity, and a performance with JAC Stringer, a trans-genderqueer activist and performance artist. Open House staff put a considerable amount of effort into bringing quality programming and discussion to the community to help students explore their gender identities and the identities of those around them. Much of this work was an effort to disrupt basic ideas about gender that students may have formed before coming to UW–Madison and Open House. On a basic level, Open House staff believed it was important for students to move toward recognizing that gender identity is formed and expressed on an individual level.

Despite the many positive aspects of the new living-learning community, Open House staff quickly realized some Open House residents were not as excited about having these conversations. In fact, several students chose Open House for its building amenities with little knowledge or interest in the gender exploration element of their living environment. This was largely attributed to the fact that any student could choose Open House as the place he or she wanted to live on the housing application.

Early in the fall semester and late in the spring, Open House staff asked the residents to complete surveys related to high-impact practices, their identities, and their experiences in the community. Conflicting opinions on Open House's climate presented a dilemma for staff when attempting to meet the mission of the community. Specifically, staff wondered if the community existed to provide a welcoming space for trans* students, or if it should be open to all students in the hope that they would want to become an active member of a gender-inclusive community. Additionally, staff wondered if there was a way to do both at the same time.

These questions represent a conflicting view of what Open House was supposed to be and how Open House staff had been pressured by various stakeholders to shape the residential learning community according to their priorities for the community (Figure 6.1). When students first approached university housing staff in 2009, the priority was to find a way to provide gender-inclusive housing to serve trans* students in a restrictive political climate in Wisconsin. However, throughout the proposal process, the original intent of Open House was transformed into a community based on gender education instead of a true gender-inclusive housing option. This was because of the housing limitations of UW System Policy 24-1(UW System, 1972), which dictated that coeducational housing in the system should separate men and women by floor or room, and because of feedback provided during the proposal writing stage. The idea that Open House should primarily be a safe space for trans* students persisted across campus the same way it has for other, identity-based, residential learning communities. Given the political atmosphere surrounding UW System Policy 24-1 and the fact that we were working at the flagship campus in our state, which was in close proximity to the state capitol, the department chose to continue to offer gender-inclusive housing on an individual basis instead of instituting a public policy, leaving Open House as an educationally focused community.

In subsequent years, Open House has been left with several spaces to fill, thus making it increasingly difficult to ensure trans* students will not face some sort of discrimination in their living environment. For the foreseeable future, it is inevitable that students with no exposure to gender or trans* contexts will end up living on the floor. This reality suggests that further difficult questions will be asked, such as: Is Open House providing a false promise of safety and comfort to trans* students? Is Open House actually better than most living communities on campus? And does Open House actually provide a safer space for trans* students than floors geared toward the general student population? These are hard but necessary to address and answer.

In Jon's work as the residence life coordinator for the residential area, Jon prioritized educational and open discussion about issues related to gender and various intersecting identities when working with the area's students and staff. Jon had a personal and professional stake in the success of the community, but at times it was difficult to know where to focus our efforts with the wide array of student needs related to gender identity and language. Jon does think it is possible to create a safe space for trans* students in Open House while also providing education about gender. Education and community-building efforts are important to this goal but are not enough to truly make Open House inclusive for all residents who live on the floor. In Jon's opinion, the first step toward creating a safer space was to make sure residents who chose Open House on their housing application know what to expect when they arrive on campus.

As a response to this issue, Open House staff have worked with partners in the university housing assignments office to make it more clear which hall or residential learning community students choose when they provide their housing assignment preferences. Open House staff have also moved the location of the community from the fourth floor (54 spaces) to the second floor (32 spaces) of Vel Phillips Hall in an effort to reduce the need to fill vacancies with residents who do not seek Open House as a living space but still want to live in the semiprivate community the hall offers. Moving Open House to the second floor, which had more community and lounge space as well as a classroom, allowed the faculty director to teach the Open House seminar on the Open House floor.

Clearly, resident recruitment was a key issue for Open House, and Open House staff created a more robust marketing plan for the residential learning community with help from campus and community partners. Open House staff worked with GSAFE to send information about Open House to high school counselors or GSA advisers who have worked with trans* students in the past. Open House also provided GSAFE with special tickets for larger events on campus so they could invite high school students to visit Open House and attend events geared toward trans* students. In the fall of 2014 Open House staff planned workshops in concert with the GWS department, including a visit from author and gender theorist Kate Bornstein. By working more with campus partners, Open House attempted to reach a broader campus audience.

REFLECTIONS ON THE FIRST YEAR OF OPEN HOUSE

After completing one year with Open House, the staff realized a programming model that started with gender identity workshops in the early fall was not as effective as hoped. Staff were excited to start discussions about gender but seemed to forget about the need to build a strong community, a critical component of life in residence halls and adjustment to campus. The discussions about gender facilitated by Open House staff exposed the knowledge and experience gap between residents, which divided—rather than united— the community. It became clear that some less knowledgeable or less experienced residents felt ostracized by residents who believed they knew more or had more experience with trans* contexts and gender diversity. Thus, the residents who might have benefitted the most from the open discussions about gender no longer wanted to participate. This also placed trans* students in a position where they had to explain, and sometimes validate, their identity to cisgender students. One student said,

> My first year, the floor was dominated by cis people, and I definitely did not feel safe talking about my experiences nor did I feel I had the space to explore my gender identity further. In my second year, the floor had a much larger group of trans people. As a result, the space felt a lot safer, and I could be more open about my identity. (Anonymous, personal communication, April 25, 2017)

The expectations for what Open House should be and what Open House turned out to be were not aligned, and Open House staff faced challenges when attempting to provide experiences for all students living in the community. The staff have learned that they cannot expose a group of students with a broad range of experiences to gender activism as early as they did. In the future, the goal for Open House is to build community and respect among students in the community first and slowly move through deeper topics while continuing to provide one-on-one support to trans* students in the community. This model is close to the current model some identity resource centers use (e.g., learning about diversity and difference and then moving on to issues related to privilege, oppression, and justice). We simply cannot expect students who have never been exposed to the idea of the gender spectra to be experts on gender theory in one semester. Furthermore, we run the risk of alienating would-be allies by not establishing a fun, respectful floor environment first.

Although Open House staff has had its share of challenges, we can say the residential learning community and its residents have had a positive impact on campus and on each other. Our residents have been able to learn about gender and how it intersects with other identities in their seminar class with the faculty director and through informal discussions and film screenings. An Open House resident shared the following:

> When I came to UW–Madison, I was both excited and terrified. I was out as trans at my high school but this would be a new start, one that included having to possibly share a floor bathroom with a group of initial strangers. After researching the dorms for Madison, I knew I needed to be in Open House so that I could have the safety of a bathroom in my dorm room. However, I have to say, after having lived in Open House for over a year now, a private bathroom is hardly noticeable compared to all that the community has done for me. (Anonymous, personal communication, April 23, 2017)

Open House residents challenged each other and staff to provide an inclusive community in Vel Phillips Hall, sometimes creating conflict and sometimes productive conversation. When asked to provide a highlight from the year, another resident wrote, "[I] really treasure some of the relationships I formed with people on my floor and felt safe expressing my identity here in ways I wouldn't have been able to in another dorm." As we moved forward with structural and programmatic changes for future classes, Open House staff continued to work toward providing a safe space where residents could engage in conversations about gender.

LONG-TERM PLANS FOR OPEN HOUSE

Some positive changes have happened on UW–Madison's campus between Open House's first and second years that have had an impact on the work of the Open House staff. Because of the diligent work of the LGBT Campus Center staff, a preferred-name policy and system were implemented, meaning every resident could provide a preferred name online, which would appear in student databases and be printed on their student identification card. Over the summer in 2014 the LGBT Campus Center and University Health Services held a Trans* Healthcare Roundtable and provided Open House staff with a wide range of support services for trans* students, including hormone replacement therapy. A trans* student who received hormone replacement therapy at UW–Madison spoke about this service in the following:

> Open House granted me the peace of mind for a private bathroom, but even more importantly, it gave me a loving and accepting family where I could be myself like never before, education about things I had never considered, and gave me the chance to take the steps I had been so desperately been waiting to take to make myself happy. (Anonymous, personal communication, April 23, 2017)

Open House staff also maintained connections with professionals at other UW System institutions who reported positive results with their gender-inclusive housing options. These developments affect the work of Open House staff and the residential learning community's long-term plans because it allows staff to rely on university systems for support rather than creating their own processes or referral networks that can quickly exhaust resources.

Spreading the word about Open House through a variety of channels will continue to be a large part of the work for Open House staff and its partners. If students do not know about the Open House program or do not want to take part in its educational activities, something has to change. Part of this effort lies in assessing the needs, satisfaction, and learning outcomes of the students who live in Open House through nationally benchmarked assessments and university housing surveys. For the time being, it seems Vel Phillips Hall is a great location for the residential learning community because it provides private restrooms, good community space, and as of spring 2014, all gender-inclusive public restrooms. Open House staff will also continue to assess the effectiveness of the programming model, including creating a peer-mentoring program with former Open House residents.

When we reflect on Open House and the process it took to open the residential learning community, we are proud of where we are but know there is more work to be done and more challenges to overcome. We know value has been added to the lives and education of the students who have participated in Open House. Open House staff have responded efficiently to the needs of the students in the residential learning community and work collaboratively with campus partners to advance gender-based initiatives on campus. This has been especially true for the support of trans* students, which has increased over the past several years because of the dedicated work of Open House's campus partners. In fact, Open House welcomed its first trans* house fellow, also a former Open House resident, into the community for the fall 2017 semester. We look forward to continued progress for the students of Open House and UW–Madison as a whole.

REFERENCES

Kaya, N. (2004). Residence hall climate: Predicting first-year students' adjustments to college. Columbia, SC: National Resource Center for the First-Year Experience and Students in Transition.

Kuh, G. D. (2008). *High-impact educational practices: What they area, who has access to them, and why they matter*. Washington, DC: American Association of Colleges and Universities.

Madison initiative for undergraduates. (2015). About the Madison initiative. Retrieved from madisoninitiative.wisc.edu

Resident assessment. (2014). Springfield, MO: Educational Benchmarking.

Simmons, J. (Director). (2005). *TransGeneration* [Motion picture]. United States of America: World of Wonder.

University of Wisconsin Madison. (2017). *UW facts and figures*. Retrieved from http://www.wisc.edu/about/facts/)[http://www.wisc.edu/about/facts

University of Wisconsin System. (1972). *Regent policy document 24-1: Coeducational housing*. Retrieved from www.wisconsin.edu/regents/policies/coeducational-housing

APPENDIX 6A
Open House Time Line

Date	Process
September 2009	Several students from the GSA present a proposal to the Department of Residence Life for a gender-inclusive housing option for students on campus.
September 2009– January 2010	Continued conversations take place with students about gender-inclusive housing. Staff and students agree that starting a residential learning community is the most feasible option.
February 2010	A listening session is conducted with GSA and gender and women's studies students to gather information for a residential learning community proposal
April 2010	An information session for the University Committee on LGBT Issues is held, and feedback from GSA and gender and women's studies students is provided. University housing staff starts forming what would become the Open House Steering Committee at this meeting.
September 2010	An additional listening session is conducted in the LGBT Campus Center and gathering student feedback is continued.
October 2010	Information on residential learning communities that focused on gender and schools where gender-inclusive housing was offered is gathered to provide more information for a residential learning community proposal.
December 2010	The final proposal for Open House, then referred to as the UW–Madison Gender Learning Community, in Vel Phillips Hall is submitted.
February 2011	The gender learning community proposal is accepted after being reviewed for funding from the Madison Initiative for Undergraduates.
March 2011– June 2012	Planning for the community continues. A faculty director from the gender and women's studies department is named.
September 2012	A program coordinator is hired by the gender and women's studies department to help recruit students for the new community and establish a program. The gender learning community is called Open House by students entering the community.

Date	Process
May 2013	A residence life coordinator is added to the residential area to help support the community.
September 2013	Open House welcomes its first 54 students on the fourth floor of Vel Phillips Hall.
June 2014	Open House is moved to the second floor of Vel Phillips Hall to accommodate a smaller community of 32 spaces.

Part Two

Initiatives Through Staff and Administration

7

Reconsidering Gender in University of Maryland Residence Halls

Deborah Grandner, Erin Iverson, and Amy Martin

GENDER-INCLUSIVE HOUSING AT THE University of Maryland (UMD) has been an important and necessary step forward in meeting the needs of our diverse resident population. The implementation of gender-inclusive housing on campus has unfolded over eight years (see Appendix 7A). In this chapter, we share our personal and professional perspectives about navigating the process of offering supportive housing options to trans* students. Prior to starting the chapter, we used a StoryCorps format (storycorps.org/about) to record our personal experiences and translate them into an in-depth account about the creation of the UMD's gender-inclusive housing program. We asked each other a series of interview questions in hopes of bringing to light the challenges and victories we experienced through this process. We also discussed the ways the unique climate and culture at the UMD influenced our collective journey.

We represent three unique perspectives in the Department of Resident Life (DRL). Deborah (Deb) Grandner, director of resident life, focuses on the big picture, political processes, and leadership challenges of introducing gender-inclusive housing to the campus. Erin Iverson, assignments manager, provides perspectives as the initial point of contact for many students during their tenure on campus and as the designated lesbian, gay, bisexual, and transgender (LGBT) liaison in the housing assignments office. Amy Martin, associate director of resident life, discusses her role in creating a safe and secure environment for students who identify as lesbian, gay, bisexual, trans*, queer, or questioning (LGBTQQ) through professional and student staff training, community building, programmatic efforts, and problem-solving.

DEPARTMENT CONTEXT

The DRL at the UMD serves a highly diverse population of about 12,000 undergraduate students living in traditional residence halls, apartments, and suites, including some public and private partnership properties. About 46% of all resident students are enrolled in living-learning programs covering a wide array of academic areas. The DRL employs a diverse workforce of more than 95 full-time and graduate staff members and about 400 undergraduate student staff members. The UMD campus is located in the greater Washington, DC, metro area, just 8 miles from downtown DC and 30 miles from Baltimore.

The DRL wants every student who chooses to live in the residence halls to feel safe and comfortable. One way the department achieves this goal is by offering a wide range of on-campus housing options. Historically, residence halls were designed to separate students into two sex-based groups, male and female. However, UMD students advocated for the residence halls to have more diverse living options as they relate to sex and gender room assignments. The DRL's shift toward providing gender-inclusive housing options is to create an inclusive and safe environment for those students who identify as LGBTQQ or who prefer to live with friends of the opposite gender. The staff of resident life also understand the importance of maintaining single-gender assignments for students who consider single-gender housing inclusive and safe. The rest of this chapter describes each of our personal journeys and walks through the details of how we implemented gender-inclusive housing on our campus.

CHALLENGING THE GENDER BINARY IN HOUSING SYSTEMS

The first leadership challenge in the development of gender-inclusive housing was creating a collective mind-set that serving trans* students was simply the right thing to do. It required a great deal of consciousness-raising, education, and commitment to make that happen. Consciousness-raising often begins because students call for a change or LGBTQQ communities advocate for students because they are acutely aware of the issues students face (Rittenberg & Tannous, 2013). For each of us, our own consciousness-raising was shaped by personal life and work experiences.

PERSONAL GROWTH AND UNDERSTANDING

For Deb, who attended college in the 1970s, this understanding came later in life and challenged her to rethink generations of gender socialization. Her experience with students, family, and friends who are gay made her aware of gay and lesbian issues earlier in life. These experiences began to break down the notion that gender is binary (the separation of sex and gender into two distinctly different groups). Learning that sexual orientation exists on a continuum helped Deb to consider that gender identity also existed on a continuum. She found that reading literature about gender and sexualities, attending conference sessions about gender and sexualities, and spending time with students were also beneficial to her understanding. Ultimately, however, the painful stories trans* students told about their experiences in housing prompted Deb's journey through understanding and led to action. In her own words, Deb described the following catalytic experience when she realized something needed to change:

> I can remember going to an LGBT forum on the campus and when I listened to how students were struggling to fit into our housing system and the challenges of being assigned to rooms by their sex and not by their gender identity, I knew that we had to do more. We had initiated mixed-gender single bedroom apartments but you had to be lucky enough to get one, and freshmen were not eligible. When I listened to the stories of bullying, prejudice, and hate, and stories of roommates and floor-mates who were insensitive, I felt when it came right down to it we were not helping students much at all.

Through Deb's experience at the campus forum, she felt compelled to advocate for and enact more substantial changes to the housing program in support of transgender students.

Erin came to the university after serving in the U.S. Army. She was hired for the assignments manager position without having the kind of experience some managers might have from a more traditional educational career path.

She did believe that every student had a rightful place in our community and was shaped by an experience in the army that was particularly challenging for her, as shown in the following:

> When I was a company commander in the Army in the late 1990s, the policy for LGBT personnel in the Army was "Don't ask, don't tell." As a company commander, I was responsible for about 200 soldiers of all different ranks. One day, a staff sergeant who had been in the Army for about 13 years—and was only seven years from full retirement—came into my office and said, "I am gay and I can't live the lie anymore and I understand that means you are going to have to process me out of the Army." While it was my duty as a company commander to uphold the policy and see that discharge through, I thought, "You give 13 years of your life to the Army and the best we can do is run you out the door?" There is an element of equity and justice in recognizing that that's just not right to do to somebody. This percolated inside me and stayed with me when I first encountered this issue in resident life. The department had clearly stated that every person has a place in the halls, period. I have never seen conditions on that and I have never seen exception statements to that. To me, that is the green light to just make decisions for students seeking housing, and that you'll trust my judgment when I do.

When Erin started in the assignments manager position, exceptions for housing trans* students were typically made at the director level. As a new staff member, Erin's instinct when trans* students approached her was to treat them like other special requests. She believed it was the right thing to do in a department that had demonstrated every student should be recognized for who he or she is and be able to live comfortably in the residence halls. However, the department did not have a published policy for handling those requests. Looking back, we realized just how hard it must have been for students to come to the director of a department to discuss such a sensitive aspect of their identity and to ask for accommodation. Handling things behind the scenes was similar to the "Don't ask, don't tell" policy. Having a transparent position that supports gender-inclusive housing takes an affirmative stance in favor of inclusion and finding positive solutions for everyone.

For Amy, her awareness of the experiences of trans* students was grounded in educational efforts at her undergraduate institution. Education in the late 1980s and early 1990s had begun to filter into resident assistant (RA) training programs. During a development session Amy attended, a faculty member presented information about sexual orientation and gender identity from a scientific and research-oriented perspective. The content of the session included a description of the continuum of trans* identity and discussed the medical aspects of gender such as anatomy, hormones, and chromosomes. Later in Amy's career, she developed a better understanding of the personal and social experiences of trans* students on a large campus. A pivotal moment in Amy's learning occurred during an encounter with an incoming first-year student, which she described in the following:

> It wasn't until our friend Jack came on my radar that it became very real for me. It was Jack who made me really think, "Here's this first-year student coming in who has decided at that point in time to change gender identity and we're suddenly scrambling to figure out how to help this student." I came to learn through the situation that Jack had been transitioning from female to male yet had been assigned to an all-female floor. While excited and happy for the student that he was able to make this change in his life, I was like, "Whoa, this assignment isn't going to work for him!"

This interaction energized Amy's desire to expand residential options for transgender students. In sum, these experiences led each of us to consider and reconsider our thoughts and practices regarding housing transgender students.

MAKING CHANGE ON CAMPUS

The DRL needed a new overall approach to transforming campus housing to support transgender students, which would include not only policy changes but also administrative, structural, and physical changes. To set the stage for transforming our housing operation, Deb met with her supervisor, students, the LGBTQ students and staff, the president's legal office staff, and the vice president for student affairs. Deb's primary goal was to communicate the housing needs expressed by trans* students on our campus and gain support for a task force to explore new residence hall options. Although potential models existed on other campuses, she wanted to design a program that would suit our campus. Because our campus had a large number of living-learning programs in multiple locations, the outcome would be to create housing options for trans* students across the campus.

Deb established a charge for the task force, which she reviewed with the vice president for student affairs to garner support and build trust in the process. The charge for the task force (goals, who should be involved, time line, and potential housing options to consider) was worth taking the time to write and review with campus administration. It also served as a guide to the committee. Deb, who asked Amy to chair the task force with Erin's assistance, said,

> When I selected a chair for the committee I wanted someone who had a passion for diversity issues, had been an advocate for change, was a patient and savvy leader who was unafraid to tackle tough issues. I wanted to be sure that we would create a program that the campus and the state could accept and that had minimal risk that anyone could step in and take it away. Not only did it need to be done right, it needed to be done well.

In addition to involving key campus leaders and creating a clear direction for the work, the campus and state political contexts must be taken into consideration. In 2012 we were fortunate to have many advantages that others might not have on their campuses. We had open-minded senior administrators ready to support trans* student housing, a campus community that took pride in serving LGBTQ students, and a state where political leaders were advocating for trans* identity protection rights (State of Maryland Commission on Civil Rights, 2014).

GENDER-INCLUSIVE TASK FORCE IMPLEMENTATION PROCESS

With a charge in hand, Deb and Amy worked on a committee structure that would help the department develop a plan for gender-inclusive housing. The committee work began in February 2012, and Deb's goal was for the task force to produce a report by July 1, 2012. The committee consisted of 18 people including the director of the LGBT Equity Center, members of the student PRIDE Alliance group, members of the Residence Hall Association, a representative from university communications, and resident life staff representing different units in the department. In five months, the committee came up with the fundamentals of the plan, but it still needed refinement.

Phased implementation of the plan (see Appendix 7A) shaped up after continued discussions with Deb, the LGBT Equity Center, students, and critical departmental staff who would have to manage the changes. Throughout the planning process, Amy checked in periodically with Deb to ensure the task force acted in ways that could be supported by campus leadership.

Terminology

At the first meeting, committee members discussed the role of the task force and what our ultimate objectives would be in the context of the charge. Members shared thoughts about gender-inclusive housing, which prompted a spirited discussion about terminology (e.g., *open housing, gender neutral, gender inclusive, gender blind, queer housing*). Our discussion of terminology took longer than expected because of generational perspectives among members of the committee. Because our charge was to establish housing options for trans* students across campus, we also had to help committee members—some of whom were unfamiliar with our housing operation—understand where buildings were located and the difference between traditional floor rooms, semisuites, suites, and apartments. Over time the committee developed fundamental definitions of each housing option (see Table 7.1) that could be applied in different settings.

While working on definitions, the committee had been calling staff members at more than 30 peer institutions (e.g., other Maryland system schools, Big 10 schools, Atlantic Coast Conference schools, and private colleges) that offered gender-inclusive housing (Beemyn, 2013). The purpose of this effort was to obtain as much information (e.g., room type, room assignment process, students served) as possible about what educators on other campuses were doing in support of gender-inclusive housing. Those conversations also reinforced the fact that our housing program was operating in a system and state environment that would support gender-inclusive housing.

Determining Housing Types

In determining various housing options, we had several challenges to wrestle with along the way. Our current building structures and administrative processes were grounded in the gender binary. Physical limitations in our buildings included lack of privacy in community bathrooms, sex-segregated traditional hall floors (wings designated as male or female), bathroom locations, and numbers of bathrooms in units. Administrative processes included

Table 7.1

DEFINITIONS OF *SINGLE-GENDER, MIXED-GENDER,* **AND** *GENDER-INCLUSIVE HOUSING*

Term	Definition
Single Gender	A housing option where floors, wings, semisuites, suites, and apartments are assigned by sex. Students residing in these assignments share a bedroom and bathroom with students of the same sex or gender.
Mixed Gender	A housing option where students live in a room with a student of the same sex or gender, but the room may be next to a room that is occupied by students of a different sex or gender. On traditional hall floors, community bathrooms are designated as male or female. Suite and apartment bathroom designations are determined by residents.
Gender Inclusive	A housing option where students, regardless of sex, gender, or gender identity, share the same bedroom. Gender-inclusive traditional hall rooms and semisuites have a private bathroom. Suite and apartment bathroom designations are determined by residents.

Note. From "Housing Availability," 2017.

separate male and female priority numbers for residents and housing infor-mation technology (IT) systems that required student sex designations to match room sex designations. These systemic barriers surfaced at various times and were resolved through patience, persistence, and heavy input by staff and students.

The committee conducted a random, 5-minute, Web-based survey of 1,500 residence hall students in spring 2012 to determine what future housing options might meet their needs. Of the 473 students who responded, 49% of students preferred to live on floors where sex or gender was not separated by wings or in mixed-gender suites and apartments. In the same survey 23% of students indicated a preference for gender-inclusive housing, and 28% indi-cated a preference for single-gender housing. We expanded on-campus housing options based on these diverse needs and preferences of our students. We cre-ated mixed-gender floors in our traditional housing so that some of our rooms with private bathrooms could become gender-inclusive rooms (see Table 7.1). In our first year, we piloted this option in one community where the layout of the floors was most conducive to offering multiple designated male and female community bathrooms. The committee also offered mixed-gender and gender-inclusive suites and apartments (see Table 7.1). These options were also in line with preferences of trans* and gender nonconforming students who indicated a preference for apartment-style living or self-contained singles in a study by Krum, Davis, and Galupo (2013).

Bathrooms

Bathroom locations and numbers became a surprisingly perplexing issue in identifying gender-inclusive housing locations. We wanted to be supportive of trans* students who needed the privacy of a personal restroom and those who wanted to use a public multiuser restroom. We also had to balance the needs of some students, staff, and faculty who had voiced concerns about transgender individuals entering the restroom of their choice. Our residence hall multiuse bathrooms lacked the privacy desired by trans* students and many other students. In the end, we decided to start by designating gender-inclusive spaces in bedrooms on traditional hall floors that had a private bathroom, preferably on a mixed-gender floor, with the intent of expanding that option over time. In suites and apartments, some of the bathrooms were also multiuse, or individual units only had one bathroom for all genders to use. This also raised concerns about privacy. Overall, bathroom privacy and accessibility are critical factors that must be accounted for in a gender-inclusive housing program.

Gender and Our Housing Priority System

As the committee considered how students would choose gender-inclusive housing, there were three major considerations. First, the task force was committed to offering gender-inclusive housing without an application process to protect student privacy and remove the obstacle of permission. Second, under the advisement of the university legal office, we believed once we offered gender-inclusive housing, all students should have access to the option. Third, we wanted the process of accessing gender-inclusive housing to be transparent and part of the overall room selection process.

The committee assumed it would designate gender-inclusive suites and apartments; however, this was incompatible with our current priority system and room selection technology. We would have had to create a separate room selection process for students to gain access to those units. This type of process would not meet the spirit and intent of our gender-inclusive housing. The committee had to work through these issues to create a more seamless process for accessing gender-inclusive spaces across campus.

Like many other campuses that have lottery or priority systems, our housing priority numbers were assigned to students based on sex designation (male or female), reinforcing the gender binary that existed in our system. Erin and our IT staff worked to understand what it would mean to take gender out of the priority system, allowing students to create mixed-gender groups to participate in room selection and to have access to spaces based on students' assigned priority number. According to Erin,

> Tom, DRL manager for software engineering, and I had figured out that instead of separate priority numbers for men and women, we could do one single list of priority numbers for all students, which we could actually leverage in room selection. At that point we realized we do not have to pre-designate spaces. We can actually let this exist within our normal process.

Deb remembers her reaction to this series of proposals to fundamentally change our processes in the following:

> I remember that as a big moment because we were going to change the process for everybody in order to accommodate gender-inclusive housing, and I remember thinking to myself that this was similar to discussions I had been involved in previously about how institutional processes perpetuate racism. You have got a process here that reinforces this binary system, and so if we are going to create gender-inclusive housing, we are going to need to change some fundamental ways we do business. And that means we may have to change things that some think are working just fine to be able to accommodate students who need this housing option. And I was interested to see how well it would go over with the students.

Amy and Erin used the committee to thoroughly examine any unintended consequences of the randomization of priority numbers that might result from removing students' sex designation from the room selection process. We provided this information to the residence hall association, and the student leaders responded by creating a resolution to advance gender-inclusive and mixed-gender housing as well as adopting this permanent change in our priority system. With these issues resolved, we were then able to incorporate the gender-inclusive housing program into the overall room selection process by allowing all students to access and designate their own units as inclusive of all genders.

Technology

IT staff can be great partners in supporting efforts to create gender-inclusive housing by overcoming technological barriers to successful implementation. Our department had an in-house system and a dedicated software development manager who could adapt our system to meet our needs. For other institutions, it is important to understand how existing student information and housing systems will interact with gender-inclusive housing efforts.

Changes to our existing technology were necessary to offer a gender-inclusive housing program that would meet our students' and campus's needs. Erin and our IT staff had been working on the ability to adapt our room assignment system to be more versatile when it came to gender. In the campus mainframe system, bed spaces were assigned as male or female, and the student's university sex designation had to match the male or female designation for the student to be assigned a bed. Erin worked with the larger campus IT division to change the student record system to allow us to designate residence hall spaces as "neutral (N)." This allowed students of any university sex designation or gender identity to be assigned to such a room.

Outreach and Education

Education was a central component of implementing gender-inclusive housing on campus (Blumenfield, 1993). The outreach efforts that were part of our charge in creating the plan also served as a way to educate the greater campus community about LGBTQ students' experiences in housing. We committed to educating different constituents across campus, including residence hall staff, student leaders, faculty, living-learning program directors, residential facilities staff, parent and family affairs staff, and university communications staff. One of the unintended consequences of implementing gender-inclusive housing was that it drew a great deal of attention from our school newspaper, which prompted greater understanding of trans* student experiences among the student body.

A unique piece of our implementation process involved creating a plan for educating students about the gender-inclusive housing options available to them through room selection. This training included descriptions and diagrams of the different housing options available, prompts to consider roommate choice and location choice, and prompts to consider the number of bathrooms in a suite or apartment. We also gave advice about having conversations with parents before move-in day and discussed how future vacancies in a unit would be managed.

During Year 1 of the pilot program, we required students to attend an in-person training session to be eligible to create mixed-gender groups in the room selection process. Four hundred students attended those sessions or an individual session with Erin. In Year 2 we created an online training program covering the same material, and 1,369 students completed the training during the spring room selection process. The Gender-Inclusive Housing Task Force believes this type of training has been critical to the success of our program.

Student Participation

In Year 1 of development we offered gender inclusive housing to returning students during room selection so we could gain some experience in this area. In Year 2 we offered gender-inclusive housing as an option on our housing application for new students. Participation has grown over the two years, as indicated in Table 7.2 and 7.3.

We conducted a survey about student experiences living in mixed-gender and gender-inclusive housing in fall 2013. Feedback from students was overwhelmingly positive, with 87% of responding students saying their needs were met with these housing options and 97% of responding students recommending it to others. We also found that students chose this type of housing for many different reasons, including feeling more comfortable with this type of housing option, being able to choose whom to live with regardless of gender, being consistent with personal values, and increasing their sense of safety and their overall sense of privacy.

Table 7.2
RESIDENTS BY GENDER, FALL 2013

Housing Options	Number of Residents
Single gender All halls	8,480
Mixed gender Traditional halls	371
Gender inclusive Traditional halls	6
Mixed gender Suites and apartments	39
Gender inclusive Suites and apartments	13

Note. From University of Maryland Department of Resident Life (2017).

Table 7.3
RESIDENTS BY GENDER, FALL 2014

Housing Options	Number of Residents
Single gender All halls	8,211
Mixed gender Traditional halls	1,067
Gender inclusive Traditional halls	6
Mixed gender Suites and apartments	38
Gender inclusive Suites and apartments	16

Note. From University of Maryland Department of Resident Life (2017).

FUTURE DIRECTIONS

As the three of us reflected on potential efforts that would help move transgender housing policies forward in the future, several areas came up in our conversation: creating coalitions with other campuses, rethinking facilities, and continuing to assess the effectiveness of various gender-inclusive options. Deb had an opportunity to work with other schools in responding to a Maryland state bill that would have blocked gender-inclusive housing on Maryland campuses. In the following, she recalled the importance of this moment and what it meant to stand with other housing directors as they spoke in support of gender-inclusive or open housing programs:

> On March 6, 2014, I gave testimony in Annapolis before the House Appropriations Committee of the House of Representatives. Campus leadership had contacted me and asked me if I would be willing to represent the campus against House Bill 1203, Institutions of Higher Education-Open Housing Policies-Prohibited Act (2014). House Bill 1203 was a bill that was designed to block universities in the state system of Maryland from allowing gender-inclusive housing on any of the state-supported institutions. I was proud that our campus was willing to take a position in support of gender-inclusive housing. It represented something very significant to me. I was also proud to present with other directors whose campuses made the same choice.

Three institutions, representing large and small state universities, presented a confident image of the program and enhanced its credibility. In the end, the bill did not move out of committee. Understanding what other campuses are doing in support of gender-inclusive housing can assist your own efforts in providing these options on your campus.

Another area is the development of new housing facility models that better support trans* students. It is important to find opportunities to involve our facilities' partners, including architects, housekeepers, and maintenance staff, about serving trans* students and how facilities that support trans* students also serve other special student populations. We traveled to Stanford University with our residential facilities architect to see how that university had created facilities that supported transgender students. Every time a facility is constructed or renovated, facilities staff can contribute to the design of new, more supportive spaces. Deb reflected on particular opportunities that we had to change our facilities as we constructed a new residence hall in the following:

> When we started to build Prince Frederick Hall in 2012 I requested that we have privacy restrooms to support trans* students and other students who needed privacy. I went to the architectural meeting, and I began to talk about how I wanted us to have gender-inclusive restrooms or privacy restrooms in this facility on every floor. They did some great design work based on our discussion and the experience of some of the architects.

As institution administrators consider long-term strategic plans, they have an opportunity to make a long-term impact by including supportive spaces in those designs in new construction and in renovations as well.

Finally, one area that is crucial for continued support of gender-inclusive housing is nationwide assessment of trans* support services and best practices (Currah & Minter, 2000). On your own campus, continual assessment can help improve and advance your program. That can come in the form of formal surveys, tracking data from room selection and assignments, and noting those more intangible identifiers described by Erin:

> Coming into this fall I felt really positive about where we landed with gender-inclusive housing and that we had students who were fully taking advantage of it. I think that's been a good marker for us too . . . a really positive response to how we rolled out the program.

CONCLUSION

In summary, three strategies ensured we could reach our goal of institution-alizing gender-inclusive housing. First, we created a plan that fit our institution. We considered the mission of our institution as well as the political climate on our campus and in our state. Second, we created a vision of where we were headed and were sensitive to the timing of the changes we wanted to implement. Sometimes making dramatic changes in sensitive areas too quickly can cause a strong reaction. Implementing our plan in stages built a foundation of success along the way to greater change. Third, we brought our institution along by building broad-based coalitional support. This process would not have been effective or successful without the help of students, staff, student leaders, administrators, faculty in living-learning communities, and representatives who are informed regarding the needs of LGBTQ students. Each of these constituents played an important role in tailoring a gender-inclusive housing program that was transparent, supportive, and safe for trans* students.

REFERENCES

Beemyn, G. (2013). *Colleges and universities that provide gender inclusive housing.* Retrieved from www.campuspride.org

Blumenfield, W. J. (1993). *Making colleges and universities safe for gay and lesbian students: Report and recommendations of the Governor's Commission on Gay and Lesbian Youth.* Boston, MA: Governor's Commission on Gay and Lesbian Youth.

Currah, P., & Minter, S. (2000) *Transgender equality: A handbook for activists and policymakers.* Retrieved from www.thetaskforce.org/downloads/reports/reports/TransgenderEquality.pdf

Housing availability. (2017). Retrieved from reslife.umd.edu/housing/mixedgenderinclusive

Institutions of Higher Education-Open Housing Policies-Prohibited Act, H.D. 1203, 2014 Leg., 434th Sess. (Md. 2014)

Krum, T. E., Davis, K. S., & Galupo, M. P. (2013). Gender inclusive housing preferences: A survey of college-aged transgender students. *Journal of LGBT Youth*, *10*(1/2), 64–82. State of Maryland Commission on Civil Rights. (2014, April 8). Gender identity protections added to state's anti-discrimination law [Press

Release]. Retrieved from www. http://mccr.maryland.gov/cgi-rumscript/csNews/ news_upload/PressMainPage_2edb.GenderIdentity0408PressRelease.pdf

Rittenberg, S., & Tannous, J. (2013). *Mitigating resistance to gender inclusive housing initiatives: Decision-making processes and implementation methods.* Retrieved from www.eab.com

University of Maryland Department of Resident Life. (2017). *Assessment and research.* Retrieved from reslife.umd.edu/aboutus/staff/assessresearch

APPENDIX 7A
Time Line for Mixed-Gender and Gender-Inclusive Housing at the University of Maryland

Date	Process
Fall 2008	Campus-affiliated apartments (12-month leases) offer mixed-gender units at the request of UMD's Residence Hall Association in 2006.
February 2011	LGBT Forum for the campus community is held. This initiated a small group in the Department of Resident Life to respond to direct feedback as quickly as possible, which then led to the formation of the Gender Inclusive Housing Task Force in January 2012 for further planning and implementation.
Spring 2012	The Gender Inclusive Housing Task Force conducts a survey to help us shape the types of gender-inclusive and mixed-gender housing we would offer.
Spring 2013	Mixed-gender and gender-inclusive pilot program is introduced and offered through the room selection process for returning residents.
Fall 2013	Residents move in to mixed-gender and gender-inclusive housing assignments.
Fall 2013	Residents in mixed-gender and gender-inclusive housing are invited to participate in the Gender Inclusive and Mixed Gender Housing Experiences Fall 2013 Survey. The results revealed how satisfied students are living in these spaces and how these options have helped meet their housing needs.
2014–2015	Program continues with expansion into new locations across campus.

8

Supporting *All* Students With Open Gender Housing Options

Chris Moody, Sara Bendoraitis, Matt Bruno, and Ryan Anderson

AMERICAN UNIVERSITY HAS EMBARKED on a multiyear transformation of open gender housing for first-year and returning or upper-class students. As institutional leaders in the campus life division, we have explored the motivation for having such an option. The use of *open gender housing* as American University's terminology, rather than *gender-neutral* or *inclusive housing* at other institutions, was our intentional choice in defiance of the notion that any genders not falling within the binary are neutral. Because words and names matter to the American University campus community, we resisted the trend of using the term *gender neutral* and instead chose *open gender* to reflect the institution's support of students who identify with a nonbinary definition of *gender*. Students' advocacy on this issue, beginning in 2010–2011, reinforced the importance for this comprehensive approach to their living experiences (McBride, Modic, & Moody, 2011). Although terminology has matured since 2010, as many campuses now describe their housing options as *gender inclusive*, American University has held strong to the use of *open gender housing*, sometimes shortened to *open housing*, as an important testament to supporting students in all their identities and genders.

Efforts to date include navigating campus politics; engaging students in strategy, design, and decision-making; addressing challenges to implementation; reviewing and updating relevant policies; assessing early results; and documenting future recommendations. Students have overwhelmingly supported the enhancement of open gender housing options, reporting that they feel it makes an important statement about inclusion at American University. Although the open gender housing option is infrequently requested, university administrators believed it was right to offer it in terms of consistency with institutional values. Housing & Residence Life and the Center for Diversity and Inclusion staff annually hear from 10 to 20 prospective self-identified trans* students, as well as an equal number of cisgender students, who are interested in an open gender housing assignment, many of whom cite the availability of inclusive housing options as a factor in their decision to attend American University. Through the use of focus groups, informal interviews, and individual conversations, students reported the convenience of roommate choice as the most frequent reason for selecting an open gender space, although most agreed that comfort and security in their living environment was equally important after further inquiry (Anderson, 2013).

In this chapter, we introduce American University's history, identity, and city context related to supporting lesbian, gay, bisexual, trans*, and queer (LGBTQ) students. After a brief overview of a few challenges faced by trans* students in collegiate housing, we describe the steps taken by American University since 2007 to develop and increase open gender housing options on campus, including more recent programmatic and facility initiatives. The chapter concludes with a discussion on future plans and recommendations for continuing to aggressively advocate for and make structural, programmatic, and facility improvements to support the experience of trans* students on campus and other students desiring to thrive in open gender housing communities.

AMERICAN UNIVERSITY AND WASHINGTON, DC

American University has a long history of supporting the LGBTQ community. There has been institutional support for the LGBTQ community since 1991, when the original GLBTA (Gay, Lesbian, Bisexual, Transgender, and Ally) Resource Center was created. The center (along with the Women's Resource Center and Multicultural Affairs) has now become the Center for Diversity and Inclusion, and serves as the main support office for LGBTQ students (in addition to first-generation students, multicultural students, and women). In addition to advising, advocacy, and education on LGBTQ topics and identities, the Center for Diversity & Inclusion also maintains a Trans* Resource Guide on the Center's website (www.american.edu/ocl/cdi/TRG.cfm) to aid the community in navigating and finding support in the university. American University received 4.5 out of 5 stars on the LGBT-friendly Campus Pride index in May 2014, and American University is included among the Best of the Best Top 20 Campuses in the Advocate College Guide for LGBT Students (Windmeyer, 2006). American University has progressively worked toward LGBTQ inclusion on campus for more than a decade. Starting with the GLBTA Resource Center, and continuing with the Center for Diversity and Inclusion and other units across campus, American University has offered numerous educational opportunities on campus, developed inclusive nondiscrimination policies (gender identity and expression was added in 2003, and sexual orientation was added around 2000), and successfully advocated for inclusive housing and medical insurance policies. We expand on this work in this chapter to describe progress and planned future actions.

American University is located in a progressive city, Washington, DC, which has created numerous laws that prohibit discrimination of a variety of identities and statuses, including LGBTQ identities. The DC Human Rights Act (1977) was amended on March 8, 2006, to add gender identity or expression to the list of illegal forms of discrimination, providing legal protection from discrimination for people who are transgender or transsexual. This protection covers individuals from discrimination in DC regarding employment, housing, public accommodations, and educational institutions, services, and programs of the DC government. The DC Office of Human Rights enforces this protection so that individuals are treated according to their gender identity and expression, not their presumed or assigned sex. The DC Human Rights Act and the Office of Human Rights provide important cultural and practical foundations to expand the university's support and advocacy for trans* students and individuals.

The chapter contributors are student affairs professionals who are currently or were previously involved in developing and implementing open gender housing at American University. Chris Moody is assistant vice president of campus life; Ryan Anderson is director of residential education at the Berklee College of Music; Sara Bendoraitis is director of programming, outreach, and advocacy for the Center for Diversity & Inclusion; and Matt Bruno is coordinator of LGBTQ programming for the Center for Diversity & Inclusion.

TRANS* STUDENTS' HOUSING CHALLENGES IN HIGHER EDUCATION

Trans* students often face unique challenges on arrival at college campuses, including self-disclosure, campus safety, and fear of isolation and marginalization (Beemyn & Rankin, 2011; Rankin, Weber, Blumenfeld, & Frazer, 2010). Regarding on-campus housing, a safe and comfortable environment that allows students to study, learn, grow, and thrive is essential (Hong & Kircher, 2010). From personal experiences and conversations with students, we understand that for some students, traditional, same-sex room assignments are not ideal or appropriate, and it is important for housing policies and facilities to evolve to meet the needs of students to create inclusive, welcoming environments (Anderson, 2013; McBride et al., 2011). In particular, trans* students may sometimes face challenges in finding housing that meets their needs in regard to their gender identity and expression, such as feeling safe with peers or roommates, wanting to be included and not isolated in residential communities, and being comfortable with privacy options in bedroom and bathroom facilities (Hong & Kircher, 2010; Sanlo 2005). Beemyn and Rankin (2011) suggested that few higher education institutions have developed policies and practices addressing the needs of trans* students. Many universities, including American University, assign housing based on an individual's legal sex designation, and most of their residence halls are designated as single-sex by building, floor, or room. As a result, trans* students often lack safe and comfortable on-campus housing options. At American University we continue working to change this problem to make on-campus housing options more accessible to all students.

EARLY DEVELOPMENTS IN OPEN GENDER HOUSING

Past housing records demonstrate that American University has been receiving and honoring requests for individual room assignments for trans* students since at least 2002 (G. S. Hanson, personal communication, February 19, 2002). In the early years of exploring housing for trans* students, the physical configurations of residence hall facilities made it challenging to systematically expand open gender housing options for trans* individuals or for any other student who wished to live with someone of a different sex. Before 2007 all efforts to provide appropriate housing placement for trans* students required individuals to self-identify as trans* to qualify for a single room, a room with a private bathroom, or a roommate of their choice. With a limited supply of single bedrooms featuring adjoining bathrooms, which were most often the room types requested by trans* students, these spaces were held separately and assigned in tandem with accommodations granted through compliance with the Americans with Disabilities Act (1990).

Starting in 2007, American University aggressively pursued residence hall renovations to meet the growing demand for increased privacy in housing for all students but particularly to address the housing needs of trans* students. Prior to 2007 less than 0.1% (about 4 beds) of American University's housing inventory was assignable to trans* students or designated as open gender housing, according to older versions of floor plans and past resident rosters. Based on national best practice recommendations, American University's residence hall construction and renovation initiatives since 2007 have created facilities with increased privacy in bedrooms and bathrooms (Beemyn, Curtis, Davis, & Tubbs, 2005; Rankin et al., 2010). American University is a campus where nearly 84% of available housing is traditional-style corridor residence halls, yet the institution has been successful in increasing the eligible open gender housing inventory to nearly 40% of rooms available in the past 7 years. From 2007 to 2013 American University increased from 0.1% (about 4 beds) to 39.3% (about 1,600 beds) of overall spaces designated as open gender housing. In 2007, 115 total bed spaces were available as an open gender housing option, yet only 16 students, or 14% of those eligible, selected to live in roommate groups of different sexes. By fall 2013, in comparison, 104 students had elected to live in an open gender roommate configuration out of the 1,600 eligible spaces. Even though the number of open gender housing spaces continued to increase annually, the results of the annual room selection process consistently demonstrated that students select open gender housing at a rate of about 10%.

Housing & Residence Life began construction in 2006 to convert an administrative building on the periphery of campus into a residence hall to assist with accommodating an increasing demand for on-campus housing. In discussion with the university's architects, Housing & Residence Life personnel expressed the need for an apartment-style residence hall on campus to retain rising junior and seniors in larger numbers and to meet the growing demand for more private accommodations, including the needs of trans* students. After demonstrating demand for privacy through survey methods and focus groups, staff from Housing & Residence Life convinced university architects that offering individual bedrooms was a more important design concept than considerations on the sizes of bedrooms as 62% of students who had moved off campus noted a single bedroom as a top-five desired amenity (Brailsford & Dunlavey, 2009). As a result, a proposal was developed by Housing & Residence Life staff highlighting the importance of building and offering single bedrooms in apartments with shared kitchens, living areas, and bathroom amenities, which included more of the amenities students who had moved off campus would have desired from a new on-campus facility (Anderson, 2013; Brailsford & Dunlavey, 2009). In 2007 Nebraska Residence Hall opened as American University's first apartment-style facility and first housing option where students could live in units with roommates of any sex or gender. The new roommate and housing option available in Nebraska Hall required several changes in administrative processes and documents, such as the Housing Room Selection Guide. In collaboration with the former GLBTA Resource Center, a statement on the Housing & Residence Life room selection website was developed to inform students of the new open gender housing option, which states,

> Nebraska Hall apartments are communities where students may select a roommate(s) regardless of sex or gender. Students who wish to request an accommodation related to gender identity or expression should contact Housing & Residence Life or the GLBTA Resource Center prior to the housing application deadline. (Housing & Residence Life, 2017)

To match the facility expansion, American University began to increase its residential programming efforts on issues of inclusion in 2008 with the creation of student-designed living-learning communities, which were called Residential Community Clusters, for returning upper-division students. One of the first cluster programs at American University was centered on LGBT identities. In 2008 and 2009 the American University student government also began advocating for increased open gender housing options for students. As a result, the percentage of campus housing eligible to be assigned as open gender housing increased to 13.2% by 2010 through the introduction of these living-learning community programs and leasing campus-adjacent apartment housing units.

Initial interest in open gender housing belonged to a very small number of students yet has increased over time as students now understand their future housing options when offered admission to the university. In conjunction with the creation of the Trans* Resource Guide, American

University administrators made it a priority to not only provide the open gender housing options but also educate students on the numerous resources available in campus housing and at the university. As a result of the new living-learning community options, new suite and apartment-style housing, and the renovations of existing residence halls, students could now participate in a housing process without indicating their sex or gender, or students could also still request individual consideration of their housing needs if they chose to self-identify as trans*. These new open gender housing options allowed students to choose whether to self-identify rather than requiring students to out themselves to have their housing needs addressed.

The physical addition of Nebraska Hall demonstrated to students at the university that the Center for Diversity & Inclusion and Housing & Residence Life had taken a step forward in accommodating trans* students' housing needs but in a limited capacity because the new apartments were only available to rising third- and fourth-year students. To address this continuing concern about the number of open gender housing beds available, Housing & Residence Life and the Center for Diversity & Inclusion worked with a group of student advocates to create a Residential Community Cluster floor in 2008, which offered students the opportunity to self-design a living community around a central topic or theme of interest with faculty or staff involvement. In its inaugural year, a group of 24 students proposed a community they named Intersections of Sexuality, Gender, and Culture, in recognition of the complexity and social construction of identities, and it was approved as a Residential Community Cluster for the 2008–2009 academic year. In the following year, 2009–2010, the community nearly tripled in size to 64 students and rebranded itself as the Over the Rainbow Residential Community Cluster. These two communities, in addition to several others also approved, were assigned to Centennial Hall, a suite-style residence hall featuring double rooms and semiprivate bathrooms. After two years of the Residential Community Clusters, with increasing participation after the first year, Housing & Residence Life decided to pilot a change to the program to test whether the driving force in student participation was the program itself or the suite-style accommodations by moving all Residential Community Clusters to a different residence hall. With the addition of a new Social Justice Living Learning Community, which is discussed later in the chapter, and the expansion of open gender housing options in other housing areas, student-led advocacy for Residential Community Clusters gradually waned.

RECENT PROGRAMMATIC INITIATIVES

With physical and program changes under way, a campus-wide Housing Options Task Force was created in 2011 to explore ways to dramatically expand student residence hall options throughout four years at American University (McBride et al., 2011). The task force was composed of representatives from administrative departments including Housing & Residence Life, the Center for Diversity & Inclusion, and the Wellness Center, as well as student organizations including the Residence Hall Association, Queers and Allies (the campus LGBTQ student group), and student government. The task force issued three recommendations that expanded open gender housing to all suite- and apartment-style residence halls, created alternatives for first-year students in open gender housing, and initiated a new advocacy-based residential theme community called the Social Justice Living Learning Community. It was recommended that the new theme community should have an open gender housing option with "the ability for students to live with the roommate with whom they are most comfortable, without consideration to the individual's sex, gender, or gender expression" (McBride et al., 2011). The task force recommendation for expanding open gender housing to all suite- and apartment-style residence halls was completed in advance of the fall 2012 semester, and the remaining two recommendations were implemented at the start of the fall 2012 semester. The Social Justice Living Learning Community, available to any new or returning student, was supervised by Housing & Residence Life in partnership with the Center for Diversity & Inclusion and located in Roper Hall, a traditional-style residence hall featuring sex-designated restrooms on each floor as well as an accessible, single-occupancy bathroom with shower dually designed to be gender inclusive and in compliance with the Americans with Disabilities Act (1990).

Choosing the right facility and creating the theme community, however, were not the only decisions made to open the Social Justice Living Learning Community. The process for marketing and assigning incoming first-year students posed a new challenge. Most incoming students interested in living in the living-learning community did not have a specific roommate request yet desired to live in a community where open gender housing was an option. To assist with roommate selection, Housing & Residence Life created an online Yahoo group and message board for students to interact with one another, share their roommate preferences, and self-match. Once students were invited into the Yahoo group, the students then created their own closed Facebook group to get to know each other and select roommates. Housing & Residence Life staff provide instructions and facilitated connections among students wishing to live in open gender housing, allowing students who want an open gender assignment to select the specific student as their roommate.

In the spring of 2013, two focus groups were conducted with students living in open gender housing, whether in the social justice community or in a suite or apartment-style rooms. Students' narratives in a report on the focus groups revealed important implications for open gender housing (Anderson, 2013). An overarching theme from the focus groups with upper-class students living in suite and apartment-style housing units was the convenience of living in open gender housing because they could choose close friends as roommates. One female-identified student stated that she generally got along better with men, thus preferring a male roommate. One issue reported by a male student was that he had experienced situations in which other students assumed he was gay or less masculine because he lived with three women. Generally, the students agreed that the advantages of living in open gender housing significantly outweighed any challenges they have experienced and that they were very pleased with having the option to live in an open gender space.

Other important themes emerged from the report; for example, as students in the Social Justice Living Learning Community saw open gender housing as an equity issue relating to the LGBTQ population (Anderson, 2013). Two roommates, one self-identified as male and the other as female, met on Facebook and decided to apply for the Social Justice Living Learning Community specifically so they could live together. They then found their third roommate, a female, through the community's private group on Facebook. The male student stated that he was gay and was afraid to live with another man through a random assignment. The students in the Social Justice Living Learning Community focus group agreed that the community made a positive statement about the university's values and level of inclusivity to have open gender housing options for all students. One student commented, "It shows the university really cares about its students and wants to create a comfortable environment for all of them." Another student highlighted the feeling of safety and "having a restroom you can go into without feeling weird" along with not having to check a male or female box, which she said leads to a feeling of more acceptance. All students agreed that having a space where they felt comfortable made transition easier in their first year and can lead to higher levels of integration into campus life. None of the students could recall negative experiences they had encountered as a result of living in an open gender housing space. The Social Justice Living Learning Community focus group members agreed there were stereotypes on campus; for example, their home, Roper Hall, was known as the gay residence hall, but they said this did not bother them. The group members also said that any roommate conflicts they had experienced were typical minor roommate issues and unrelated to the open gender aspect of their living situation.

Students in the Social Justice Living Learning Community focus group expressed the desire to expand open gender housing to all first-year areas (Anderson, 2013). Because the Social Justice Living Learning Community was the only open gender option for first-year students, it restricted access because it forced new students to choose between living in the Social Justice Living Learning Community or in other first-year housing options not designated as open gender. One student stated, "Just because you are trans* doesn't mean you should have to give up opportunities like University College or Honors housing," referring to two other successful and highly sought-after living-learning communities. The focus group students also said there was tension between those wanting to live in open gender housing and others wanting the theme community to be more broadly focused on a range of social justice issues.

The Social Justice Living Learning Community in Roper Hall was shown through Mapworks, a student retention and success software system, assessment data to have high student satisfaction scores in factors associated with connecting with other students and community development. Specifically, the Social Justice Living Learning Community reported 5% higher factor scores than the rest of campus for connecting with students with whom they shared common interests, 7% higher on satisfaction with connecting with students who include them in their activities, and 6% higher on satisfaction with connecting with students whom they like. The Social Justice Living Learning Community residents also had the highest scores across campus on questions related to spending time with other residents (10% higher), the extent to which they are able to study in their room (8% higher), and their intentions to hold campus leadership positions in student organizations (17% higher).

RECENT CAMPUS FACILITIES INITIATIVES

In addition to programmatic initiatives, we have been vigilant in our commitment to continue expanding the styles and types of housing available to students, including room types that support trans* student needs and requests for increased privacy. The expansion of campus housing with increased privacy for students has been a driving force in the institution's current Strategic Plan and Campus Facility Master Plan (American University, 2017). By 2017 American University added more than 1,600 new beds to the campus housing inventory to meet enrollment demands and to improve retention of juniors and seniors in campus housing. In planning for this expansion, particular emphasis was placed on housing types that support more private bedroom and bathroom accommodations to meet the desires of upper-division students as well as the needs of the growing population of students requesting gender-inclusive roommate options. After years of planning and construction, in August 2013 American University opened Cassell Hall, a new 358-bed suite-style residence hall, in which all units offer open gender roommate assignments, and it expanded Nebraska Hall apartments by 150 beds. The university also made all campus suite- and apartment-style residence halls completely open gender, regardless of the existence of a living-learning community. Recognizing that much of the effort toward open gender housing has focused on housing types most commonly assigned to returning students, the university also converted a number of double rooms into single-occupancy rooms in the traditional-style residence halls where first-year students most commonly reside. In terms of bathroom improvements, every renovation of a traditional-style residence hall now includes lockable shower stalls to provide students with increased privacy and furniture storage rooms that have been converted into single-user, full-amenity bathrooms that comply with the Americans with Disabilities Act (1990). The combination of these bathroom enhancements and the conversion of traditional-style housing double rooms into single rooms has enabled American University to more consistently meet the demand for living-learning community participation from first-year students so that no student is denied an academic or other learning opportunity because of housing needs.

FUTURE PLANS

Based on positive feedback from students, it has been evident that the creation of an open gender housing option for first-year students and the expansion of housing options for returning students were necessary and well-received enhancements to the residential experience.

American University continues to work on the renovation of residential facilities to increase the number and types of spaces available for open gender housing and has developed a commitment statement that describes the university's ongoing support and plan for expanding open gender housing; implementing training programs for housing staff and workshops for floor communities; and taking the lead in the national and campus conversations on trans*-inclusive policies, services, and benefits. Related to continued facility expansion, American University's residence hall renovations and new construction since 2007 have significantly increased its ability to be responsive to trans* students and many other student needs to maximize the educational experience. However, more work is still needed, particularly for students in their first and second year of campus housing. In first-year student communities, which are increasingly becoming cohort-driven based on academic courses, Housing & Residence Life staff plan to create more single rooms in traditional-style residence halls out of double-occupancy rooms to increase the number of students who can participate in first-year academic-based living-learning communities. In addition, Housing & Residence Life staff will continue to convert furniture storage rooms on residence hall floors into single-user, full-amenity restrooms.

American University currently offers a number of open gender housing living accommodations, yet no public statement exists for recruiting or retaining students interested in these living alternatives. A commitment statement would demonstrate the importance of each student's gender identity or expression and provide the Center for Diversity & Inclusion and Housing & Residence Life staff with common text for communicating with students. The statement should relate to American University's strategic plan as well as to its nondiscrimination policy. Additionally, regular training should be implemented for staff charged with recruiting, retaining, and providing students with an inclusive living and learning experience. Advancing the facilities and increasing the number of programs will fall short if additional student and professional staff training to support trans* student success is not a priority. Finally, American University continues to be a national leader in expanding programs, benefits, and services to trans* students, faculty, and staff. Among ongoing efforts are allowing students to have a chosen name on internal documents, creation of a Trans* Resource Guide, continued faculty and staff trans*-inclusive health insurance benefits, coverage for students in the student health insurance plan, changes in student identification cards, training across campus such as Trans* 101, and efforts to make university computing and software programs more inclusive and accessible.

CONCLUSION

Although trans* students directly benefit from the changes American University has made, all students now have more access to living options on campus. Open gender housing allows students the flexibility to live with the roommate of their choice, including students who are comfortable living with someone of any sex, gender, or gender expression. Open gender housing also allows students to construct the relationships that are most meaningful to them (Hong & Kircher, 2010). Implementing open gender housing demonstrates to those interested in the university (including potential students, faculty, donors, National Merit Scholars, and summer conference guests) that American University has a serious commitment to diversity and the needs of students.

Prior to the creation of an open gender housing option for first-year students, much of the conversation among staff responsible for its design and implementation centered on providing a space where students felt comfortable in hopes that increased open gender housing options would lead to greater levels of success, satisfaction, and retention. Over time it has become apparent that some students make their enrollment decisions based on the institution's commitment to open gender housing. Although a small percentage of students may see open gender housing as a deciding factor in where they choose to attend college, it illustrates the importance of making its availability well publicized in housing materials, print and online.

Working together on developing, improving, and increasing American University's open gender housing program has been an educational experience. We learned that student demand for enhanced services or resources are important for an institution to attend to because of the significance of supporting each student but also because a college's response to what the right thing to do is as champions of student success and social justice advocates sends a broad message about the value of inclusion on that campus and to the external community. It is important for campuses, specifically housing and residence life professionals, to advocate for students' needs in the practical areas and not just in the theoretical ones. For example, we were contacted by two incoming students in summer 2012, one who identified as trans* and the other who identified as genderqueer. Both students stated that the availability of the open gender housing option for first-year students was the reason they had chosen to attend American University. The students also commented on the difficulty they had in finding schools that had such an option for first-year students and said they were excited to live in the community after having experienced some level of anxiety at the prospect of having to live in a traditional-style, first-year residence hall. Although the percentage of students who select an open gender housing roommate group is only 10% (300–400 students) annually, it is still important for facilities and programs to use universal design concepts as if this demand percentage were much higher, simply because it is the right thing to do.

When working with student activists or young professionals, student affairs professionals should continuously remind them that they might not see the fruits of their labor, but that does not mean the advocacy is not worth their effort. We have noticed an increase in individual conversations about open gender housing options with incoming trans* students compared to discussions on this topic with currently enrolled students. This should be kept in mind when making sure to include first-year and transfer options or at least have options available for first-year and transfer trans* students when they inquire, but it does not mean that education and training is not needed for returning students or staff at the institution. As mentioned throughout this chapter, American University has been evolving in terms of trans*-inclusive housing for many years, and the students who have pushed and questioned campus policies and practices led American University to make great strides when space and opportunity aligned.

REFERENCES

American University. (2017). *Strategic plan*. Retrieved from www.american.edu/strategicplan

Americans with Disabilities Act of 1990, Pub. L. No. 101-336, 104 Stat. 328 (1990).

Anderson, R. (2012). *MAP-Works responses by hall—fall 2012*. Washington, DC: American University.

Anderson, R. (2013). *Housing & Dining Programs open gender housing focus group report*. Washington, DC: American University.

Beemyn, G., Curtis, B., Davis, M., & Tubbs, N. J. (2005). Transgender issues on college campuses. *New Directions for Student Services*, 111, pp. 49–60.

Beemyn, G., & Rankin, S. (2011). *The lives of transgender people*. New York, NY: Columbia University Press.

DC Human Rights Act of 1977, Section 1150 of D.C. Law 18-111 (1977).

Hong, C., & Kircher, A. (2010). *Gender neutral housing: Key considerations, implementation strategies, and assessment*. Washington, DC: Education Advisory Board.

Housing & Residence Life. (2017). *Room selection guide.* Retrieved from www .american.edu/ocl/housing/roomselection/room-selection-guide.cfm

McBride, S., Modic, K., & Moody, C. (2011). *Housing options task force report.* Washington, DC: American University.

Rankin, S., Weber, G., Blumenfeld, W., & Frazer, M. S. (2010). *State of higher education for lesbian, gay, bisexual, & transgender people.* Charlotte, NC: Campus Pride.

Sanlo, R. (Ed.). (2005). *Gender identity and sexual orientation: Research, policy, and personal perspectives. New Directions for Student Services,* 111.

Windmeyer, S. (2006). *The advocate college guide for LGBT students.* New York, NY: Alyson Books.

APPENDIX 8A
Supporting *All* Students With Open Gender Housing Options

Date	Process
1994	AU opens a volunteer-run GLBTA Resource Center on campus.
2000	AU adds sexual orientation to institution's nondiscrimination policies.
2001	GLBTA Resource Center employs first full-time staff member.
2002	The earliest recorded history of AU making housing accommodations or arrangements for trans* students. AU creates a formal agreement (passed by the board of trustees) to design at least one single-user restroom in all new or renovated facilites hereafter.
2003	AU adds gender identity and expression to institution's nondiscrimination policies.
2006–2007	AU Housing Room Selection Guide is revised with the GLBTA Resource Center to include a statement of the expanded opportunity to live in an open gender housing assignment.
August 2007	AU opens Nebraska Hall, including the open gender housing option for all residents of that community.
2008–2009	AU develops and pilots residential community clusters, which are living-learning communities, for returning students, including a floor wing available for open gender housing
2008–2009	AU adds benefits to health insurance for transgender faculty and staff.
Summer 2009	Anderson Hall (traditional-style residence hall) is renovated to provide lockable shower compartments in community-style bathrooms; all future renovations of traditional-style residence halls followed suit in subsequent summer renovations.
2009–2010	The second residential community cluster is initiated, featuring double the number of student residents than in the inaugural year.

Date	Process
2011	AU Housing Options Task Force convened to develop a strategic direction for future of open gender housing programs and options.
August 2012	AU Social Justice Living Learning Community opens, offering the option for first-year and new students to live in open gender housing.
Spring 2013	Focus groups are conducted with student participants living in open gender housing roommate pairs and groups.
Summer 2013	AU adds benefits to the student health insurance policy for transgender students.
August 2013	AU opens Cassell Hall Suites, which includes the open gender housing option for all residents of that community; AU builds an addition to Nebraska Hall, expanding the availability of open gender housing. All existing suite-style and apartment-style accommodations in other parts of campus are included in the option to be open gender.
August 2016	Three new semisuite-style residence halls open, housing 590 students, with the open gender housing option.

9

Transforming the Transgender Housing Process

A Tailored Approach

Luca Maurer and Bonnie Solt Prunty

THE WORK TOWARD AND creation of the trans* housing policy at Ithaca College became the starting place of something much bigger: the opportunity to think differently about the housing options offered on campus and how they could better meet the needs of all our students. Although not planned at the time, the conceptualization and implementation of the policy became the cornerstone for creating more diverse housing choices for cisgender students as well. This chapter describes Ithaca College's experience with creating a housing policy for trans* students to identify and obtain the on-campus housing option that best meets their individual needs. It outlines the process of becoming aware of unaddressed student needs, collaborating to develop the policy, navigating campus culture and politics, responding to unexpected challenges and opportunities, and the ways the experience of creating the policy ultimately resulted in the creation of new housing options for all students.

Ithaca College is a private, independent institution located in Ithaca, New York, in the heart of the Finger Lakes region. Originally founded in 1892 as a conservatory of music, it expanded to include courses of study in the humanities and sciences, business, communications, health sciences, and human performance. The college enrolls about 6,500 full-time students, has a strong liberal arts core, and offers several preprofessional and graduate programs. Ithaca College has been designated by Campus Pride, a national organization working to create safer college environments for lesbian, gay, bisexual, and transgender (LGBT) students, as one of the top 25 LGBT-friendly campuses in the nation (Nicholas, 2013). The criteria used for this distinction are measured via an index that assesses campus climate through a set of more than 50 questions, corresponding to 8 different areas that include LGBT policy inclusion, LGBT support and institutional commitment, LGBT student life, and LGBT housing, among others. This is especially relevant as this chapter relates to several of these areas, most specifically inclusive policy, institutional commitment, and housing as they affect trans* students at Ithaca College. The chapter contributors are Bonnie Solt Prunty, director of residential life and judicial affairs, and Luca Maurer, program director of the Center for LGBT Education, Outreach, and Services. Bonnie and Luca, with residential life staff, have collaborated for many years to create the trans* housing policy and to continually improve, expand, and diversify residence hall opportunities for students.

Ithaca College is a comprehensive residential institution with more than 70% of students living in on-campus housing. In addition, Ithaca College has an energetic student population with more than 200 registered student organizations on campus and many additional academic and cocurricular initiatives. Students living, learning, and working on campus have easy access to countless opportunities on campus; thus, residing on campus is central to the Ithaca College educational experience. Therefore, welcoming, safe, and inclusive residence halls are critical to contributing to Ithaca College's campus environment.

All students have different needs, wishes, and goals when it comes to housing. Just because students identify as trans* does not mean they will want to live in LGBT-specific housing or a gender-neutral floor, or any other one-size-fits-all placement (Beemyn, Curtis, Davis, & Tubbs, 2005). Ithaca College's trans* housing policy was first established in 2004. Since the time it was put into place, more requests to use the policy are coming in from students every year.

HISTORY AND OVERVIEW OF GENDER-RELATED HOUSING PROPOSALS AND POLICIES

When Ithaca College obtained an existing apartment complex in 2002, the Circle Apartments, it allowed mixed-sex units. Unlike other campus apartment-style housing options at the time, students could live in these three- and four-bedroom apartments in mixed groups of males and females rather than each apartment being restricted to only students of the same birth sex. This mixed-sex housing in the Circle Apartment complex was the closest option to a gender-neutral housing practice until 2003.

In 2003 Ithaca College developed its first gender-neutral housing proposal, which sought to allow mixed groups of men and women to live together in all college housing units. The proposal was a response to LGBT students who were looking for more supportive roommate experiences in the residence halls. The proposal was not approved because of concerns related to parental reactions. In particular, one type of concern involved heterosexual students using the policy to work around a no cohabitation policy that prohibited heterosexual students from living with their significant others.

In 2004 the college created a trans* housing policy that allows any student who identifies as trans* to live in whatever housing arrangement is the best fit for the student's individual needs. At this time students of different birth sexes were not allowed to share a bedroom for any other reason. Building on the success of the trans* housing policy and the mixed-sex units in the Circle Apartments, gender-neutral housing options allowing students of a different sex to live in the same apartment unit were expanded in 2007 to include the college's Garden Apartments, which house two, four, or six students in double bedrooms. In 2008 a pilot gender-neutral housing floor was established in a traditional residence hall, and an LGBT residential learning community came shortly after. Both these options were short lived as students indicated they could have their needs or interests met in other existing housing options.

THE TRANSGENDER HOUSING POLICY

Formulating the trans* housing policy required a number of steps and addressed a previously unmet student need. It also ultimately resulted, over time, in the creation of several new housing options for all students. In 2004 the college created its foundational residence life policy to address the needs of trans* students. The Transgender Housing Policy was instituted in response to specific needs identified by trans* students at the time. In the policy, the term *transgender* is used to describe a person whose gender identity differs from the biological sex the individual was assigned at birth. The policy uses *transgender* as an umbrella term to refer to the range and diversity of identities in transgender communities (which may include people who identify as *transgender, transsexual, trans*, genderqueer, gender nonconforming, nonbinary,* and other terms) because it is currently the most used and recognized term on campus and among prospective students. Recognizing that language used within trans* communities continues to evolve and change, different people use terms in different ways, and each term has a complex history and meaning that has evolved over time, staff invested significant energy into intentionally naming the end policy. The staff wanted to balance the need for the policy's name to be the most inclusive while also addressing the likelihood that those unfamiliar with Ithaca College would seek information online about policies, programs, and services of interest to transgender students by using the term *transgender.* Residential life and the Center for LGBT Education, Outreach, and Services staff have revisited the issue of whether the policy should be renamed several times since it was instituted to make sure *transgender* is still the most inclusive and most searched term on the college's website. Based on feedback from current and prospective students and their families as well as the search terms visitors most commonly use on the college website when seeking information related to transgender student housing, the policy's name has remained the same.

Under this policy, trans* students can indicate their preferred living option, and the college accommodates their request. To make a request, students download a trans* housing accommodation form from the Office of Residential Life website, complete it, and submit it to the assistant director for housing services in residential life, who has been specially designated for this role, or to the LGBT center program director.

Students may also contact the LGBT center or residential life to request consultation or assistance when considering or completing the request. The student then meets individually with a specially trained designated staff person in residential life (since the inception of this policy, this has been the assistant director for housing services) and the LGBT center program director. During these meetings, the student's unique needs can be explored and clarified, and all housing options are described to the student to find the most appropriate housing solution.

The trans* housing policy is open to all who identify as trans* in any way, and with this policy a student may live anywhere on campus. It provides personalized housing not merely relegated to only one specific hall or floor on campus but wherever the best fit is for each individual student's needs, throughout all campus housing options (an approach supported by Williamsen-Garvey, K. & Wisener, 2006). This can be a single, double, apartment, on a single-gender floor, mixed-gender floor, mixed-gender apartment, or in specialty residential learning communities, and in each individual case, with the exact room, restroom, or roommates of their choosing.

Students can find out about the policy and how to request accommodation in several ways. Information about the policy and the request form are provided on the college website in several places including the residential life and LGBT center Web pages and on social media. Information about the policy is also provided to all first-year, transfer, and international students at summer orientation, in presentations by residential life staff about housing and roommate selection. The college's dedicated online social networking site for accepted students also provides this information in the residential life and LGBT life forums, where prospective students, current students, staff, and faculty can interact. Students, prospective students, and their parents can also contact residential life or LGBT center staff directly to inquire about how housing needs of trans* students are met.

DEVELOPING THE POLICY

Residential life and LGBT center staff members were committed to creating a policy that would provide the widest variety of options for trans* students. Staff members recognized that students gain key interpersonal skills and participate in experiences that support their academic development (outcomes noted by Robison, 1998) as well as contribute to the vibrancy of a residence hall environment. At the time the policy was being developed, the book containing Robison's (1998) work was the only resource available specifically about LGBT college students. This text contributed to this policy work because it reinforced what staff recognized through observation to be true and because it served as an important reference and external source of credibility colleagues and supervisors could turn to as residential life and LGBT center staff sought to discuss, create, and shepherd this new policy toward approval.

Thus, housing can firmly establish (or detract from) trans* students' feelings of safety and having their needs met (Beemyn, 2005; Rankin, Millar & Matheis, 2007). A policy allows trans* students to experience these benefits while living safely in community with their peers in the housing configuration that best addresses their needs. Staff members also shared the conviction that trans* students should have their needs met, even if at the time few institutions had adopted housing policies or other supports for trans* students on college campuses (Beemyn & Rankin, 2011).

The discussion about having a transgender housing policy began in an effort to meet the needs of a student who began the transition process while living on campus. In the first year at the college, a student had been serving as a volunteer in the LGBT center, and since that time the student had also become involved in a number of student organizations while also pursuing academic and leadership opportunities across many disciplines and interests. At the beginning of this student's junior year, the student said that following a deeply introspective process over the summer, he had come to the understanding that he identifies as a trans* person, and that he had chosen the new name Justin. He had a list of questions about services available on campus and in the community to support him in his transition.

He was also delighted that his roommate was unwaveringly supportive and remained one of his closest friends and fiercest allies. They had been matched through a random assignment process the summer before they became first-year students. They had become fast friends, developed a strong bond, and chose to remain living together in subsequent years on campus. Justin's roommate was completely supportive of Justin's gender identity, and she enthusiastically wanted to continue rooming with him.

Justin decided to be increasingly open in sharing his gender identity with others on campus, including volunteering to be interviewed by the campus press and participating in LGBT student panel discussions for classes and residence halls as an out transgender person. Over time, Justin had achieved a number of goals related to his transition. He had engaged in a supportive and helpful counseling relationship with one of the campus psychologists to clarify what he envisioned his transition to be. He legally changed his name and had begun hormone therapy. He had also changed some of his identity documents to reflect his new name and gender marker, and was just about to have his records updated with the college's registrar when he encountered a roadblock.

The conversation about trans* housing options started when Justin had just learned that because he was about to change his gender marker on his records with the registrar, he would not be able to continue in the same campus housing arrangement with the same roommate. At that time, all rooms on campus had a coded sex-designation field in the housing software (male, female, or coed). The sex field used by the software corresponded to the student's gender marker on record with the college (M or F) as per their identity documents when they were admitted. Rooms that were coded *coed* automatically adopted the gender marker of the first student who selected to live in that room. A must-match feature then required for the next student signing into the room to have the same gender marker on his or her record. At the time, if students changed their gender marker with the registrar, it could cause their campus housing options to change because college policy did not allow cohabitation, which meant on-campus students could not live in mixed-sex placements. Thus, a student's options would include moving to an apartment, a single room on a coed-by-door (single-sex rooms with men and women living on the same floor), living with only roommates with the same gender marker on their records, or considering off-campus housing. It would not allow Justin to continue living with the same female roommate, even though they both wanted to continue in their same living arrangement. According to Bonnie,

> I had the opportunity to get to know Justin and work with him as a student leader prior to the time he began his transition. When he came to the Residential Life Office to discuss his desire to continue to live with the same roommate during his transition, it was the first opportunity I had to work with an out trans* student. Hearing from Justin about the challenges he was facing on campus really helped clarify for me the importance of making sure that trans* students can live in accommodations that provide them with a safe space. If Justin could navigate all of the challenges facing him in transition, surely we could figure out how to work around the limitations of our current computer system.

There was no policy at the time to address the needs of trans* students regarding housing options. The director of residential life and the assistant director for housing were interested in helping in any way possible. They invited Justin and the LGBT center program director to discuss his needs with them so they could assist in finding the best possible outcome. There had been discussions in the past about how best to accommodate transgender students in the residence halls, but this was the first request by a current student. Because the request involved two people who had already been living together on campus for three years and who wanted to continue living together in the same unit, Justin's scenario became a prime opportunity for strategy and discussion.

The director of residential life and the LGBT center program director identified several issues that would need to be carefully considered as a policy was drafted. First, they anticipated the need to address the same concerns about parental reaction and student manipulation of the policy that derailed approval for the gender-neutral housing proposal in 2003. They also knew that a technology work-around would need to be identified in the automated housing selection process that would allow two students of different genders to be assigned to live in the same room. Also they would need to work closely with the student and professional staff living in residence halls to train them about the needs of transgender students as well as how to respond to parent or student concerns regarding where transgender students may live.

Before becoming mired in the logistical details, the director of residential life and the LGBT center program director wanted to make sure to find a shared philosophy that would become the basis of the policy. In the following, Luca recalls discussing the philosophy that would form the basis of a transgender housing policy:

> As program director of the LGBT Center, I felt it was nonnegotiable that the policy allows the student to self-identify—the required meeting of the student and LGBT Center program director would not have an evaluative component to determine student's gender identity in any way. The purpose of the meeting would be to clarify each student's specific needs so that the best possible housing could be individually determined. Additionally, it was essential that the best housing would be provided to the student, regardless of the cohabitation policy and other issues such as traditional room/floor, roommate, and bathroom configurations.

Once those two underlying tenets (no evaluative component and any housing placement and configuration would be available) were agreed on, a policy proposal was drafted and submitted to the vice president for student affairs. It was easier to get approval for the transgender housing policy than it was for the gender-neutral housing proposal because it involved smaller numbers of students and each request would be processed individually. The administration also had confidence in the professionals slated to work with the trans* students to find solutions that would meet the needs of the student and the institution.

Once the new policy was approved, the director of residential life met with the assistant director for housing services to discuss the implementation of the new policy. The assistant director created the housing accommodation form used by transgender students to submit a request. The assistant director put information about the new policy and the accommodation request process on the departmental website and integrated information about it into presentations for students and parents during summer orientation. Residential life staff could not find an automated way for the housing assignment system to allow different gender students to share a room, so the office staff developed a manual method.

The college newspaper also announced the policy to the campus community in a feature story highlighting the change and ways it would benefit trans* students. Once news of the policy was announced through these methods, the program director of the LGBT center played a critical role in training residential life staff regarding supporting the needs of transgender students and addressing questions or concerns from parents and students about the new policy.

The policy was further tested several years later when an incoming first-year student did not want to live in a single room on a coed-by-door floor. The singles and apartment options had previously been requested by students using the policy. However, Sam, an entering student, wanted to live in a double room with a roommate in a first-year-only residence hall. Sam was transitioning from female to male and wanted to be housed on an all-women's floor with shared bathrooms with a woman as a roommate. Although Sam was transitioning, he stated he would still feel most comfortable and safe on a women's floor. This tested the institutional commitment to meeting the individual needs of transgender students because of significant concern about how other first-year women, and their parents, might react to Sam's living on the floor.

Bonnie worked with the program director of the LGBT center to review the challenges they had encountered during past proposals for gender-inclusive housing. They met knowing that parental concerns were a major barrier to the initial gender-neutral housing proposal in 2003 and expected similar concerns with the transgender housing policy. According to Bonnie, they discussed proactive steps that could be taken to address these concerns,

> I can remember attending a series of challenging meetings with the vice-president for student affairs, the college attorney, and our compliance officer. At those meetings we spent a great deal of time talking about the differences between what kind of accommodation would be required by law versus what kind of accommodation would be best for the student. We discussed the anticipated negative parent and student reaction that might occur if we honored the transgender student's request, as well as the negative impact it would have on the transgender student and the transgender housing policy if we denied the request. We ultimately granted Sam's housing request because the policy had been clearly formulated and rested upon the commitment to individually meet the specific needs of each transgender student. Staff members were made available at opening move-in day to respond to any questions or concerns that might come up, but the institution never heard from a single parent or student.

ASSESSMENT

Students, alumni, and parents have consistently provided positive feedback about the policy through personal communications as well as program evaluations and focus groups. In a 2008 program evaluation of all LGBT-themed programs and services at Ithaca College, student and alumni respondents ranked the policy as one of the most important offerings at the college. A senior student said, "It really eased my mind when I found out I could live in the exact kind of room I needed, and with the roommate I felt most comfortable with." The roommate of a junior student said, "I've known my roommate since we were both at Orientation. It's amazing to see how she can use all her energy on her classes now. She feels at home and safe here, and it really shows." The parent of a first-year student commented, "When we heard about Ithaca College's housing policy, and all the services for transgender students, we knew [Ithaca College] was the right choice for our son's education." (Maurer, 2008). Efforts continue to monitor satisfaction with and effectiveness of the policy.

TIME LINE FOR TRANSGENDER HOUSING POLICY

Appendix 9A presents a chronology of the major events and decisions that led to the creation of the trans* housing policy and provides a reference for the progression of work toward the policy, from the factors put into place that assisted with its conception and discussion through implementation. The adoption of the trans* policy ultimately resulted in changes to the gender-neutral housing options for all campus residents, as a foundation for further work toward expanded gender-neutral housing options, and a possible open housing policy in the future. After several proposals, and attempts that spanned more than 13 years, an open housing policy was approved in winter 2016 for all returning students.

CHANGING TIMES, CHANGING REQUESTS

Requests under the policy have steadily increased over the past decade from 1 request in 2004 to 10 requests in 2013 to 10 more requests in 2014. As the number of trans* students on campus has grown, requests are becoming more nuanced and at times reflect societal changes compared to a decade ago. For instance, we have received requests from first-year students who transitioned while still in high school but who have not yet been able to change their gender identity on identity documents because of varying and restrictive state requirements. Also, we have had requests from students who want to obtain appropriate housing but sometimes also want to maintain their privacy or be *stealth* (i.e., not disclose their transgender status) with the entire campus community. Under Ithaca College's policy, students only have to share information with two people, the assistant director for housing services and the program director of the LGBT center who must be told to secure students' housing needs. For requesting students, disclosing their status to anyone else is entirely their decision. The student request process was further refined in 2016, when the request form was made voluntary rather than required. Students only had to communicate their housing needs to the assistant director for housing services or the program director of the LGBT center. Students' housing needs will be met regardless of whether they decide to fill out the form.

College staff are also increasingly encountering parents who are supportive and involved and want to assist their transgender students with navigating the housing process. Parents may contact the LGBT center or residential life to try to select housing for their transgender student. Sometimes, however, the wishes of the students and the good intentions of their parents may be in direct conflict. Parents may have different ideas about the most suitable housing for their student. For example, parents may be interested in their student living in a single room in a coed hall because they are focused on safety, whereas the student may be interested in entirely different housing options.

RECOMMENDED STEPS AND STRATEGIES

Based on the experience at Ithaca College with implementing the trans* housing policy, the following are recommended strategies and steps for creating a policy:

- When possible, describe real-life student situations (being mindful to preserve confidentiality) to help illustrate the importance of adopting a transgender housing assignment policy.
- Avoid the temptation to adopt a one-size-fits-all approach.
- Know or learn the process at your institution for getting a major proposal reviewed and approved.

- Work to build allies among key stakeholders who will be involved in the approval process.
- Identify obstacles to implementing your policy, and make sure the proposal addresses how you will work around these obstacles.
- Provide information on what other institutions are doing to accommodate transgender students.
- Create a communication plan that addresses how to disseminate the plan internally and externally.
- Be prepared to review the policy and adapt it as new situations arise.

Ithaca College created a policy centered on exploring, and then meeting, the specific needs of each individual trans* student who can have unique housing needs that require a more individualized process. Transgender students are also as diverse in terms of backgrounds, dimensions of diversity, and process and stages of gender identity development (Bilodeau, 2005) as all other students (Beemyn et al., 2005). Like all students, trans* students must balance multiple identities including not only gender but also race, ethnicity, class, ability, orientation, faith tradition, and others. They must also consider whether or when to transition, what transition means to them, and decisions about whether and with whom to share their trans* status. Some trans* students may have socially or medically transitioned while still in high school; their needs may be quite different from students who do so while in college. Other trans* students may choose not to medically transition or may not have access to do so. Some may have obtained identity documents reflecting their chosen name and correct gender marker, whereas others, because of state laws or issues of economic access or family support, may not have been able to do so. In each of these situations, a student's needs may be very different.

At the time Ithaca College developed its trans* housing policy, few resources were available. Today a variety of resources exist that can assist with benchmarking, identifying best practices, and evaluating basic, intermediate, and advanced levels of inclusive policies and practices (Beemyn, Domingue, Pettitt, & Smith, 2005), including the following:

- Campus Pride LGBT-Friendly Index benchmarks and standards for inclusion in higher education assessment tool, and
- Suggested Best Practices for Supporting Trans* Students, developed by the Consortium of Higher Education LGBT Resource Professionals (2014).

Remember that once your policy is put in place, you will likely need to revisit it frequently. For example, now that Ithaca College is known for being transgender friendly, current and prospective students and their parents feel more empowered to take advantage of all the opportunities the institution provides. With this comes new opportunities to examine housing and placements outside traditional on-site residence halls and academic semester frameworks. For instance, administrators should examine housing and placements for summer student employees who are required to live in campus residence halls during specialized programs, and housing and fieldwork placements in various off-campus and study abroad programs.

CONCLUSION

With the increasing awareness of an evolving and increasingly diverse student population, it is incumbent on colleges and universities to meet the needs of trans* students. In today's environment, transgender students and their families expect colleges and universities to meet their needs (Beemyn & Rankin, 2011). Strategizing about a policy, or working toward developing a policy, may help advance other initiatives that support trans* students, and this is work institutions should undertake to provide inclusive, safe, and welcoming residential facilities for *all* students.

REFERENCES

Beemyn, B. G. (2005) Making campuses more inclusive of transgender students. *Journal of Gay & Lesbian Issues in Education, 3*(1), 77–87.

Beemyn, B., Curtis, B., Davis, M., & Tubbs, N. J. (2005). Transgender issues on college campuses. *New Directions for Student Services*, 111, 49–60.

Beemyn, B. G., Domingue, A., Pettitt, J., & Smith, T. (2005). Suggested steps to make campuses more trans-inclusive. *Journal of Gay & Lesbian Issues in Education, 3*(1), 89–94.

Beemyn, G., & Rankin, S. (2011). *The lives of transgender people.* New York, NY: Columbia University Press.

Bilodeau, B. (2005). Beyond the gender binary: New perspectives on transgender student identity development. *Journal of Gay & Lesbian Issues in Education, 3*(1), 29–44.

Consortium of Higher Education LGBT Resource Professionals. (2014). *Suggested best practices for supporting trans* students*. Retrieved from lgbtcampus .memberclicks.net/assets/consortium%20suggested%20trans%20policy%20 recommendations-compressed.pdf

Maurer, L. (2008). *LGBT Center Program evaluation*. Unpublished manuscript, Ithaca College, Ithaca NY.

Nichols, J. (2013, August 20). Campus Pride releases 2013 "Top 25 LGBT-friendly universities and colleges" listing. *Huffington Post*. Retrieved from www.huffingtonpost.com/2013/08/20/campus-pride-lgbt-colleges-2013_n _3781950.html

Rankin, S., Millar, E., & Matheis, C. (2007). Safe campuses for students. In J. Jackson & M. Terrell (Eds.), *Creating and maintaining safe college campuses: A sourcebook for enhancing and evaluating safety programs* (pp. 75–98). Sterling, VA: Stylus.

Robison, M. (1998). The residence hall: A home away from home. In R. Sanlo (Ed.), *Working with lesbian, gay, bisexual and transgender college students: A handbook for faculty and administrators* (pp. 53–66). Westport, CT: Greenwood Press.

Williamsen-Garvey, K., & Wisener, S. (2006). 8 steps to improve campus housing for LGBT students. In S. Windmeyer (Ed.), *The Advocate college guide for LGBT students* (pp. 363–365). New York, NY: Alyson Books.

APPENDIX 9A
Time Line for Gender-Inclusive Housing Policies at Ithaca College

Date	Process
October 2001	Luca Maurer arrives on campus as founding director of the Center for LGBT Education, Outreach, and Services.
August 2002	Ithaca College acquires new apartment complex (Circle Apartments) and allows students to live in mixed-gender apartment units.
Fall 2003	The first gender-neutral housing proposal is not approved by the president's council.
Fall 2004	The transgender housing policy request process are determined, which are still in place today.
Fall 2007	Gender-neutral housing options are expanded to include units in a second college apartment complex (Garden Apartments). Office of Residential Life submits a new gender-neutral housing proposal, which is approved by the president's council to implement a pilot program.
Fall 2008, Fall 2009	Attempt to pilot a gender-neutral housing floor in a traditional residence hall does not get off the ground because of the lack of students signing up.
Fall 2010	An LGBT residential learning community is established.
Spring 2011– Winter 2016	Work continues toward a possible open housing policy for all students.
Winter 2016	The open housing proposal, written by residential life staff and members of the Student Government Association with input from the LGBT center, is approved by the provost, presidents council, and college president. Beginning in fall 2016, it allows returning students to live with whomever they wish, regardless of sex or gender, in a number of residence halls and other campus housing. In light of this development, the transgender housing policy is reviewed to determine if it is still of use, and it remains in place to meet the needs of first-year students and students of any year should the open housing policy not meet their needs.

10

Our Journey Toward Justice

Gender-Inclusive Housing at the University of Arizona

Jennifer Hoefle Olson and Hannah Lozon

THIS CHAPTER DESCRIBES HOW in 2010 the University of Arizona (UA) created two new housing options in our residence halls intended to directly support lesbian, gay, bisexual, transgender, and queer (LGBTQ) students. Both options were created in a little under three months during fall semester 2010. The first option was an LGBTQ and allied living-learning community (LLC) with single-gender and gender-inclusive roommate pairings, which ultimately came to be called the Social Justice Wing. The second option was a gender-inclusive housing (GIH) policy that included the option of gender-inclusive roommate pairings and private bathrooms throughout our residence hall system and the first publically articulated commitment on the residence life website to individually support students who identified as transgender, genderqueer, gender variant, or nonbinary to help find a housing placement that was right for them.

At the time we created our GIH policy, we followed the lead of one of our peer institutions, Pennsylvania State University. We modeled our policy on the language it was using at the time, which included *transgender* and *gender variant* as identity classifications for students. We later added *genderqueer* and *nonbinary* to better reflect the diversity of our students and the language they use for their own identities. For the purposes of this chapter we use the umbrella term *trans** to refer to this student population and to encompass all gender identities previously mentioned.

This chapter describes the process we undertook to bring our two newly developed housing options to fruition, paying particular attention to the impact on trans* students. Evidence for our chapter comes from three primary sources. First, we include institutional data primarily from LGBTQ needs assessment surveys (UA LGBTQ Affairs, 2008, 2014), which illuminate the experience of trans* students in our halls today. Second, we discuss how we conducted qualitative interviews with trans* students currently living in our residence halls. Third, we use our personal anecdotes as pillars to our narrative, at times describing past students' experiences that described the need for institutional change. We close with some lessons learned.

Our journey toward more inclusive housing practices for trans* students began in the spring of 2010 when we were both hired by UA. Jen Hoefle Olson is director for LGBTQ affairs, and Hannah Lozon was the residence life coordinator of social justice education.

We are both cisgender White women; Jen identifies as queer and Hannah as heterosexual, and we both continually work to be allies to the trans* community. We work to be aware of the privileges that accompany cisgender identities, where our assigned sex has aligned with our gender identity and expression throughout our lives, and have worked to approach advocacy for trans*-inclusive policies with careful consideration and attention to the experiences of trans* students. From our first meeting, we committed to make the creation of more inclusive housing practices for LGBTQ students, and particularly trans* students, a priority in our work.

CONTEXT MATTERS: THE STATE OF ARIZONA AND THE UA

We are uniquely situated in an institution that has a strong history of supporting LGBTQ inclusion but is located in a conservative state. Arizona is widely known for its controversial immigration legislation, a ban on ethnic studies and Affirmative Action programs, English-only legislation, a repeal of domestic partner benefits for state employees, and the proposal of a bill that would support a business's right to discriminate against patrons.

At the same time, the UA has a strong history of supporting LGBTQ inclusion. Historically, the president's LGBTQ Advisory Council worked closely with the university president to better serve LGBTQ-identified students, staff, and faculty. The UA has a particularly strong history of trans* and gender identity–inclusive policies. For example, the university's non-discrimination policy has been inclusive of gender identity since 2008. The UA created a restroom-access statement that affirms individuals in using the restroom that corresponds to their gender identity and expresses the university's commitment to designate and maintain "a gender-neutral restroom in as many of its buildings as is reasonably feasible" (UA Office of Institutional Equity, n.d.). Beginning in 2012 the university's student health insurance began offering a trans* benefit inclusive of hormone therapy and sex reassignment surgeries.

WHERE WE STARTED

From the beginning, our journey to create GIH policies resulted from a larger process to make our residence halls safer and more inclusive environments for LGBTQ students in general. This stemmed from the fact that there were vocal queer student leaders at the time, one in particular, who had personal experience with overt homophobia from multiple roommates and were advocating for more inclusive policies. We worked closely with these students as we advocated for more LGBTQ-inclusive policies in our residence halls.

It was important to us that the needs of trans* students were forefront in the conversation. Although sexual orientation and gender identity are inextricably linked, they are at the same time unique identities that deserve their own focus and attention. As described by Beemyn and Rankin (2011), experiences of trans* people are unique from those of LGBQ people and merit their own attention, understanding, and policy-making. For these reasons, it was imperative for us to ensure that the issues particular to trans* students were addressed with a GIH policy and that these issues were not subsumed by the larger focus on LGBTQ inclusion. Thus, we made sure our GIH policy included strategies outlined in research by Beemyn, Dominique, Pettitt, and Smith (2005), including the option of gender-inclusive roommate pairings, private bathrooms throughout our residence halls, an LGBTQ wing, and support for trans* students to find a housing placement best suited for their needs.

At the time, the common practice in residence life was to work with each trans* student on a case-by-case basis, much like it is today. However, without a specific policy, the practice was not inclusive or consistent. With no publicly available information, the responsibility was placed solely on the student to contact residence life to seek support, forcing trans* students to out themselves to residence life staff with no indication that it would be safe to do so. When support was sought, it was common practice to place trans* students in single rooms with private bathrooms, which many students found isolating and cost significantly more than living in a double room. In addition to the isolation many students felt, most trans* students were placed on wings that did not align with their gender identity. The need for institutional change was clear.

There was much anecdotal evidence about the negative experiences trans* students were having in the residence halls. To provide a context for our readers, we present vignettes from two students we worked with. Their names have been changed for privacy. In the following, Jen recalls an experience of Everett, a student whom she met in the summer of 2009:

> One striking example occurred in the summer of 2009 when I met Everett, who identified as MtF [male to female] and planned on beginning her transition later that summer. She was an incoming student going through summer orientation and had been placed in one of our residence halls on a male wing. She and her parents, who were completely supportive of her gender identity, advocated for her to be placed in a female wing. Residence life suggested a single room, but Everett wanted a roommate her first year, fearing a single room would contribute to isolation. Ultimately, residence life administrators said they could not put someone on a female wing until they had completed transition and required Everett to stay on the male wing. Everett found a male roommate she knew and they moved into the male wing in the fall. Everett dropped out her first semester and never returned.

For Jen, requiring a student to complete transition to be housed in alignment with the student's gender identity was extremely problematic. Foremost, who determines when someone's transition is complete, and what criteria is that based on? Without any articulated policies or guidance, these decisions were left to the discretion of residence life staff to make on a case-by-case basis with no commitment to act in the best interest of trans* students. In Everett's case, even with her own advocacy and the support of her parents and Jen, she was still told she had to live on a male wing. Jen recalls another interaction with a student named Mark in the following:

> Another poignant example of the immediate need for change was Mark, who identified as FtM [female to male] and who changed his pronouns and started taking hormones at the beginning of fall semester 2010. The previous

summer he had lived in an all-female wing in a residence hall, which he liked. In the fall he requested to move to a single room in the same hall, to have a male RA [resident adviser], and to use the male restrooms. Residence life granted Mark's request but told him that he should continue to use the women's restroom and that they would reassess as the semester progressed. (Administrators were concerned about other residents or their parents having a problem with a FtM student using the male bathroom.) Mark was understandably distraught and frustrated; he didn't feel safe using a restroom that didn't correspond with his gender identity and it didn't make sense to be introduced to other residents as Mark and then use the women's bathroom. It was humiliating to be made to feel that he needed permission in the first place. This situation caused Mark to lose sleep and created undue stress during an already vulnerable time. Finally, his community director told him he could use the male bathroom.

Mark's and Everett's experiences elucidated the need for better policies for serving trans* students and were crucial to the case we made for GIH options and policies. Mark's community director allowed him to use the male bathroom without getting permission from residence life administrators and was considered a lapse in protocol. This mistake became a cornerstone in the case we built for our GIH policy.

As a whole, the process that guided residence life staff's handling of Everett's and Mark's experiences felt archaic and transphobic. This was especially striking to Hannah, who came to UA from the University of Vermont, which had numerous housing options and campus-wide support structures for trans* and LGBQ students. To not have trans-affirming practices or information publicly available to students and their families sent a message that residence life did not value trans* students.

THE CASE WE BUILT AND THE STEPS IN OUR PROCESS

As stated in the beginning of this chapter, the LLC and the GIH policy were created in a little under three months. Along the way, we worked with students to build a case for these options and included their comments alongside institutional and national data about the need for more inclusive options. Appendix 10A contains a time line that chronicles the steps in our process.

As we built the case to support these initiatives and sought the support of our university president, student government, and Residence Hall Association, it was crucial to place our initiative in a national context and support it with data from our own institution. For example, on the needs assessment survey (UA LGBTQ Affairs, 2008) almost 40% of LGBTQ student respondents (26 total) indicated they were (or had been in the past 5 years) living in a residence hall and would support a wing specifically for the LGBTQ community. At that time, Campus Pride had just released its report on the state of higher education for LGBT people, which revealed a "chilly" campus climate for LGBTQ people on college campuses across the nation, with particularly high numbers of trans* and gender nonconforming respondents reporting harassment based on their gender expression (Rankin, Weber, Blumenfeld, & Frazer, 2010, p. 9). These findings were echoed on our own campus, where UA Campus Health (2010) found that LGBTQ students were experiencing more harassment and violence than their heterosexual and cisgender counterparts. In fact, according to the survey, 32.1% of LGBTQ students experienced some type of violence in the previous 3 months compared to 15.6% of non-LGBTQ students (UA Campus Health, 2010). Rankin and colleagues (2010) identified many best practices for institutions that offer on-campus residences, including gender-neutral housing and a housing option or LLC focused on LGBTQs and allies, further building our case for support of these initiatives.

Although our campus data were important to building our case, it was also important to provide a national context for institutions implementing similar policies. At that time, 54 colleges and universities nationwide had gender-neutral housing options, and dozens had LGBTQA-themed communities, including fellow Pacific-Ten Conference (now Pacific-Twelve Conference) institutions including Oregon State University, Stanford University, University of California at Berkley, and the University of Oregon.

A strong case can be made about the benefits of living on campus and why it is imperative to make that experience accessible to all students. Longitudinal data from residence life showed that on-campus students outperform off-campus students in all academic success measures, from grade point averages (10% higher) to retention rates (8.7% higher) to four-year graduation rates (46% higher; UA Residence Life, 2014). All of these data, along with student voices at public forums, made a clear case that ultimately convinced residence life administrators that offering GIH and an LLC was in the best interest of students.

WHERE WE ARE NOW AND THE IMPACT ON STUDENTS

Today when trans* students apply for housing, they can indicate their gender identities on the housing application. For any student who identifies as trans*, the system provides a pop-up box that tells the student a staff member will be in contact to discuss the best housing options. At that point, Hannah contacts the student directly. In addition to discussing their housing options, this is a time for Hannah to build a relationship with the students and also explain the many services available for LGBTQ students across UA if the student is interested. It is our hope that these conversations will leave students feeling like they know someone in residence life if they have any concerns or questions at a later time. This personal touch seems to make all the difference, as first-year student Michael said in the following:

> I didn't expect anyone to actually call once I applied for housing. And then once Hannah did, it was a really personal approach . . . I really appreciated this, because being transgender was something I really wanted to talk about. I would be at UA for four years, so being able to talk about that early on made me feel safe and validated. (M., personal communication, May 19, 2014)

Michael went on to have a positive experience with residence life overall. He felt supported by all the staff in his residence hall, was involved in residence life and LGBTQ student organizations, and has been a support to other trans* students on campus.

Abby was another student who lived in our residence halls for three years, and for two of those years she was in GIH. The following is what she had to say about her experience:

> How was I feeling about moving into a residence hall? I was scared. At that time, I wasn't passing as my desired gender. So, I wasn't sure which gender I would be placed with, and I didn't know how to handle my gender with my new roommate. I questioned whether or not I would need to tell my roommate about my trans status . . . Speaking with Hannah was helpful. I found out that one option I had was that I could room with another trans student AND be on the Social Justice Wing, which made me feel relieved. I was excited to room with someone who would better understand what I was going through. My third year in the halls, I roomed with a cisgender person which I was excited about because it felt like I was finally being seen as a normal girl. Living in the halls really allowed me to begin my new life. (A., personal communication, May 27, 2014)

In addition to these students' stories, data have allowed us to be confident that we have improved the experiences of trans* students in our residence halls. According to a survey with a total of 589 student respondents, representing the largest survey of its kind at UA, of trans* students living on campus, 86% (6) indicated that they felt somewhat to very safe living in their residence hall (UA LGBTQ Affairs, 2014). Only one student indicated an issue with a roommate who did not accept the respondent's gender identity, but the respondent received the necessary support from staff, and the roommate moved out.

It is amazing to think of how far we have come from just four years ago with the addition of UA's GIH policy and LLC. Housing applications from trans* students have grown steadily since we implemented our GIH policy and LLC. We began with three trans* students living in the LLC in 2011 to nine students (including a resident adviser) living throughout our halls in 2014. Michael and Abby's experiences offer anecdotal evidence about the improvement in support we have been able to offer trans* students compared to Everett's and Mark's time on campus. Evidence from the needs assessment survey highlights the critical importance of having articulated policies and practices for trans* students (UA LGBTQ Affairs, 2014).

WHAT WE LEARNED

Throughout this journey, we have learned a number of lessons about how to best support trans* students living at UA. Although more work is necessary to make our campus as welcoming as possible, the following are lessons learned that helped make our efforts successful.

Remain United During Resistance

Initially, some residence life administrators were cautiously supportive of the need for GIH and an LLC but expressed concern about what one called balancing safety and inclusivity. Some administrators feared the state legislature might try to stop the GIH option, and these administrators wanted to be careful moving forward so they and other staff at the UA would not attract attention to GIH and UA during implementation. We replied by saying we would prefer not to be secretive or subversive about the GIH and LLC initiatives; we felt it was important to be visible and not send a message that trans* inclusion in residence life needs to be kept a secret.

Staff at residence life then suggested starting with a GIH option for upper-class students as a pilot, as this was the approach numerous housing departments were taking across the nation. Again, we were stalwart in our desire to offer GIH for all students, especially because the vast majority of students who live in UA residence halls are first-year students. We insisted that GIH was not just a residence life issue but a university issue. We drew attention to how GIH options benefit not only LGBTQ students but also families, siblings, and international students and that there was a need to offer these resources to first-year students (particularly first-year trans* students). We remained united and were ultimately able to win over residence life administrators.

Work as a Collective

Throughout our work in developing GIH and the LLC, these initiatives strengthened the connection between our offices of residence life and LGBTQ affairs. We are convinced that our success came from working together, whether garnering support from the UA president or working with student government or the Residence Hall Association. We did not put residence life out in the front alone; instead, we worked as a collective with leadership from the Office of LGBTQ Affairs and from student organizations. By working together and representing the voice of the students, we were able to push for change as a united collective.

Have a Nimble Practice

Hannah quickly found that it served students best if we allowed for flexible practice and handled everything case by case. Framing that with an ethos of service and making it about a student making the transition to college, and not about gender identity, allowed us to build personal relationships that ultimately improved our service to trans* students. We have specific spaces set aside for GIH, but we are willing to make other arrangements as needed. On three occasions now we have had trans* students live in double rooms in other halls with a random roommate and have not had any problems. Bottom line: Flexibility is key. Our goal is always to allow trans* students to determine what is best for them and then to work according to their needs.

Student Voice Is Critical Even When They Are Not in the Room

Students' stories were the most effective tool to help people understand why GIH initiatives were necessary at UA. Residence life administrators who attended the student forums said that hearing the students' stories helped them explain to senior UA administrators why GIH and an LLC were necessary. As we have said, our initiative for GIH grew out of a larger process to make our residence halls safer and more inclusive for LGBTQ students in general. When we began our journey, the main students who sat on our committee and were vocal at the open forums were LGBQ students. Only one trans* student ever attended an open forum, and that student was very quiet.

We are deeply grateful to the trans* students over the years with whom we have worked and whose stories and experiences we have come to know. As detailed throughout this chapter, many of their experiences guided our advocacy. Still, we wonder what we may have missed in the absence of more active participation of trans* students in the process. It was important to us to keep the needs of trans* students at the forefront of conversations about GIH, but we cannot help but wonder what may have been different with more trans* voices present. Was there something we missed or overlooked?

IN CLOSING

As we reflect on where we are now, we are proud that GIH and the LLC are institutionalized on our campus and that our process paved the way for our sister institutions, Arizona State University and Northern Arizona University, to do the same. Four years ago, students like Michael and Abby would have been forced to live on a wing that did not align with their gender identities. Today, we work individually with each trans* student who lives in our halls to find the best housing option. We feel the personal approach we take is paramount to our success. Through articulated policies of support, designated housing options, competent staff, and multiple gender options on applications, UA sends a strong message about how it actualizes a commitment to social justice and inclusion. Still, as we write this, we wonder what the next step toward inclusion will be and realize that we must never stop asking ourselves this question: How can we continue to work toward justice for trans* students?

REFERENCES

Beemyn, B. G., Dominique, D., Pettitt, J., & Smith, T. (2005). Suggested steps to make campuses more trans-inclusive. *Journal of Gay & Lesbian Issues in Education, 3*(2), 89–94.

Beemyn, G., & Rankin, S. (2011). *The lives of transgender people*. New York, NY: Columbia University Press.

Rankin, S., Weber, G., Blumenfeld, W., & Frazer, S. (2010). *2010 state of higher education for lesbian, gay, bisexual, and transgender people*. Charlotte, NC: Campus Pride.

University of Arizona Campus Health. (2010). *Health and wellness survey*. Available from www.assessment.arizona.edu/campus_health/Annual_Health_and_Wellness_Survey

University of Arizona LGBTQ Affairs. (2008). *Needs assessment survey for UA LGBTQ and allied students, staff, and faculty*. Retrieved from lgbtq.arizona.edu/2008-needs-assessment-survey

University of Arizona LGBTQ Affairs. (2014). *LGBTQA+ needs assessment report*. Retrieved from lgbtq.arizona.edu/lgbtqa-needs-assessment-report

University of Arizona Office of Institutional Equity. (n.d.). *Statement on restroom access*. Retrieved from equity.arizona.edu/restroom_access

University of Arizona residence life. (2014). Retrieved from housing.arizona.edu

APPENDIX 10A
Our Journey Toward Justice: Gender-Inclusive Housing at the University of Arizona

Date	Process
September 21, 2010	Initial meeting takes place between LGBTQ affairs and residence life to discuss the need for safer housing options for LGBTQ students.
October 20, 2010	Thirty students attend an open forum to provide student feedback to residence life administrators about the proposed GIH and an LLC.
October 29, 2010	The directors of residence life and LGBTQ affairs submitted a joint letter to the President's LGBTQ Advisory Council, asking it to recommend the president support the GIH and LLC initiatives.
November 2, 2010	The UA president gives his support at the LGBTQ Advisory Council meeting and asks that the programs be cost neutral, meaning that no rooms go unfilled as residence life was preparing to be over capacity at the start of fall 2011.
November 3, 2010	UA student government passes a resolution in support of GIH and the LLC.
November 18, 2010	The Residential Housing Association passes a resolution in support of GIH and the LLC.
November 20, 2010	A second student forum takes place to solicit feedback on hall locations for both the LLC and GIH options and the name for the LLC. A 22-bed wing is chosen in a hall at the center of campus, at the lower price point for rent, with two community bathrooms, and it is decided that the residents would determine the gender of the bathrooms after moving in.
November 22, 2010	A Tucson newspaper publishes a story on GIH and the LLC that is balanced and accurate. Five other news stations run the story for the evening news. Much of the coverage is inaccurate, suggesting that residence life would be randomly assigning students of all genders to live together, and that the LLC is self-segregation.
	Hannah and Jen put together talking points for the residence life central office staff, as the media stories generate a number of phone calls from confused students and parents.

Date	Process
December 15, 2010	A statement is posted on residence life's and LGBTQ affair's websites outlining the housing application process for trans* students, affirming UA's commitment to the self-identity of every student, and committing to find an on-campus housing option that is right for every transgender student.

11

Centering the Student Experience

Chicora Martin, Lori Lander, and Maure Smith-Benanti

IN THE SUMMER OF 2004 the University of Oregon added the terms *gender identity* and *gender expression* to its policy on prohibited discrimination, discriminatory harassment, and sexual harassment. Shortly afterward, a public hearing was held so comments could be taken on this new rule. The most significant public question asked during the hearing was why we had waited so long to do what was clearly the right thing. When the leadership of the University of Oregon's Lesbian, Gay, Bisexual, Transgender, Education, and Support Services Program (LGBTESSP) and residence life sat down in the fall of 2008 to propose gender-inclusive housing, the conversation began with that very same question: Why have we waited so long to do the right thing? Sitting at the table were student affairs professionals who were committed to the success of every student and who were willing to take the first initial unknown steps. In writing this chapter, we want to emphasize that we think of ourselves as student advocates first and administrators second. We care deeply about the student experience and are committed to constant reevaluation and redevelopment to best connect with our student community.

In this chapter, we document the process of creating gender-inclusive living at the University of Oregon over the past decade, including our Gender Equity Hall as well as other gender-inclusive spaces. We use anecdotes from student experiences with their names changed to protect student privacy. We also use the personal pronouns *they*, *them*, and *theirs* to respect the

179

diverse and ever-changing process of identity development for some of our students and colleagues. We also acknowledge dozens of other staff and students who were fundamental to this process and we are just documenting the efforts of many. Most important, we aim to be as transparent as possible so our experiences can serve as a resource for other readers, scholars, and practitioners.

ABOUT THE UNIVERSITY OF OREGON

The University of Oregon was founded in 1876 and is the state's flagship institution. Since 2000, it has been ranked among the top 25 LGBT-friendly campuses in the nation. The University of Oregon was also named in Campus Pride's 2012 list of the top 10 trans-friendly colleges and universities and recognized as the "Best of the Best" colleges and universities leading the way for transgender inclusion in higher education. These characteristics, even more than the nondiscrimination statement that was amended in the summer of 2004 to include gender identity and gender expression as protected characteristics, are what encouraged professionals like Maure and Lori to apply for positions at such a progressive institution.

Having laid the groundwork for gender-inclusive housing, Chicora describes the changes that sparked a campus dialogue on gender-inclusive spaces in the following:

> I remember vividly the first time I met Chance. As the director of the LGBT center, an important part of my job is to reach out to students during orientation who have questions about our services and support. I was asked by an orientation staff member if I could please meet with a student who had questions they were not sure they could answer correctly. It was summer orientation, and on the second morning, all students head to the computer lab to register for classes. The entrance to the lab is right next to a wall of windows, and as I approached, I could see new students feverishly searching for the perfect schedule. I immediately noticed this one student, standing right in the middle of the room, staring intently at a piece of paper, and looking uncertain about whether they were even in the right place. As I entered the computer lab, the student looked up.

Chance offered a slight smile and extended their hand. "Hi, I'm . . . ," a tense slight pause ensued, "Chance." I said, "I am Chicora. How about a walk?" We walked around our student union that morning talking about how the LGBTESSP could be helpful, but we also talked about coming to college, living with a roommate, being away from home. Chance was due at the next session in a few minutes, and I passed on my card.

Something struck me about Chance in that moment. Maybe it was the way Chance spoke: patient, focused, and with crystal clear intention. Maybe it was being so open to trusting someone they had just met. But Chance's demeanor evoked a sense of courageousness. Chance took my card, and with a quick glance up, shared "Chance isn't my birth name." I nodded. "How do I fix that?" Chance asked, almost in a whisper. "I would love to help you get that all worked out. E-mail me, and we can take care of it before fall term begins," I replied. Chance smiled and walked away, and I remember thinking that it was the kind of smile that normally happens over birthday candles, a different, more authentic smile. I knew Chance was a different kind of student, but I could not have predicted how Chance would change all of us over the next four years.

THE INFORMAL PROCESS

Chance had also asked how they could change their gender marker and their name on their university records. As with some of our students, Chance was not sure how their parents would accept this change and was concerned about not having support for completing their college degree. Chance was not sure how open and honest they could be about their identity. They had come out as gay to their family in high school and things had gone better than expected. However, coming out as trans and telling their family they were now their son seemed a little risky. We talked via e-mail during the summer to brainstorm some options. We shared a mutual frustration about how many systems are so bureaucratic at a large institution, but we found creative ways to plan for a transition of gender markers and name once Chance arrived on campus. Many of the processes were difficult to navigate then, including university housing's application and the university's student identification process. Students who were able to connect to the LGBTESSP could be assisted in name changes, gender marker changes, and specialized room assignments. However, some students did not know to make a connection with the LGBTESSP or had negative experiences with other offices and were deterred from these resources.

We offered opportunities wherever laws and database flexibility allowed. The staff in the LGBTESSP worked on a case-by-case basis and advocated with the registrar's office on behalf of students to get paperwork filed for name changes. The staff also asked for exceptions to e-mail assignments to change e-mail addresses associated with birth names and gender. Other concerns included working with individual faculty members so they would respect names provided by students that were different from the names in our student database, advocating for assignments in residence halls by gender identity, and increasing the number of gender-inclusive spaces like bathrooms and locker rooms available on campus.

The University of Oregon did not have gender-inclusive housing spaces in 2003–2004. The only options were to put students on a floor based on the gender listed in their official records or to put them in housing options that included in-room private bathrooms. Unfortunately, most of those spaces were reserved for upper-class students or were located in our most distant campus buildings, where students felt they were being relegated to the outskirts of our campus community. Our trans and gender-fluid students opted to live in various communities and hoped it would all go well. However, as we know because of the lack of education and experience with diverse expressions of gender, some individuals faced subtle and more overt experiences of gender bias (Beemyn & Rankin, 2011). One of our most concerning challenges was the negative impact the extended community's homophobia and gender bias had on the safety and health of our differently gendered students. These students were often faced with roommates who were not welcoming, with being outed by well-meaning staff who were trying to be supportive, and with physical spaces and restrooms that felt unsafe or where their ability to access these spaces felt unclear.

Chance's experience living in their residence hall space as a first-year student illustrates some of those exact concerns. Chicora ran into Chance the first few weeks of fall term at an event for new first-year students to get involved. Chance was living in an all-women's residence hall and had the same patient, polite demeanor, and yet Chicora was still able to sense some underlying tension.

> Chance and I walked together across campus and about halfway to the residence hall community, Chance shared that they had decided to come out to their roommate. "How did it go?" I asked, holding my breath a little. I know when my students struggle—to this day, 20 years into this work, I feel

it. Chance shared they were better than Chance expected. "It was still a little weird, but we get along so well that it should be okay," Chance said with the kind of optimism that continues to inspire me. The next day, Chance and the roommate told the other women in the shared space. With the roommate's support, Chance felt that things were settled enough to stay there. I think we both let out a collective breath. In my head I thought, "It should not have to be this way." Not ironically, Chance said that the first question the women asked was, "If you identify as a guy, why are you living on this floor?" Chance did not say a word to me in that moment but did not have to. We both nodded in acknowledgement; this was a broken system and it had to change. As soon as I got back to my office I sent an e-mail to the director of residence life. "RE: hey it's been a while since we talked but let's connect again about that gender inclusive housing." The body of my e-mail was short. It said, "I think it's time that we really get serious about gender-inclusive housing. In fact, it's more than time."

Also at this time the practice of placing students based on gender identity and not on birth assigned sex was formalized. Before the fall of 2011, the handful of students who approached residence life and identified as trans were given the option of a single room at an additional cost or of living with a self-selected roommate and only in residence halls rooms that included bathrooms in the actual residence hall room. In these situations, students would have to out themselves, advocate for a reduced cost, or request a special roommate assignment. Thus, it became clear the current policy created an unwelcoming environment that reinforced systemic trans oppression (Catalano, McCarthy, & Slasko, 2007).

ADMINISTRATIVE AND LEADERSHIP-BASED CHANGE

In October 2004 the University of Oregon began the first changes related to gender identity in the housing process, modifying the 2005–2006 application by removing a question that specifically asked the sex of a student, allowing only two binary sex responses (i.e., male and female). It was replaced with a gender question with the option to provide a fill-in-the-blank short answer. This modification was made in collaboration with the LGBTESSP and university housing to assign students to their room choices and roommate selections by gender identity.

Some housing employees were concerned this option might invite negative or inappropriate responses, such as "Gender: yes," or men indicating "woman" to get a woman roommate. LGBTESSP staff offered to contact any student who used this new demographic question as a forum for inappropriate responses, thus ensuring that the housing staff responsible for reviewing applications would not have an additional workload. However, despite the initial concern of staff members, there was never a need to contact anyone on a large scale, as the concerning answers that housing staff anticipated were simply not a problem. The only people who required follow-up were those who identified outside the categories of male or female or man or woman, and follow-up was simply to ensure they received supportive and welcoming housing options. Students were then assigned housing based on their self-identified gender rather than their assigned sex at birth.

At this time we did not have any students opt into university housing who also selected identities outside the gender binary of man or woman. However, LGBTESSP staff regularly worked with students who self-identified outside that binary, and we expected another important conversation with university housing about how best to begin thinking about serving students who may eventually identify themselves outside the gender binary and also have the desire to live on campus.

About the third week in May, Chicora ran into Chance again and described the meeting as follows:

> I asked Chance how the year was wrapping up. "Great!" Chance replied. "I am going to be a resident assistant (RA) next year. I just found out today!" I offered my heartfelt congratulations to Chance; their excitement was definitely contagious. I also knew that another e-mail was brewing. In my head I knew that RAs were assigned by sex to sex-segregated floors. I was mired in the overall implications of Chance's announcement. In my e-mail inbox, serendipitously, I see the unread message "Assigning RAs based on gender," from residence life.

From our collaborative conversations about housing placement and gender identity, it only made sense that RAs would be assigned in the same way. However, we all knew that what should make sense was not always what happened. Residence life and the LGBTESSP staff met over the next few weeks and prepared a policy that assigned RAs based on their gender identity. By the time Chance completed the RA class, the policy had been approved, meaning Chance could be placed on a floor in line with their gender identity rather than their assigned sex at birth. To clarify, our practice at the time was still a binary system, and we were well aware that although this worked for Chance, it would not work for many of our other students with nonbinary trans identities. Often our policy development is not as forward-thinking as our need to have inclusive practices. What we really learned was that we had to be more innovative in policy development and implementation. We could not be deliberately indifferent to our emerging campus communities by waiting for students to advocate for or demand inclusive services on our campus.

CREATING GENDER-INCLUSIVE HOUSING

We began conversations in the fall of 2006 about the creation of a gender-inclusive housing space. We worked continuously over the next three years, finalizing our comprehensive proposal that included information about the few schools—most of which were private—that included gender-inclusive housing. Chance and dozens of other students attended our focus groups to provide feedback on our proposal. From this feedback, we developed a frequently asked questions document to address myths and stereotypes about gender-inclusive housing. But most important, we met with everyone who might be in the policy chain of approval, especially those who might have concerns that would keep our proposal from moving forward, such as the vice presidents for administration and student affairs, staff in the Office of Disability Services, staff in facilities management for housing and the overall campus, admissions staff, and staff who worked with parents and families. We were well aware that changing a practice and policy for our current students required a more expansive lens regarding what it means to be a stakeholder in policy, practice, and reputation. We knew from other campus activism and from the work of the small private colleges that had already made this change that proactively addressing the myths and stereotypes of gender-inclusive spaces was important. We wrote lengthy proposal materials focused on educating our community about gender-inclusive housing and distributed these broadly. We also held informational open meetings for campus partners to address myths, stereotypes, and assumptions about gender-inclusive spaces.

The proposal inched forward through hours of dialogue as it made headway through our formal campus policy-making process. In these meetings and information sessions we answered all the "What if?" questions from participants. What if someone is sexually harassed in the space? What if parents get upset? What if we cannot fill the spaces? We answered these questions by encouraging dialogue, and we were specific about not just dismissing their concerns. The experiences of women who self-identified as survivors of sexual assault and the misperception that gender-inclusive spaces might contribute to more incidents of assault had to be discussed. Although we may have been able to intellectualize this conversation, we also had to directly respond to apprehension and concern.

In the overall policy proposal conversation, we countered with our own questions: What if we are not serving our students? What if our students need these spaces to live and learn safely? What if we are unprepared to serve all our students into the future? We reminded campus decision makers of their role as policy makers and emphasized the concept that policies are designed to operate broadly and do the most good for the most students.

Throughout this whole process, Chicora could not stop thinking about what this would mean for students like Chance. What if caring about one student's experience was all it took to create positive and inclusive systemic change? We have no doubt that in this case, and in the cases of hundreds of students who have come after Chance, it did. Creating inclusive policy serves not just that one student but all the students (Bergerson & Huftalin, 2011) at the university. The final proposal was released in winter 2009.

The following summer, the university president retired. He was adamant that communities like the one we had proposed created environments that he called *new tribalism* and were not to be approved. He commented in his speeches about his concern over political viewpoints and ideological discourse, and said that "we must find our common ground" and "we must let no single-issue demagogue dominate our thinking" (Frohnmayer, 2008). With his retirement, we felt this was a new opportunity for new leadership with a different perspective. Residence life as a unit in university housing began the new and dynamic logistical planning process, which included how roommates would be assigned, where the specific residential rooms might be located, and how professional and student staff would be selected to oversee and interact with this specific community of students.

We knew if we had these spaces, students like Chance would have more options. Moreover, the conversation about having a gender-inclusive housing option changed to more broadly reflect what many of us had known all along. If we offered these options, all students would have more opportunities for residential communities that could accommodate their needs and desires.

Placement of the community in the residence hall system was an important consideration. Although the conversation about gender-inclusive housing supersedes discussion about bathroom spaces, this has been where we often began the conversation at the University of Oregon. Currently the gender-inclusive community is on two floors with shared bathrooms that include showers separated by curtains as well as showers separated by partial stalls. This configuration does not allow the utmost privacy, and practitioners might think this is counterintuitive. But when members of the community were asked if they would like to move to a hall that would provide three private bathrooms per floor, residents said they would like to stay where they were because the shared bathroom is part of the experience. Usually students are the first to criticize our 1960s-style bathrooms. In fact, we cannot remember the last time we had heard a positive comment about these facilities. And yet we think the lesson here is clear: Do not let a perceived lack of the perfect bathroom design limit the possibility of moving forward. Always allow students to participate in guiding the process, as each campus is unique.

As we began the placement process in the fall of 2011, every student was given the option of applying for space in the Gender Equity Hall. Then, residence life staff called each student who opted in to discuss the intention of the community as a space that was not about sexual orientation. It was a space where anyone could live with anyone else regardless of one's gender identity. These phone conversations resulted in a few students adjusting their application preference. The time spent, although intensive, helped to ensure the community's success by proactively creating a supportive and caring environment for all students. We knew the success of this community would rely heavily on the quality of the community created, and a big part of that puzzle was the student staffing. Staff training and staff placement in the community were critical. Optimal staff placement can be achieved by identifying interest from potential candidates or, better yet, recruiting from the returning staff. The ongoing goal is to be intentional and create a high level of investment from the live-in professional staff and the resident assistants.

CONCLUSION

Our work regarding gender-inclusive spaces is not static at the University of Oregon. We are continuously interacting with our students to ensure we are evolving to meet and exceed their needs, learning opportunities, and sense of belonging. What started out as a simple process of matching roommates regardless of students' gender identities now includes residential student staff with academic expertise in queer studies. It includes a student organization engaged in connecting resident's experiences in this space to their academic experiences and their personal identity development. It includes a core partnership with residence life and the staff in the LGBTESSP to mentor and connect in fundamentally deeper and more meaningful ways than we had before this community existed. As Mary, one of our student leaders, stated, "[The Gender Equity] floor is about so much—but you know what it's not about? It's not about the bathrooms."

Colleagues from across the nation have asked us how to provide support to the trans community and begin the process of creating a gender-inclusive residential community. We encourage all our colleagues, regardless of position or years of experience in higher education, to take on the responsibility of learning about the trans community and the concerns members of this community have about living in the residence halls on their campuses. Take the active step of educating yourselves about trans issues. Do not rely on students to bridge the gap of knowledge for you; read a book, follow a blog, and really listen when students share their experiences with you. Do something, but do not just think about it.

A collaborative effort has resulted in the successes summarized in Appendix 11A. As educators, we each bring a unique perspective and knowledge base to our work. Together we have developed a strong foundation that each could never have achieved alone. As student advocates, we encourage all practitioners to set aside their own biases and be open to new ways of thinking. We need to listen to students and collaborate in our care for a trans student population that is often minimized and overlooked because they do not fit into traditionally narrow definitions and expectations. It is worth it to start small and build on the successes of other universities. We suggest educators work to alter their paradigms to be more about making change for students and less about what negative things might happen or who might not support the community or how much it might cost. Students like Chance are on every campus and in every state. We are better off as an institution and as a community with alumni like Chance who embody what it means to be a Duck (the University of Oregon's mascot) in all our unique ways.

Most important, as student affairs professionals, we must remember this work is not about us. We must move beyond where we get stuck in our process, where we feel powerless, and beyond the barriers that seem insurmountable. We must extract the desire to move forward and forget the fear of criticism, the fear of failure, and even the fear of those calls to (or from) the president. We must do this because the conclusion of our work will result in a community where we can care for all its members equitably, even when some of our campus partners and local communities are unsure how or why it is important. We must do this because the conclusion of our work could even result in a more global iteration of "the beloved community" as Martin Luther King Jr. (1957, p. 162) envisioned it, a creative, collaborative space to live and learn where all stories can be true and all experiences can be authentic.

REFERENCES

Beemyn, G. & Rankin, S. (2011). *The lives of transgender people.* New York, NY: Columbia University Press.

Bergerson, A., & Huftalin, D. (2011). Becoming more open to social identity-based difference: Understanding the meaning college students make of this movement. *Journal of College Student Development, 52*(4), 377–395.

Campus Pride. (2014). *Campus pride releases first ever list of the top ten trans friendly colleges universities across the nation.* Retrieved from www.advocate.com/politics/transgender/2012/08/15/top-10-trans-friendly-colleges-and-universities

Campus Pride. (2017). *Top 25 list of LGBT-friendly colleges & universities.* Retrieved from www.campuspride.org/2015-top-25/

Catalano, C., McCarthy, L., & Shlasko, D. (2007). Transgender oppression curriculum design. In M. Adams, L. A. Bell, & P. Griffin (Eds.), *Teaching for diversity and social justice* (2nd ed., pp. 219–245). New York, NY: Routledge.

Frohnmayer, D. (2008). *The new tribalism.* Retrieved from http://frohnmayer.uoregon.edu/speeches/newtribalism/

King, M. L. (1957). *The birth of a new nation.* Retrieved from kingencyclopedia.stanford.edu/encyclopedia/encyclopedia_contents.html

University of Oregon Office of Affirmative Action & Equal Opportunity. (n.d.). *UO equal opportunity, non-discrimination and affirmative action policy statement.* Retrieved from aaeo.uoregon.edu/content/uo-equal-opportunity-non-discrimination-and-affirmative-action-policy-statement

APPENDIX 11A
University of Oregon Success Time Line

Summer 2004	UO adds *gender identity* and *gender expression* to the prohibited discrimination, discriminatory harassment, and sexual harassment policy.
	Trans students advocate for themselves and are assigned to rooms with private bathrooms at a higher cost.
	Trans students are able to change their gender marker and name on university records and some other services (e.g. e-mail, bathrooms, locker rooms) with assistance from LGBTESSP staff.
Fall 2004	University housing changes a demographic application question that asked an applicant's sex and only allowed "male" or "female" as the response to one that asks an applicant's gender and allows an open-ended response.
	LGBTESSP staff contact by phone students identifying outside the male or female or man or woman categories on the housing application.
	One student questions the policies and procedures.
Summer 2005	Students are assigned housing and roommates based on their self-identified gender, connecting the process to the student's identity rather than the binary male and female indicators.
Winter 2006	A trans student is hired as an RA.
	Residence life and LGBTESSP staff collaboratively develop a policy that assigns RAs based on their gender identity and not their assigned sex at birth.
Fall 2006	Conversation begins among residence life and LGBTESSP staff about the creation of a gender-inclusive housing space.
	Focus groups with students are conducted.
	LGBTESSP and residence life staff met with everyone and anyone who might be in the policy chain of approval, for example, vice presidents for administration and student affairs, Office of Disability Services, university housing, facilities staff, admissions, and so on.

Winter 2009	A formal proposal is submitted.
Summer 2009	The university's president retires.
Fall 2009	Residence life staff develops the new process of roommate assignments, residential room locations, professional and student staff selection, and community expectations and programs.
Fall 2010	The university housing application includes assignment to the Gender Inclusive Hall as an option.
	Residence life staff contacts by phone students who indicated a preference for the Gender Inclusive Hall on their housing application.
Summer 2011	Students are assigned to the Gender Inclusive Hall.

When Policies Are Not Enough

Z Nicolazzo

Wㅤ HAT HAPPENS ON A college campus after a residence life department has adopted a gender-inclusive housing policy? Are these policies effective in bringing about the cultural change their advocates intend, namely, increasing the livability of lives for trans* college students on campus? Although such policies may be an important symbolic marker of inclusion, Spade (2015) argued that viewing administrative policies (e.g., gender-inclusive housing policies) as a panacea to institutionalized trans* oppression (Catalano & Griffin, 2016) can have a marginalizing effect on the community it purports to help (i.e., trans* college students). In this epilogue, I explore how gender-inclusive housing policies may create the facade of inclusion while concurrently not changing the basic cultural assumptions in which trans* oppression is rooted.[1] Although the efforts to develop trans*-inclusive housing throughout this book are laudatory and are indeed necessary, I propose that they are simultaneously insufficient in addressing systemic trans* oppression and how it pervades not only all campus housing but also entire campus environments. Specifically, I raise questions that expose the illogical basic assumptions about gender that guide how trans* college students' lives are regulated on college campuses and, in turn, offer alternative possibilities for how one may expand possibilities for how to work alongside trans* college students that extend beyond gender-inclusive housing policies.

BEGINNINGS: TWO CASE STUDIES

In elucidating the complex ways gender-inclusive housing policies may not increase the livability of trans* college students' lives, it may be best to consider two case studies. The first is a fictional situation that asks educators to question the basic assumptions in understanding who trans* college students are. Although this case is fictional, it encompasses many of the realities of gender-inclusive housing policies discussed throughout this book, and it should be understood to have some significance in thinking about the limits and potential harm done by these policies. The second is a real situation that emerged at Miami University during the spring 2012 semester, when I was a doctoral student in the student affairs and higher education program at the institution.

CASE 1: NELL

Nell just completed hir first year at Metropolitan State University, a midsize public institution in the coastal Atlantic region of the United States. During the spring semester of hir first year at college, Nell decided to come out as trans*. For Nell, this meant identifying as gender nonconforming, using a proper name different from hir legal name, having people use the pronouns *ze* and *hir* when referring to hir, and seeking gender-inclusive housing. In coming out as trans*, Nell had also made the decision that ze was uninterested in seeking hormone treatments, using a voice coach to modify hir voice, or otherwise modifying hir body morphology. Nell knew hir identity as gender nonconforming may not be well understood by others on campus, be they cisgender or perhaps even other members of the trans* community. Nell also knew that although there were several faculty members who identified as trans*, no staff members in the Division of Student Affairs, which included the Office of Residence Life (ORL), identified as trans*. Because of this, Nell was hesitant to speak to an ORL staff member about gender-inclusive housing options.

After talking to some friends, Nell found out ORL recently adopted a gender-inclusive housing policy. Encouraged by this, Nell set up a meeting with hir residence hall director to discuss the possibility of securing a spot in gender-inclusive housing for hir sophomore year in college. When Nell walked into hir director's office, ze was met by a confused look. When Nell asked if ze was in the right office, the director replied, "Yes, you are, but you just don't look like what I expected you to." Already on edge, Nell asked about gender-inclusive housing options, mentioning there was not much on the ORL website. The director told Nell there was one floor in one of the new residence halls on campus that was designated as a gender-inclusive community. Also, Nell learned that ze would have to submit an application to be considered for this community, which included answering questions about hir trans* identity and hir intent in being a member of the gender-inclusive community. The director then explained that members of the ORL staff would determine who would get the spots in this community as a way to "make sure the right people are getting access." The director also stated that all the rooms on the floor were singles, which carried an additional cost. Furthermore, because the gender-inclusive community was in a new building, the overall cost of rooms was already elevated from what Nell had been paying during hir first year in school. Nell also realized the new building was in an area of campus that ze did not feel comfortable in, which made hir hesitant to apply for the gender-inclusive community.

At the end of hir meeting, the residence hall director told Nell not to get hir hopes up, because preference was given to students who identified as trans*. Nell was confused by this, and asked the director, who identified as a cisgender woman, what she meant by this comment. She looked at Nell and said, "Well, you know, the floor is for trans* people, not people who just want to be expressive or provocative in their appearance." She told Nell ze could still submit an application but that Nell may want to think about other possibilities for housing on campus. Nell left the meeting deflated and upset, knowing ze had not been seen as "trans* enough" to potentially enter the gender-inclusive community on campus. Given the fact that Metro State had a two-year live-on-campus residency requirement, Nell wondered about the potential of getting out of hir housing contract so ze could live off campus. However, if this meant having to come out as trans* and sit through future meetings with other ORL staff members like the meeting ze had just had, ze was reticent to pursue that option. "Maybe I'll just suck it up and hope for the best," Nell thought.

CASE 2: MIAMI UNIVERSITY

As I and my colleague Susan B. Marine have written about elsewhere (Nicolazzo & Marine, 2015), the case of Kaeden Kass, a transmasculine student who applied to become a resident assistant (RA) in the Office of Residence Life at Miami University, provides another useful example to think about trans* inclusion in housing and residential life settings. Kass, who was open about his gender identity throughout the application process, was ultimately offered a position as an RA in a suite-style residence hall. Although this hall housed any student regardless of their gender identity, as an RA in this hall, he would have had to live in a women's suite and have women roommates, thereby erasing his identity as transmasculine. Because of this outcome, the trans* student who saw this decision as being in contrast with the university's policy prohibiting harassment and discrimination,

> filed a charge of discrimination . . . against three Miami officials: . . . [the] dean of students; . . . director of the Office of Residence Life; and . . . general counsel for the Office of the President. (Conrad, 2012, para. 6)

Following this series of events, Miami's campus became a focal point for gender activism. With local and national media coverage of the case, I coordinated a teach-in on trans* inclusion that was well attended by faculty, staff, and students on campus, and, as a result, more people began talking about what equity for trans* people might actually look like at Miami. Because of the upswell of activism, many people agreed with a sentiment best articulated by the coordinator of Gay, Lesbian, Bisexual, Transgender, and Questioning Services on campus at the time, who stated, "I personally feel that we should be able to house people on the basis of their gender identity . . . and not just their sex" (Kingkade, 2012, para. 15).

In response to these events, Miami University released a formal statement regarding gender-neutral housing options offered on campus,[2] which, for a campus of more than 16,000 undergraduate students, were described as being "limited to two suites in two halls (four students per suite) and one apartment" (Conrad, 2012, para. 11). Kass also said gender-inclusive housing was "only available for second-year students and up [and] . . . it's very small, secretive, and hard to get into. You have to be interviewed and basically out yourself to do it" (Kingkade, 2012, para. 11). Although the discrimination lawsuit was eventually dropped because of an apparent lack of evidentiary support, Kass suggested his case was a microcosm of the larger specter of gender-based inequity on campus, and specifically in housing and residence life, stating, "'My case was a symptom of the real problem . . . People can't forget about it. It will change if people keep talking'" (Taylor, 2012, para. 38).

TRANS* OPPRESSIVE ASSUMPTIONS EXPOSED

Writing about organizational culture, Edgar Schein (2010) elucidated three levels of culture: artifacts, espoused values and beliefs, and basic assumptions.

Artifacts are the physical elements that help one make sense of cultures. Often, these artifacts are manifestations of the values and beliefs of an organization. For example, a gender-inclusive housing policy may represent an office's values of gender equity. However, a more in-depth look at these policies may uncover the basic assumptions of an office (e.g., residence life office) or a campus regarding trans* students. Basic assumptions are ideas that are so deeply embedded in a culture they are taken for granted. One often hears about basic assumptions when people in an organization answer questions by saying something to the effect of, "That's just the way we do things around here." The assumptions are so basic, and so culturally embedded, that they go unquestioned, and thus, are not interrogated. Therefore, despite these policies espousing the value of gender equity, many gender-inclusive housing options are deeply rooted in trans* oppression, or a type of systemic oppression negatively affecting "people whose gender identity or expression do not conform to binary cultural norms and expectations" (Catalano & Griffin, 2016, p. 183).

Looking closer at the case of Nell, one is able to see a number of trans*-oppressive assumptions; most notably, that as a nonbinary individual, Nell's residence hall director sees hir as an anomaly. An example of the supposed anomalousness of Nell's nonbinary identity is evident when Nell's director describes it in terms of Nell's desire to be "provocative" in appearance. Although the campus has taken the first step to recognizing trans* students and their unique housing needs, the basic assumption being made by the residence hall director is that there are still *two distinct gender identities with which one must ascribe*. Because Nell identifies as gender nonconforming and has chosen to not biomedically transition, hir gender identity is culturally unintelligible (Butler, 2006) and Nell is deemed not trans* enough (Catalano, 2015) by the cisgender ORL staff member. Thus, the cisgender ORL staff person's active unknowing of Nell's identity as trans* makes hir life less livable on campus. Although a variety of scholars have called for greater awareness and understanding of nonbinary trans* identities (Bilodeau, 2005; Butler, 2006; Califia, 2003; Feinberg, 1998; Mattilda, 2006; Stewart, 2017), it is clear many gender-inclusive housing policies are constructed on the false assumption that to be trans* is only synonymous with biomedical transition and being legible as one of two supposedly binary genders.

Another assumption evident in both case studies is the apparent need to accommodate trans* students. By only having one area—or in the case of

Miami University, several rooms—available for gender-inclusive housing, the basic assumptions being made are (a) there are not many trans* students on campus, and (b) an office can accommodate the few who are on campus by just setting aside a few rooms for them. However, the problem with this approach is that genderism as an overarching system of marginalization does not change. Instead, a buffer zone (Kivel, 2007; Spade, 2010) is created whereby trans* students are tolerated, and trans* oppression is still the prevailing notion of how one constructs, understands, and functions in relation to gender on campus. In other words, gender-inclusive housing policies that only set aside a few rooms, a floor, or even just one residential building do not encompass the whole campus, do little to challenge the trans*-oppressive idea that there are two and only two genders (i.e., masculine and feminine) that comport with two and only two sexes assigned at birth (i.e., male and female), and nowhere in between shall the two meet (or not meet as the case may be for students who identify as agender). Thus, there may be an espoused value of gender equity, but the basic assumption underlying the separation of one specific area for gender-inclusive housing belies this notion.

When taken at face value, gender-inclusive housing policies may do little to increase the life chances (Spade, 2015) of trans* college students. Although this accommodation may be welcomed by trans* faculty, students, and staff alike, these policies do little to address the ethos and effects of institutional trans* oppression that research has shown to be present on college and university campuses (Nicolazzo, 2017). Additionally, because these policies are typically seen as a desired end rather than the start of prolonged conversations regarding gender and trans* equity, they may do harm to trans* students, faculty, and staff. For example, having a gender-inclusive housing policy may improve an institution's score on something like Campus Pride's index of campuses that are friendly to lesbian, gay, bisexual, and transgender people (www.campusprideindex.org). However, including gender identity or expression in an antidiscrimination policy or offering gender-inclusive housing in one area on campus may only provide the facade of inclusion. As seen in the case study about Miami University, the residence life office had (and still has) "gender, [and] gender identity expression [sic]" listed in the office nondiscrimination policy (Office of Residence Life, 2017, para. 8). These policies suggest offices are safer spaces for trans* students. However, when trans* students seek these spaces on campus and find a far different reality exists, there is an increased possibility of trauma and harm, a point made clear in Nell's thinking that ze will have to "suck it up and hope for the best" and in Kaeden's frustration, which led to his seeking—and being granted approval—to get out of his housing contract.

IMAGINING POSSIBILITIES FOR WORKING ALONGSIDE TRANS* STUDENTS IN RESIDENCE LIFE

Often, when I am approached by student affairs educators to discuss trans* college students, I am asked what the staff of offices, departments, and campuses should do to be more inclusive. However, I have grown wary of answering this question, as it seems to suggest that if educators meet several best practices, their campuses will be transformed. It also suggests that once best practices are met, the work of creating a gender-inclusive campus is done, which, as I stated earlier, is a highly dubious claim (Nicolazzo, 2017). Instead, I agree with Spade (2015), who said that any progress one hopes to make toward trans* equity should be "about practice and process rather than arrival at a singular point of 'liberation'" (p. 2). Thus, I will not end by providing a list of things staff of an office, department, or campus can do to meet the needs of trans* students, as I do not think these lists bring one closer to trans* liberation. Instead, I offer several questions I hope will be a catalyst for ongoing conversations about one's basic assumptions about gender, trans* students, and one's role as an educator on a college campus. I break these questions into three categories: personal, office or departmental, and campus culture. Thus, educators will be able to engage in self-reflection while also finding questions they can ask to examine gender on broader mezzo- and macrolevels on campus. Additionally, these lists should not be understood as exhaustive but should be read as a beginning from which other questions can be developed.

Personal Questions

Individuals can use the following questions to think through their own personal feelings and investments related to increasing trans* equity on campus:

- How do I collude with or resist trans* oppression through my beliefs, behaviors, and practices as an educator?
- How do I feel about trans* students? How might my feelings be harmful or helpful in achieving trans* equity?

- Do I have a role in furthering trans* equity? If so, what is my role? If not, why not?
- How can I gain a more in-depth understanding of trans* identities without asking trans* people to teach me?
- What assumptions do I make about other people's gender identity and gender expression that may limit possibilities for gender diversity?
- What steps can I begin to take in the coming semester to learn more and improve my own beliefs, behaviors, and practices as an educator as they relate to trans* equity?

Office or Departmental Questions

The following questions can be used by office and department staffs to think deeply about how office policies and practices may or may not increase trans* equity:

- How do the policies and practices of my office or department collude with or resist trans*-oppressive assumptions?
- For residence life offices or departments that use gender or sex assigned at birth as a basis for any housing decisions, why is this an important factor?
- What would it look like *not* to use gender or sex assigned at birth as a category as a basis for office policies and practices (e.g., housing assignments)?
- What is holding our office back from making this decision? Who might object? Who might support our decision?
- How can our office create partnerships across campus and with external stakeholders to support our choice not to use gender or sex assigned at birth as a basis for office policies and practices (e.g., housing assignments)?
- When our office staff think about creating policies regarding trans* students, how can we make sure to do so in a way that does not limit the possibilities for one's gender identity or expression?
- What literature could we use to support moving in this direction?
- What are the steps our office can begin to make in the coming semester to move toward trans* equity?

Campus Culture Questions

Although they can often be hard to formulate, the following questions can help individuals understand better the basic assumptions in which campus cultures are rooted:

- What are the basic assumptions about gender on my campus? What evidence can I find to support my claim?
- Who are the students, faculty, and staff across campus I can join to promote trans* equity?
- What are small and measureable goals I can create to make change in the coming semester or year?
- Based on my goals, what other campus groups, organizations, or marginalized populations can I collaborate with to advance equity? For example, advocating for gender-inclusive restrooms is beneficial for students with disabilities whose personal care attendants' gender or sex assigned at birth differs from their gender or sex assigned at birth and for other people who may not identify as trans* but who do not always pass as the sex assigned at birth or gender with which they identify.
- What are ways I can increase trans* equity that are not dependent on (or go beyond) the institutionalization of new policies?

CONCLUSION

It is imperative for student affairs educators to not assume that the creation of a more inclusive policy or practice means the work of gender equity and trans* inclusion is done. Although it is true that such policies are necessary when creating the conditions for structural diversity, it is also the case that such policies are not sufficient for the creation of trans*-inclusive campus environments (Nicolazzo, 2017). Furthermore, trans* housing policies are just the start of what student affairs educators need to be thinking about in terms of gender equity. For example, the underrepresentation of trans* staff members signals an overwhelming absence that needs to be addressed. This absence can even be seen anecdotally throughout this book, as many of the chapters are written by people who do not identify as trans*.

This is not to say the efforts detailed throughout this book are without merit or efficacy. Indeed, trans*-inclusive housing is an important and necessary feature of providing physical spaces that affirm students' gender identities. Moreover, the professionals who lead these efforts often do so from a desire to increase equity and justice for marginalized students, which is noble and illustrates the current thrust of the field of student affairs moving in this same direction. However, although these efforts are necessary, they are also insufficient in dismantling the overwhelming pervasiveness of trans* oppression on college campuses. Therefore, although the creation of more inclusive housing policies is a positive step, there are many more issues student affairs educators should address in the coming years, especially if those in the field are to take seriously their mission toward equity and inclusion for all marginalized student populations.

NOTES

1. It is important for me to acknowledge the good work undertaken by those educators who have worked tirelessly to implement gender-inclusive housing policies. Although I see these as a good first step in working toward trans* equity, I believe they are just that: a first step. Furthermore, it is important not to think an office, department, or campus has done everything it can or should do to promote trans* equity by instituting such a policy. Therefore, the purpose of this epilogue is not to suggest gender-inclusive housing policies should *not* be undertaken. Instead, I suggest ways that educators can and should do more, with gender-inclusive policies being the start of further conversations about trans* equity on campus. Additionally, this epilogue also encourages reflection on whether gender-inclusive housing policies as they are written are as inclusive and equitable as one may want to believe (I propose they may not be).

2. Although this epilogue uses the term *gender neutral*, I find it to be highly problematic, as it suggests gender is something one should mask or wipe away through policies. Therefore, although I use this term to reflect Conrad's (2012) choice, I prefer to use the term *gender inclusive*, which focuses on recognizing the multiple possibilities for how individuals may choose to identify and express their genders.

REFERENCES

Bilodeau, B. (2005). Beyond the gender binary: A case study of two transgender students at a midwestern research university. *Journal of Gay & Lesbian Issues in Education, 3*(1), 29–44.

Butler, J. (2006). *Gender trouble: Feminism and the subversion of identity.* New York, NY: Routledge.

Califia, P. (2003). *Sex changes: the politics of transgenderism* (2nd ed.). San Francisco, CA: Cleis Press.

Catalano, D. C. J. (2015). "Trans enough?": The pressures trans men negotiate in higher education. *TSQ: Transgender Studies Quarterly, 2*, 411–430.

Catalano, D. C. J., & Griffin, P. (2016). Sexism, heterosexism, and trans* oppression. In M. Adams, L. A. Bell, D. J. Goodman, & K. Y. Joshi (Eds.), *Teaching for diversity and social justice* (3rd ed., pp. 183–211). New York, NY: Routledge.

Conrad, P. (2012, March 21). Male student files discrimination charge. *Journal-News*. Retrieved from www.middletownjournal.com/news/news/local/miami-student-files-discrimination-charge/nNYtH

Feinberg, L. (1998). *Trans liberation: Beyond pink or blue.* Boston, MA: Beacon Press.

Kingkade, T. (2012, March 23). Kaeden Kass, transgender student, alleges housing discrimination at Miami University of Ohio. *Huff Post College*. Retrieved from www.huffingtonpost.com/2012/03/21/kaedan-kass-transgender-housing-discrimination_n_1370431.html

Kivel, P. (2007). Social service or social change? In Incite! Women of Color Against Violence (Ed.), *The revolution will not be funded: Beyond the non-profit industrial complex* (pp. 129–149). Cambridge, MA: South End Press.

Mattilda. (2006). Reaching too far: An introduction. In Mattilda (Ed.), *Nobody passes: Rejecting the rules of gender and conformity* (pp. 7–19). Berkeley, CA: Seal Press.

Nicolazzo, Z. (2017). *Trans* in college: Transgender students' strategies for navigating campus life and the institutional politics of inclusion.* Sterling, VA: Stylus.

Nicolazzo, Z, & Marine, S. B. (2015). "It will change if people keep talking": Trans* students in college and university housing. *Journal of College and University Student Housing, 42*, 160–177.

Office of Residence Life. (2017). *About the Office of Residence Life.* Retrieved from miamioh.edu/student-life/residence-life/about/index.html

Schein, E. H. (2010). *Organizational culture and leadership* (4th ed.). San Francisco, CA: Jossey-Bass.

Spade, D. (2010). Be professional! *Harvard Journal of Law & Gender, 33*, 71–84.

Spade, D. (2015). *Normal life: Administrative violence, critical trans politics, and the limits of law* (2nd ed.). Durham, NC: Duke University Press..

Stewart, D-L. (2017). Trans*versing the DMZ: A non-binary autoethnographic exploration of gender and masculinity. *International Journal of Qualitative Studies in Education, 30*, 285–304.

Taylor, K. (2012). Discussing diversity: Lawyer rules actions of Miami officials non-discriminatory. *Miami Student*. Retrieved from issuu.com/miamistudent/docs/09-07-12/1

Editors and Contributors

EDITORS

STEPHANIE H. CHANG is a PhD candidate in the college student personnel administration program at the University of Maryland, College Park. Her research interests are in culture, critical theories, and equity and social justice in higher education. She serves as an adjunct faculty member in New England College's master of science higher education and administration program. She is also the director of student diversity and inclusion at the University of Delaware.

Prior to this role, Stephanie served as director for education with the American College Personnel Association Standing Committee for LGBT Awareness from 2011 to 2013. She has also served on the executive board of the National Consortium of Directors of LGBT Resources in Higher Education. Stephanie has taught undergraduate and graduate courses in student development theory, intergroup dialogues, diversity and multicultural competency, and leadership development. Stephanie has professional student affairs experience in LGBT, multicultural, leadership development, and student activities functional areas.

JASON C. GARVEY is assistant professor of higher education and student affairs in the Department of Leadership and Developmental Sciences at the University of Vermont and a research associate with Campus Pride's Q Research Institute for Higher Education. He received his PhD in college student personnel administration from the University of Maryland with a certificate in measurement, statistics, and evaluation. Garvey is the recipient of the 2014 Scholar-Activist Dissertation of the Year Award from the Queer Studies Special Interest Group of the American Educational Researcher Association. His research examines student affairs and college classroom contexts with focus on assessing and quantifying student experiences across social identities, with particular attention to people with marginalized sexual and gender identities.

Prior to his faculty appointment, Jay worked in student services across a variety of functional areas, including academic advising, LGBT student advocacy, undergraduate research, and residence life. He has taught graduate and undergraduate courses in student development theory, counseling, research methods, diversity and social justice, and student affairs, among others. Jay formerly served as director of education for the Coalition for LGBT Awareness and on the Commission for Professional Preparation Directorate, both of which are in ACPA: College Student Educators International.

REX JACKSON is the associate director for residence life at Southern Illinois University Edwardsville where he develops and implements the vision and direction of the residence life program and residential curriculum, serves as part of the central management team for university housing, and leads the department's assessment efforts. He previously served as community director and as assistant director of residence life for the first-year communities at Southern Illinois University Edwardsville. Rex is a past vice chair for social responsibility, civic engagement, pluralism, and inclusion on the directorate body for ACPA: College Student Educators International's Commission for Housing and Residential Life. Rex received his master's degree in college student affairs leadership from Grand Valley State University and his bachelor's degree in fisheries and wildlife from the University of Missouri–Columbia.

Z NICOLAZZO is assistant professor in the Department of Counseling, Adult, and Higher Education and a faculty associate in the Center for the Study of Women, Gender, and Sexuality at Northern Illinois University. Z received hir PhD from the student affairs in higher education program at Miami University with a certificate in women's, gender, and sexuality studies. Z's research centers on the lives and livelihoods of trans* collegians and pays particular attention to the intersections of gender, sexuality, race, and disability through critical and queer theoretical lenses. Z has published widely on hir research alongside trans* college students and is the author of *Trans* In College: Transgender Students' Strategies for Navigating Campus Life and the Institutional Politics of Inclusion* (Stylus, 2017). Prior to hir faculty appointment, Z worked in student affairs administration in a variety of functional areas, including residence life, fraternity and sorority life, and sexual violence prevention education. Z has taught undergraduate and graduate courses on gender and sexuality, student development theory, critical and feminist peda-gogies, and research methods.

CONTRIBUTORS

RYAN ANDERSON is director of residential education at the Berklee College of Music. He received his master's in higher education and student affairs administration from Indiana University in 2008. Ryan served as assistant director for learning communities and assessment at American University from 2011 to 2013 and has also worked in residential life at California Poly-technic State University and Northeastern University.

ADRIAN BAUTISTA is assistant vice president of student life and senior associate dean for strategic initiatives at Oberlin College. Adrian helps manage a residential-administrative space for Oberlin College trans* students and allies named the Edmonia Lewis Center for Women & Transgender People. Prior to his current role, Adrian was director of residential education at Oberlin College. Adrian holds a doctorate in American culture studies with a women's studies certificate from Bowling Green State University.

SARA BENDORAITIS is the director of programming, outreach, and advocacy in the Center for Diversity & Inclusion at American University. She received her master's in student affairs administration in higher education from Texas A&M University in 2005. Sara has presented at national conferences on LGBTQ student support and advocacy, gender-neutral housing best prac-tices, academic and student affairs collaboration, assessing Safe Zone pro-grams, leadership, and women's and gender centers. Sara has also been a consultant for various federal government agencies, national and interna-tional nonprofits, higher education institutions, and the U.S. Naval Academy. She has served as a board member for the National Association of Student Personnel Administrators' (NASPA) Center for Scholarship, Research, and Professional Development for Women; as a NASPA regional representative; education, advocacy, and outreach chair and cochair for the Consortium of Higher Education Lesbian Gay Bisexual Transgender Resource Professionals; and is a member of the Council on the Advancement of Standards in Higher Education Board of Directors.

BOB BROPHY has a master's degree in college student development. He has served as director of residence life at the University Center Chicago since January of 2010 and has been involved with residence life in some capacity for more than 25 years.

MATT BRUNO is assistant director of education and training in the Center for Diversity & Inclusion at American University (AU). Matt received a master's in higher education administration from George Mason University (GMU) and has worked in higher education settings for close to 10 years, primarily in diversity, inclusion, and LGBTQ-based centers. Matt's work at AU has primarily consisted of curriculum development, policy advocacy, and student advising. Matt has served as cochair and treasurer of the Consortium of Higher Education LGBT Resource Professionals. Matt has also taught in the Department of Women, Gender, and Sexuality Studies at AU; the School of Education at AU; and the School of Integrative Studies at GMU. In addition, Matt has facilitated LGBTQ inclusion trainings for government agencies, nonprofits, universities, and high schools in the Washington, DC, metropolitan area.

ANDREW J. ERDMANN is associate director of residential education in the Office of Residential Living at Georgetown University, as well as a PhD candidate in the Department of Educational Leadership and Policy Analysis at the University of Wisconsin–Madison. Before working at Georgetown, Andrew received his master's degree in educational leadership and policy analysis from the University of Wisconsin–Madison where he was residence life coordinator. During this time, he had the opportunity to work with the proposal team to develop the vision of Open House through the proposal writing stage. Andrew was involved with Open House throughout the proposal stage.

KRISTEN FRANKLIN is associate director of housing at George Washington University where she works with the gender-inclusive housing program and serves as a liaison between housing and LGBTQA+ students. She has worked in housing and residence life for more than10 years and holds a master of education in educational policy and leadership from Marquette University.

DEBORAH GRANDNER has more than 30 years' experience in the housing profession. She currently serves as director of resident life at the University of Maryland where she earned her PhD in college student personnel and administration. During her career Deb served in diverse roles in the housing profession including leadership, research, and program development positions. An active member of the Association of College and University Housing Officers–International (ACUHO–I) and the National Association of Student Personnel Administrators, she has served on the ACUHO-I Executive board, and cochaired the James C. Grimm National Housing Training Institute, teaching and mentoring housing professionals for a decade. She has a special interest in global learning opportunities and partnerships with academic affairs in the development of living-learning programs. Deb is an affiliate faculty member in the College of Education. Deb is also the proud mother of a University of Maryland graduate.

Angie M. Harris is associate dean of students and director of residence life and housing at Dickinson College. She has spent more than 15 years in residence life and housing at various institutions including the University of South Carolina, Southern Methodist University, University of Richmond, Texas A&M University, and Dickinson. Angie is currently a doctoral student at the University of Virginia in higher education administration, and her research interests are focused on issues related to gender in the college experience.

Jennifer Hoefle Olson has more than 18 years of experience in higher education as a faculty member and a student affairs professional. She has served as director for LGBTQ affairs through the dean of students office at the University of Arizona (UA) since 2010. In this role, she serves as a hub for LGBTQ+ work on the UA campus, runs the LGBTQ+ Student Resource Center, directs the Safe Zone Training Program, supports the many affiliated LGBTQ+ student organizations, and collaborates with residence life, counseling and psych services, and other departments across campus. Prior to this role, she was program director for social justice education programs through the Center for Student Involvement and Leadership at the UA. She earned a master of arts in applied sociology from Northern Arizona University in 2001.

Erin Iverson is manager of assignments and public inquiry for the Department of Resident Life at the University of Maryland where she supervises the administrative and assignment functions for the department. In her capacity as assignments manager, she serves as the department's lesbian, gay, bisexual, and trans* liaison, working directly with students who have concerns about housing needs, particularly as they relate to gender identity, expression, and trans* student needs. Erin was cochair of the task force that developed the mixed-gender and gender-inclusive housing program for the University of Maryland to provide housing options that are most welcoming to lesbian, gay, bisexual, and trans* students. She is involved throughout campus, most notably as a member of the President's Commission on Lesbian, Gay, Bisexual, and Trans Issues and the Campus Assessment Working Group, and serves as the faculty adviser to the Phi Sigma Pi National Honor Fraternity. In 2014 Erin received the Champion of the Community award from the Lesbian, Gay, Bisexual, and Trans Staff and Faculty Association for her work supporting lesbian, gay, bisexual, and trans* students on campus.

TIMOTHY KANE is associate director for inclusion initiatives at George Washington University (GW), where he directs the LGBTQIA Resource Center and oversees religious life. Timothy is also president and founder of Niche2Norm Consulting. Timothy received his bachelor of arts from Hamilton College, his master of divinity from Harvard University, and his master of theology in justice and peace studies from Maryknoll School of Theology. As a certified instructor of Teaching English to Speakers of Other Languages, Timothy also holds a certificate in international development from the Monterey Institute of International Studies and a graduate certificate in HIV/AIDS studies and in international education from GW. Currently, Timothy is also pursuing a graduate certificate in Islamic studies in the GW Department of Religion.

KATHLEEN G. KERR serves as associate vice president for student life and executive director of residence life and housing at the University of Delaware. She has leadership responsibilities in the Division of Student Life and oversight for the residence halls and associated operations, new student orientation, and the student centers. She has a secondary appointment as assistant professor in the College of Education and Human Development. Kathleen attended Indiana University in Bloomington, where she received her BA in psychology and her MS in college student personnel administration. In 1998 she earned her EdD in educational leadership from the University of Delaware. She resides in Newark, Delaware, with her husband, where they raised their four daughters.

LORI LANDER is assistant vice chancellor for campus life and associate dean of students at the University of Arkansas. Lori is a student affairs practitioner with more than 20 years of experience creating programs that contribute to the success of all students. Most of Lori's career has been spent in residence life at the University of Colorado, which led to the role of director of residence life and academic initiatives at the University of Oregon. Throughout this time, Lori developed the belief that gender-inclusive housing should be a fundamental part of any residential campus community because all students need to feel supported. Lori's work on gender-inclusive communities is not static, and she understands that the physical spaces are just a small part of the evolving conversation regarding the living-learning experience. Lori strives to engage in conversations among academic and student affairs colleagues to create politically active, socially responsible learning communities. Lori earned her BS at Lyon College in economics, MEd at the University of Arkansas in higher education administration, and PhD at Colorado State University in education and human resource studies.

BRIDGET LE LOUP COLLIER is associate provost and director for equal opportunity programs at the University of Chicago. Prior to joining UChicago in May of 2015, Collier served in a number of roles at Roosevelt University, including chief of staff to the president, Title IX coordinator, assistant provost for student success, and assistant vice president for residence life. She is the founder and chair of the Chicagoland Title IX Consortium, an organization of more than 40 higher education institutions in the Chicago area that seeks to enhance knowledge, understanding, and application of Title IX policies and resources to advance gender parity and reduce sexual misconduct. Bridget holds a doctorate of education from the University of Southern California, a master of education in counseling and student affairs from Northern Arizona University, and a bachelor of science in psychology from Ball State University.

CRAIG LEETS JR. has been engaged in queer advocacy work on college campuses since 2006. He has been director of Queer Student Services and the Queer Resource Center at Portland State University since October 2013. His accomplishments on this campus include advanced preferred name options for trans students, an all-gender restroom policy, and supporting the implementation of an all-gender housing option for students. Before this, Craig worked at Pennsylvania State University as assistant director for the Lesbian, Gay, Bisexual, Transgender, Queer, and Ally Student Resource Center. Before working at Penn State, Craig was resident director at the University of Maryland, College Park, where he worked on gender-inclusive housing, an inclusive language campaign, and a coming-out support group for students.

Also, he completed his master of arts degree in counseling and personnel services with a focus in college student personnel while at Maryland, focusing his thesis research on leadership and activism among lesbian, gay, and bisexual undergraduates.

HANNAH LOZON works in human resources and operations for the Opportunity Hub at the University of Michigan's College of Literature, Science, and the Arts. She previously served as coordinator of social justice education for housing and residential life at the University of Arizona, where she worked with the director for lesbian, gay, bisexual, transgender, and queer affairs to bring about the first gender-inclusive housing program to the public higher education system in Arizona. Hannah received her master's degree in higher education student affairs administration from the University of Vermont and her bachelor's degree in English and communications studies from the University of Michigan.

AMY MARTIN serves as assistant dean for undergraduate student success initiatives, Office of the Provost, at Michigan State University. Amy has 25 years of progressive leadership experience at three large public research institutions, including the University of Maryland, College Park where she served as cochair of the Gender-Inclusive Housing Committee.

Amy has dedicated her career to developing strong student-centered academic communities on large, diverse campuses; tackling complex campus crises; researching women and leadership in higher education; and improving persistence and graduation outcomes for lower income, first-generation, or minoritized (e.g., Black, Latinx, Native American, LGBTQ) students. Amy has particularly enjoyed teaching, developing, and learning from multiple levels of student and professional staff members throughout her career. Her graduate degrees are from Eastern Michigan University and the University of Maryland, College Park.

In July 2016, Amy joined 63 women leaders across the United States as part of the HERS Institute at Bryn Mawr College. Institute sessions included *Managing and Leading Change: Your Role in Re-inventing Higher Education, Negotiation Strategies, Leaning Into Turbulent Times,* and *Diversity and Inclusion and Reframing: Work-Life to Living Well.* Visit www.HERSnet .org for more information about HERS.

CHICORA MARTIN is vice president and dean of students for Mills College in Oakland, California. Before coming to Mills, Chicora was at the University of

Oregon for 14 years serving as the assistant dean of students and director of the Lesbian, Gay, Bisexual, Transgender Education and Support Services Program while also leading the Center for Multicultural Academic Excellence and Bias Response Team. Chicora's national leadership positions include past cochair for the National Consortium of LGBT Resource Professionals, member of the ACPA: College Student Educators International, Senior Student Affairs Officer Advisory Board, and former member of the Standing Committee for LGBT Concerns and Region V knowledge community chair for LGBT issues for the National Association of Student Personnel Administrators. Chicora's research interests include the intersections of higher education policy, gender identity, and ethnic identity. Past presentations have focused on gender identity, LGBTQ+ engagement and support, Title IX and policy development, multiethnic and queer identity, bystander intervention, and campus climate.

LUCA MAURER, program director of the Center for LGBT Education, Outreach, and Services, arrived at Ithaca College in 2001 as its founding director. Luca has collaborated for many years with valued colleagues in residential life to create the trans* housing policy and LGBT residential learning community and to continually improve, expand, and diversify residence hall opportunities for students. Luca is coauthor of *The Teaching Transgender Toolkit* (Out for Health, 2015).

CHRIS MOODY is assistant vice president of campus life at American University and a doctoral student in the higher education administration program at George Washington University. In this role, he oversees the Departments of Housing and Residence Life, One Card and Dining Services, and University Conferences and Guest Services. Chris received his bachelor's degree in psychology from Wake Forest University and his master's degree in college student development from Appalachian State University. Previous employment experiences include roles at the University of North Carolina at Chapel Hill, Appalachian State University, the University of Memphis, and the Semester at Sea program. In professional circles, Chris has been an active member of the ACPA-College Student Educators, the National Association of Student Personnel Administrators, and the Association of College and University Residence Halls–International (ACUHO–I). He served as chairperson for the ACPA 2016 Convention in Montréal, Canada, which was the first comprehensive student affairs in higher education organization to host its annual meeting outside the United States, and is a former ACPA Governing Board member.

CHANTAL (CHAMPALOUX) MOSELLEN graduated from George Washington University with a master's in higher education administration in 2015. She became interested in gender-inclusive policies and practices in residence life while working as a resident adviser at the University of Vermont. Chantal currently works in the GW School of Medicine and Health Sciences.

REBECCA MOSELY is director of the Office of Equity, Diversity, and Inclusion and is coordinator for Title IX and the Americans with Disabilities Act at Oberlin College. Before taking this position Rebecca worked in residential education at Oberlin for 11 years. Prior to Oberlin, she worked in housing at Texas Tech University and the University of Arizona. Rebecca holds a doctorate in higher education from Bowling Green State University, and her main interest in higher education is studying issues of social justice and access.

ELLEN O'BRIEN is associate professor of English and women and gender studies at Roosevelt University and has served as director of the women and gender studies program.

BRENDEN PARADIES is a graduate of the master of urban planning and policy program at the University of Illinois Chicago, with concentrations in transportation planning and community development. He also holds a bachelor of arts in integrated marketing communications and a minor in women's and gender studies from Roosevelt University. While at Roosevelt, Brenden was an active LGBTQ activist and helped to implement gender-inclusive housing as an on-campus housing option for Roosevelt students. He has delivered guest lectures and led conference presentations covering topics related to gender and LGBTQ issues.

Driven by his passion for women's and gender studies, Brenden was eager to pursue a master's degree in urban planning and policy to focus on building inclusive communities by improving accessibility to various resources for low-income and LGBTQ-identified residents. His master's thesis was the creation of an LGBTQ Education Advocacy Action Plan for high school educators in the Chicago area to provide awareness, resources, and education about LGBTQ topics at an early and preventative stage in hopes of lowering LGBTQ teen suicide rates. Brenden now lives and works in Denver, Colorado, and he continues to be an advocate for underserved communities.

BRIAN J. PATCHCOSKI is associate dean and director of the LGBT Resource Center at Cornell University. He was also founding director of the Office of LGBTQ Services at Dickinson College. He joined Dickinson after working at Pennsylvania State University where he served as assistant director of the LGBTA Student Resource Center. He has participated in several national research projects examining student identity development and campus climate and has served as the mid-Atlantic representative for the Consortium of Higher Education LGBT Resource Professionals. Brian has worked extensively providing training and conducting discussions exploring issues of sexuality and gender identity and has made presentations at several national conferences.

BRANDON ROHLWING received a bachelor of arts with honors from Roosevelt University, majoring in integrated marketing communications. He is a media analyst at Starcom and serves as a national youth council member with the Inspire USA Foundation.

JAMES C. SMITH is associate director for residential life at University of California, Riverside. In this role, James has direct oversight of student programming, academic initiatives, and staff recruitment for the department. His portfolio also includes training and development, student success programs, special-interest communities and large-scale student events. James has also worked in other student affairs positions at the University of California, Santa Cruz and University of the Pacific. James earned an EdD from University of California, Los Angeles, where his research focused on LGB-identified student affairs professionals and their personal perspectives on career trajectory. He also holds an MA in student affairs administration from Michigan State University and a BS in telecommunications and film from Eastern Michigan University.

MAURE SMITH-BENANTI is associate dean of students and director of intercultural affairs at Grinnell College. Prior to this, Maure came to the University of Oregon in 2011 as assistant director of the lesbian, gay, bisexual, transgender, education, and support services office and was promoted to director in 2015. During her time at the University of Oregon, she served as the Northwest regional representative for the Consortium of Higher Education LGBT Resource Professionals. Maure began work with lesbian, gay, bisexual, and transgender students in 2007 as the first program coordinator of Utah State University's GLBTA Services after many years of student leadership and activism. Maure brings a wealth of experience and enthusiasm for developing inclusive and safer learning environments built on the principles of equity, activism, and authenticity.

ROBERT SNYDER is executive director of planning and outreach in the Division of Student Affairs at George Washington University (GW), where he oversees planning and assessment, development and alumni relations, communications and outreach, and staff professional development initiatives for the division. Robert also directs the university's Presidential Administrative Fellowship Program. A GW staff member since 2004, Robert previously held positions in the Office of the Dean of Freshmen, Mount Vernon Campus, and the Office of the President, where he represented the president on the university-wide committee that created recommendations to introduce a gender-neutral housing program at GW. Robert earned a bachelor's degree in business administration from GW and master's degrees in education and business administration from the University of Delaware, where he worked for nine years before returning to GW. He is currently a doctoral candidate in higher education administration at GW.

BONNIE SOLT PRUNTY, director of residential life and judicial affairs, arrived at Ithaca College in 1988, where she first worked as the housing assignments coordinator. She has worked in various positions in the Office of Residential Life since. During her time at Ithaca College, Bonnie has been committed to creating housing policies, programs, and procedures that create an inclusive and welcoming residential environment for all Ithaca College students.

ANDREW SONN is director of military and veteran student services at George Washington University (GW). Andy has worked in GW's student affairs division for 18 years in several roles relating to housing, parent services, international student services, assessment, and professional development. He also teaches courses in GW's higher education administration program as a visiting professor. Prior to GW, Andy worked in residence life and housing roles at the University of Maryland at College Park and Georgetown University.

MAURA STERNBERG is a 2014 graduate of Oberlin College with a degree in dance and comparative American studies. While at Oberlin, Maura spent three years as the resident assistant for a women's and trans* collective in a housing unit named Baldwin Cottage. Maura is currently teaching dance, dancing in the community-oriented hip-hop company Hip Hop ConnXion, and pursuing a master's degree in secondary education with a social justice focus. In 2017 Maura completed her master's degree in English language and literature and letters at Northwestern University.

JENNIFER TANI currently serves as director of Posse Chicago at the Posse Foundation, which is one of the most comprehensive and renowned college access and youth leadership development programs in the nation. Jennifer has an extensive background in government and community relations and civic engagement. She holds a master's in public service management from DePaul University, and a bachelor of arts in sociology and anthropology from Carleton College.

JON TINGLEY is assistant director for housing facilities in the housing and residence life department at Tulane University. Jon had worked as a residence life coordinator at the University of Wisconsin–Madison when Open House, the gender-focused learning community, welcomed its incoming class of students. Previously he worked with students in the LGBT Resource Center and residence life departments at Minnesota State University, Mankato, where he received a master's degree in counseling and student personnel.

NANCY JEAN TUBBS has directed the University of California, Riverside's (UCR) Lesbian Gay Bisexual Transgender Resource Center since 2000. She holds a master's degree in educational administration from Texas A&M University. Working with colleagues and students, Nancy Jean helped implement best practices at UCR, including gender-inclusive housing, trans-inclusive student health insurance, gender-inclusive restrooms campus-wide, a student preferred name policy and procedures, and gender identity demographic information in the campus student information system. She cofounded T*Camp, an intercampus retreat for transgender and gender-questioning college students. Working with Asterisk of UCR, she's taken the lead on hosting the Asterisk Trans* Conference for several years. Nancy Jean is also cofounder of the Campus LGBTQ Centers Directory, an online resource cataloguing professionally staffed centers in the United States and Canada.

SETH WEINSHEL has worked in university housing for more than 17 years. He currently is asistant dean of students for housing and financial services at George Washington University, where he earned a master's in tourism administration. Seth has presented nationally on gender-neutral housing, planning and construction, and housing revenue generation.

Open House
  gender identities continuum at, 105
  high school GSAs contacted by, 104
  learning community with focus on
    allies, 105
  name changes eased at, 105
  stakeholder perspectives in, 103–4
  for trans* safety concerns, 104–5,
    107–8
  UW-Madison accepting and
    funding, 103
  UW-Madison first year experiences
    of, 105–10
  UW-Madison learning communities
    as, 100–112
  UW-Madison time line for, 113–14

Paradies, Brenden, 22, 24
parents, 26–27
  consent required or not from, 30,
    40–41
  Dickinson policy for consent from,
    91
  Ithaca and trans* housing reactions
    from, 153, 159–61, 163
  Oberlin and concern by, 56
  stakeholder group including, 38, 40
  UCR inclusive housing influenced
    by, 68, 75
PGP. See preferred gender pronouns
policies
  American University needing written
    inclusive, 145
  development of housing, 26–31
  Dickinson and inclusive housing,
    86–91
  Dickinson history leading to, 82–83
  GW stages of developing, 37–41
  for inclusive housing as furthered,
    202n1
  Ithaca and trans* housing, 155–59,
    161–63

Ithaca newspaper on trans*, 159
  UMD previous coming out, 120
  UO needing gender identity, 184–86
  of UW-Madison coeducational
    housing, 104, 107
politics
  Dickinson LGBTQ office utilizing,
    85–86
  gender-inclusive bathrooms and, 12
  for GW trans* housing, 36–37
  Oberlin and gender, 48–52
  Oberlin and racial, 57–59
  trans* housing and, 11, 13
  UA in context of government, 167
  UMD inclusive housing and, 122,
    129–30
  university staff assisted with trans*,
    viii
preferred gender pronouns (PGP)
  Oberlin utilizing, 54
  trans* student utilizing, 194–95
  UCR trans* students utilizing, 64
  UW-Madison allowing identity cards
    with, 110
proposal team. See task force

racial identity, 50
  ELC for, 57–59
  gender identity solutions akin to,
    126
  Oberlin and politics of, 57–59
  Oberlin segregation by, 51
religion questions, 69
residence practitioners, 22, 194, 201–2
  as allies, 53
  at American University for inclusive
    housing, 137, 141
  gender diversity and identities
    training for, 53
  at Ithaca advocating for trans*
    housing, 155
  LGBTQ education for, 72–73